T0282766

PRAISE FOR *Shadows of Tyranny*

"It takes a very rare skill to make history read like a propulsive novel you can't put down, but that is what Ken McGoogan has done for years, and he has done it again with *Shadows of Tyranny*. Is this the twilight of democracy? Does history tell us we are on the precipice of an age of darkness? These are the urgent and fearless questions McGoogan poses so well."

EVAN SOLOMON, political journalist, radio host and special correspondent to CTV *News*

"We all need to read Ken McGoogan's book. It is prescient, terrifying, sober—a clarion call for us to wake up and see the totalitarian monster clanking toward us."

PATRICK CREAN, CM, editor and publisher

"When fascism was cooked up in the embers of the First World War, brilliant celebrity writers and activists saw the danger and took awful personal risks to tell their stories. McGoogan's book introduces readers to these courageous, talented people and raises the question: 'Where are they now?' As a new fascism emerges in the West, will intellectuals have the skill and the platforms to push back against authoritarians the way Matthew Halton, George Orwell, Hannah Arendt, Ernest Hemingway and Norman Bethune did in the interwar years? And, if the new fascism succeeds in undermining democracy and the rule of law, will individuals have the courage to resist, following the example of the women and men who fought back in occupied Europe?"

MARK BOURRIE, lawyer, journalist and author

"*Shadows of Tyranny* is, in part, a celebration of those brave souls in the twentieth century who resisted autocrats and plutocrats, dictators and 'devil kings' in order to save us from unimaginable calamity. But it is also an urgent call for the rest of us in the here and now. In his always engaging, inimitable style, Ken McGoogan has created a 'pointillist' historical narrative that paints a larger picture we all not only need to see clearly but also act upon—like those earlier resisters. It's a must-read."

STEPHEN KIMBER, author, journalist and professor of journalism at University of King's College

KEN McGOOGAN

SHADOWS OF TYRANNY

DEFENDING DEMOCRACY IN AN AGE OF DICTATORSHIP

Douglas & McIntyre

Douglas and McIntyre (2013) Ltd.
P.O. Box 219, Madeira Park, BC, VON 2H0
www.douglas-mcintyre.com

Edited by Derek Fairbridge
Indexed by Lisa Fedorak
Jacket and text design by Naomi MacDougall | DSGN Dept.
Printed and bound in Canada
Text printed on 100% recycled and FSC® certified paper

Douglas and McIntyre acknowledges the support of the Canada Council
for the Arts, the Government of Canada, and the Province of British
Columbia through the BC Arts Council.

Library and Archives Canada Cataloguing in Publication
Title: Shadows of tyranny : defending democracy in an age of dictatorship
/ Ken McGoogan.
Names: McGoogan, Ken, author.
Description: Includes bibliographical references and index.
Identifiers: Canadiana (print) 20240380711 | Canadiana (ebook)
20240380789 | ISBN 9781771624244 (hardcover) |
ISBN 9781771624251 (EPUB)
Subjects: LCSH: Totalitarianism—History—20th century. | LCSH:
Dictators—History—20th century. | LCSH: Democracy—Forecasting.
Classification: LCC JC480 .M34 2024 | DDC 320.5309/04—dc23

For Sheena
The Love of my Life

Contents

Timeline

THE RISE AND FALL
OF THE FIRST AGE OF DICTATORSHIP

DONALD TRUMP HAS made no secret of his dictatorial tendencies or his admiration for the "genius" of Vladimir Putin. Besides those two, today we have Ali Khamenei in Iran, Victor Orbán in Hungary, Kim Jong Un in North Korea, Xi Jinping in China, Recep Tayyip Erdoğan in Turkey, Narendra Modi in India, and serial dictators in several African and South American countries. History doesn't repeat, as the saying goes, but it does often rhyme. Does the rise and fall of the first Age of Dictatorship have anything to teach us? "What place is this? Where are we now?"

1917–1929

1917   Russian Revolution—Vladimir Lenin and Bolsheviks seize power

1918   First World War ends with German surrender; Allies occupy German Rhineland

1919   Treaty of Versailles limits German armed forces, stipulates reparations

German army sends corporal Adolf Hitler to spy on German Workers' Party

1920s   *Les années folles* in Paris—café society, surrealism, expatriate writers, Josephine Baker

1922   Fascist leader Benito Mussolini marches on Rome, becomes prime minister of Italy

1923   France and Belgium occupy Germany's Ruhr Valley to compel war reparations

Adolf Hitler leads the Beer Hall Putsch, fails to overthrow government, caught and jailed

1924   Hitler uses trial as a platform, sentenced to five years, serves eight months

1924   Vladimir Lenin dies, Joseph Stalin starts purging rivals

1925   Hitler's anti-Semitic rant, *Mein Kampf*, is published

1927   Joseph Stalin expels Leon Trotsky, gains undisputed control of Soviet Union

1929   Winston Churchill preaches disarmament in Canada and the US

Great Depression begins after October stock-market crash in New York

1930–1939

1930 France withdraws from Rhineland—Nazis become second-largest party in the Reichstag

1931 Under attack for anti-totalitarian novel *We*, Yevgeny Zamyatin leaves Russia for exile

1933 German president Paul von Hindenburg appoints Hitler chancellor

Germany builds first concentration camp, Dachau, dispatches homeless, alcoholic, unemployed

Reichstag fire leads to *Enabling Act*, giving Hitler dictatorial powers

Germans told to boycott Jewish shops and businesses

Journalists Matthew Halton and Dorothy Thompson raise alarm about rise of dictatorship

1934 Germany and Poland sign ten-year non-aggression pact

Night of the Long Knives—Hitler assassinates at least eighty-five potential rivals

German president Hindenburg dies; Hitler makes himself all-powerful Führer

1935 Reichstag passes Nuremberg Laws, legalizing persecution of Jews in Germany

1936 Flouting Treaty of Versailles, Hitler rearms Rhineland

1936 Spanish Nationalists under Francisco Franco revolt against democratic government

Germany and Italy aid General Franco, while France and England stand aside

George Orwell, Andre Malraux, and Norman Bethune join Spanish fighting for democracy

1936 Russia: Stalin launches the Great Purge (1936–1938), killing 600,000 to eliminate opposition

1937 Canadian prime minister William Lyon Mackenzie King judges Hitler a man of peace

1938 The Anschluss—Germany annexes Austria

Chamberlain hails Munich Agreement, Churchill denounces it; Hitler annexes Sudetenland

Nazis smash thousands of Jewish shops and synagogues during *Kristallnacht* (November 9-10)

1939 Right-wing Spanish Nationalists defeat democratic Republicans; Franco becomes a dictator

1939 Canada follows US and UK in refusing entry to more German Jewish refugees

Germany and Soviet Union sign a non-aggression pact featuring joint occupation of Poland

Nazis invade Poland; UK and France declare war on September 3, Canada follows on September 10

1940–1975

1940 Churchill becomes British prime minister on May 10, leads fight against Nazis

Nazis invade western Europe, win Battle of France, occupy Paris on June 14

Evacuation of 338,000 soldiers from French port of Dunkirk in May–June

Battle of Britain, July–October—Royal Air Force beats back Luftwaffe attacks

1940–1944
French Resistance uses spies and sabotage to disrupt Nazi war effort

1941 Soviet Union repulses massive Nazi attack

1942–1944
During Holocaust, Nazis deliberately murder six million European Jews

1944 Allies liberate Paris on August 25

1945 Benito Mussolini captured and shot on April 28 while fleeing to Switzerland

Hitler kills himself on April 30

Nazis surrender on May 7

George Orwell's *Animal Farm* is published

1949 George Orwell's *Nineteen Eighty-Four* is published

1953 Joseph Stalin dies after suffering a stroke at age 74

1975 Francisco Franco, having remained as dictator, dies of heart failure at age 82

The View from Canada

"And what rough beast, its hour come round at last,
slouches towards Bethlehem to be born?"
—W.B. Yeats

NOT LONG AGO, Thomas Homer-Dixon, a prominent public intellectual, warned Canadians that a terrible storm was coming our way
out of the United States. The headline over his opinion piece, which
appeared in the *Globe and Mail* early in 2022, read, THE AMERICAN
POLITY IS CRACKED, AND MIGHT COLLAPSE. CANADA MUST
PREPARE.

Homer-Dixon, founding director of the Cascade Institute at Royal
Roads University, argued that, all through 2021, Canadians had been
preoccupied with COVID-19, healing the wounds of colonization,
and climate change. But now, as we entered 2022, "we must focus
on the urgent problem of what to do about the likely unravelling of
democracy in the United States."

As a self-described "scholar of violent conflict" for more than four
decades and leader for more than twenty years of a centre on peace
and conflict studies at the University of Toronto, Homer-Dixon is
arguably the most authoritative Canadian to sound the alarm. He
drew attention to an especially dire portent: the Weimar Republic
that governed Germany in the 1920s and early 1930s, and then gave
way to the Third Reich of Adolf Hitler.

Homer-Dixon discerned worrisome parallels between Hitler's
Germany and Donald Trump's America. In both worlds, a charismatic

leader or demagogue was able to unify right-wing extremists around a political program to seize control of the state. To mobilize followers, that leader told barefaced lies about how internal enemies had betrayed the country. Homer-Dixon might have added that both Trump and Hitler sought to win over less extreme segments of the populace with specious claims about restoring their countries to some mythical past glory.

In both cases conventional conservatives believed they could contain their demagogic leaders, and in both cases their ideological opponents squabbled among themselves and focused on marginal issues that served only to provoke extremism. In Germany, polarization and demagoguery led to systemic collapse and dictatorship. Donald Trump could be the wrecking ball that demolishes American democracy and clears the way for a different autocrat.

Homer-Dixon has called for the creation of a non-partisan standing committee charged with preparing the Canadian government for democratic failure south of the border. We have yet to hear of any such body—though in August 2023, foreign affairs minister Melanie Joly said the government had been considering a "game plan" in case the US were to elect an authoritarian government in 2024. Other senior Liberals have since indicated that they are actively considering how to cope in the event of another Trump presidency. Still, despite the spillover of American rhetoric, most Canadians do not regard the rise of the far right in the US as representing a threat to Canada. Like the French in the 1930s, most of us might occasionally raise an eyebrow, but otherwise we just go on about our business.

Yet Homer-Dixon is not the first Canadian to worry. Forty years ago—incredible to think—Canadian novelist Margaret Atwood began warning of the rising threat of totalitarianism. As it happens, I interviewed her in 1985, when she published *The Handmaid's Tale*. The story she tells, having been amplified by a TV adaptation, is now world famous: In a not-too-distant future, religious fanatics have taken control of the US Congress and turned much of the country into a patriarchal theocracy called Gilead. Women are powerless, third-class citizens, some of whom, the so-called handmaids, are made to serve as sex slaves and baby-makers.

Canadian novelist and poet Margaret Atwood in 1990, five years after she published *The Handmaid's Tale*. *Alamy*

"It's an extrapolation of present trends set in the US," Atwood told me. "It's as much about the past as about the present. There's nothing in it that hasn't actually happened somewhere. Polygamy? Check out the Mormon Church. Public hangings? They were standard in the 19th century." Atwood offered a hypothetical: "If you were planning to take over the US," she asked, "what line would you take? . . . My gang says, 'Let's have a theocracy.'" She added: "Nothing in my book is pure invention or has been cooked up out of my fevered brain . . . The seeds of my scenario are not lacking."

Atwood characterized *The Handmaid's Tale* as "speculative fiction of the George Orwell variety." It springs from a subset in "a long tradition of utopias—although in the twentieth century, the vision is much bleaker and utopias have become dystopias." In this book, I reference visionary works by Atwood and Orwell, and by H.G. Wells, Yevgeny Zamyatin, Jack London, Sinclair Lewis, and Philip Roth.

People have told me that you can't use the past to predict the future. Fair enough. But I think also of an observation attributed to both historian George Santayana and Winston Churchill: "Those that fail to learn from history are doomed to repeat it." *Shadows of*

Tyranny notes the growth of alt-right fascism in the US while telling the story of what happened in Europe in the early to mid-twentieth century.

In the 1920s and early 1930s, a few people *did* see fascism rising. A few sounded the alarm, warned that fascist dictatorship posed a threat to the democratic way of life. But too many remained blind until shamefully late in the day—among them Canadian prime minister William Lyon Mackenzie King. Others said yes to the totalitarian juggernaut, took to scapegoating, and fanned the embers of anti-Semitism into a conflagration.

Collective hysteria has been known to arise closer to home, as war correspondent Martha Gellhorn pointed out in her 1988 book *The View from the Ground*. Looking back at the 1950s, she wrote that, for four years, Republican senator Joseph McCarthy ran the US like "a devil king." She likened his American purges to those of Joseph Stalin in the Soviet Union in the 1930s—though where McCarthy destroyed livelihoods, reputations, and careers, Stalin had people murdered. His purges were more like those of Adolf Hitler, whose "Night of the Long Knives" in 1934 saw at least eighty-five men executed without trial.

Against that background, the narrative of this book celebrates those people who refused, rejected, and opposed—those who resisted. It follows them from the obliviousness of the 1920s through the stunned awakening of the 1930s, and on into the nightmare horror of the 1940s. It honours those who defied the would-be dictators—heroic men and women of all nationalities who risked their lives to fight fascism, Nazism, communism—in brief, to battle totalitarianism in all its forms.

We track George Orwell, of course, but also journalists like Matthew Halton, Dorothy Thompson, and Martha Gellhorn, philosophers like Walter Benjamin and Hannah Arendt, and such hard-to-classify, multi-faceted figures as Winston Churchill, André Malraux, Norman Bethune, and William Stephenson. And we do so in the hope that a generation of equally courageous people will step forward in the days ahead should the need arise.

Framed by events of the present day, the main narrative comes to us not *ex cathedra*, not through a single omniscient voice, but via the stories of heroes and heroines who fought the rise of fascism through the Spanish Civil War and the Second World War. They had to contend with Franco, Mussolini, Hitler, and Stalin, who together constituted what I think of as the first Age of Dictatorship. Today we have entered a second such age, a period in which tyrants rule Russia, China, North Korea, and Hungary, among other countries—an era in which Donald Trump has never had dealings with an autocrat he did not publicly admire.

In this book, against this backdrop, we take a biographical approach to history, highlighting personal impact and resistance and inviting the reader to engage more fully than usual—indeed to participate in turning a collage into an overarching narrative. *Shadows of Tyranny* incorporates conventional history, political commentary, literary reflection, and biographical sketches into a work of future-facing or speculative non-fiction.

Part One, "Slouching toward Bethlehem," finds people realizing that fascism poses an existential threat. Part Two, "The Spanish Dress Rehearsal," looks at the Spanish Civil War, when more than forty thousand international volunteers flocked to Spain to fight for democracy. In Part Three, "Invaders, Collaborators, and Scapegoats," Adolf Hitler overruns countries that neighbour Germany and finds collaborators willing to join him in targeting innocent Jews. Part Four, "Here Come the Canadians," tracks the stories of those who, while not themselves immediately threatened, took up the fight against the Nazis. Part Five, "The French Resistance," celebrates the French citizens who laid their lives on the line. And Part Six intertwines contemporary events and historical narrative while highlighting the need for constant vigilance: "What, Me Worry?"

PART ONE

Slouching toward Bethlehem

1 / Overture:
What Rough Beast?

IN THE AUTUMN of 2016, a wealthy American woman told me during a private conversation at a public event in Toronto that she was surprised to see Canadians taking such an interest in the US presidential election. We could not vote in it, after all. And presidents come and go every four years. Why would Canadians concern themselves? I had expressed a worry that Donald Trump might get elected, and she was indicating that, as a Canadian, I should keep my opinions to myself. I observed mildly that whatever happened in the US affected the whole world and especially Canada. But then I let the matter drop. Canadian *politesse*, eh?

After Trump won that 2016 election, I, like many other Canadians, started watching more closely. Installed in the White House in January 2017, Trump moved immediately to ban immigration from seven Muslim-majority countries. He fired acting attorney general Sally Yates when she ordered the Justice Department not to defend that illegal ban. For those who had eyes to see, Trump made no secret of his racism. And his rhetoric found a sympathetic audience.

In August, seven months into his presidency, far-right groups mounted a Unite the Right rally in Charlottesville, Virginia. The two-day demonstration attracted self-identified members of the alt-right: neo-Confederates, neo-fascists, white nationalists, neo-Nazis, Klansmen, and various right-wing militias. Some brought weapons. Many wore Nazi and Ku Klux Klan insignia. Others carried neo-Nazi artifacts, Confederate battle flags, and items featuring anti-Islamic and anti-Semitic symbols. They chanted slogans like "Blood and Soil," a rallying cry born in Hitler's Germany.

The Charlottesville event turned violent. Protesters clashed with counter-protesters, and more than thirty people were injured. Early in the afternoon of August 12, a self-identified white supremacist deliberately drove his car into a crowd of counter-protesters, killing a thirty-two-year-old woman and injuring nineteen other people. He would be arrested, tried, and convicted of first-degree murder. But that came later.

Reacting immediately, Donald Trump condemned "this egregious display of hatred, bigotry, and violence, on many sides . . . This has been going on for a long, long time." He then observed that "you also had people that were very fine people, on both sides." With those words, as Joe Biden remarked later, the president was assigning "a moral equivalence between those spreading hate and those with the courage to stand against it."

Ten months after Charlottesville, in June 2018, Trump's policy of separating migrant children from their parents at the US border began making headlines. Children were transported to special holding facilities, including a shuttered Walmart. During one six-week period, nearly two thousand children were taken from their parents. Trump claimed falsely that a law enacted by Democrats was forcing family separations: "We have to break up families. The Democrats gave us that law, and they don't want us to do anything about it."

A year later, hundreds of children were still being held. Two days before Trump celebrated the Fourth of July with a martial "Salute to America" featuring tanks, military flyovers, and a fireworks display in Washington, the Department of Homeland Security made public an urgent report on conditions in migrant detention centres in the Rio Grande Valley. Published photos showed adults and children crowded into cages. Some held signs up in windows, pleading for help. The report spoke of "serious overcrowding" and detentions so prolonged that they violated federal guidelines.

Children, separated from their parents, were denied access to showers and received no hot meals. At one location, adults were confined in spaces that were standing room only. Many had gone without showers for as long as one month. A diet of bologna sandwiches made some of them sick. On MSNBC's *Rachel Maddow Show*, Democratic congresswoman Alexandria Ocasio-Cortez observed that Trump "has systematically engaged in the violation of international human rights on our border." She noted that one child died while in custody. And she charged that Trump was trying to restrict every form of legal immigration: "This is systemic, it is wrong, and it is anti-American."

July 23, 2015: Donald Trump speaks to the media at the Paseo Real Reception Hall in Laredo, Texas. *Alamy*

Trump shrugged off this criticism. He never let up. Early in 2022, when Russian president Vladimir Putin announced, just before he invaded Ukraine, that he would recognize two regions of that country as independent, Trump hailed the move as a stroke of genius. Speaking on a syndicated conservative talk radio show on February 22, Trump said, "So, Putin is now saying, 'It's independent,' a large section of Ukraine. I said, 'How smart is that?' And he's gonna go in and be a peacekeeper . . . We could use that on our southern border. That's the strongest peace force I've ever seen."

Next day, at a Florida fundraiser, he reiterated that the Russian dictator was "pretty smart." After all, "he's taken over a country for two dollars worth of sanctions . . . taken over a country—really a vast, vast location, a great piece of land with a lot of people—and just walking right in." Trump would continue to celebrate Putin though the rest of his presidency and beyond.

This brings me back to that naïve American woman who wondered at my unseemly interest in the US political process and thought I should mind my own Canadian business. I could have asked her what she thought the French should have done in the mid-1930s. Should they have remained silent while, next door in Germany, the Nazis took power and began furiously rearming? Oblivious, self-absorbed, the French did not start seriously mobilizing for war until September 1, 1939, after Germany invaded Poland and launched the Second World War.

Early in May 1940, the Nazis bombed Dutch and Belgian airfields. They circumvented the vaunted Maginot Line and rolled over the French army. On June 14, motorcyclists led the invaders into Paris, roaring up the Champs-Élysées followed by German cameramen and broadcasters. Then came the Nazi troops, goose-stepping up that splendid boulevard while Parisians watched, sick with shock and disbelief. So began the occupation of France by its powerful next-door neighbour—a subjugation that lasted four years.

Given this historical precedent, and Donald Trump's tendency to praise dictators and admire invasions, I might have asked that friendly American how Canadians could *not* worry about what happens in the United States? Some will argue that Canada's contemporary situation is nothing like that of France in the early decades of the twentieth century. Fact remains that the US has already invaded Canada more than once. Even if we discount the splinter-group incursions of 1837–38 and 1866–71, we have to recognize two significant invasions. In 1775, during the American Revolutionary War, rebels marched north, occupied Montreal, and besieged Quebec. Then, between 1812 and 1814, American forces invaded Upper Canada repeatedly, managing even to sack York (now Toronto).

But now, in the twenty-first century, such crude approaches would appear to be unnecessary. Canadians have a habit of emulating the worst that comes out of the United States. Consider the insurrection of January 6, 2021, when a mob of Trump supporters attacked the Capitol Building in Washington, DC, bent on overthrowing the democratic process and keeping their man in power. They were delusional, convinced that the 2020 election had been stolen by radical-left Democrats. Five people died that day, many were injured—including 138 police officers—and damages totalled more than $2.7 million.

Surely, it would not be far-fetched to suggest that the "Freedom Convoy" siege of Ottawa in 2022 was inspired by the storming of the US Capitol? And so we arrive at a provisional answer to anyone who might not understand my keen interest in events that brought Donald Trump to power. Given his legal troubles, the man may be less of a threat than he was. But the dark forces that raised him up—the ignorance, the racism, the rage—are alive and thriving. They bear an uncanny resemblance to the anti-democratic forces that led to Francisco Franco, Benito Mussolini, Adolf Hitler, and the Second World War.

Totalitarian governments are centralized, dictatorial, and want more of everything. Hitler wanted *Lebensraum*, or living space. Joseph Stalin wanted world revolution. Since the mid-nineteenth century, a subset of Americans have frequently invoked "Manifest Destiny," the doctrine which insists that the United States is destined to rule all North America.

In today's world of climate catastrophes and ruthless autocrats, is it paranoid to suggest that some Future Trump, whoever he may be, will look north and cast a rapacious eye over Canada's abundant water and other natural resources? Canadian author and activist Maude Barlow has been warning about this through book after book. Three of her titles summarize her battle: *Blue Gold: The Fight to Stop the Corporate Theft of the World's Water; Blue Future: Protecting Water for People and the Planet Forever; Whose Water Is It, Anyway: Taking Water Protection into Public Hands.*

But threats come also from within. Certainly, we have more than enough white-supremacist or neo-Nazi groups functioning in this country. Barbara Perry, director of the Centre on Hate, Bias and Extremism at Ontario Tech University, has put the number as high as three hundred. Jonathan Kay, editor of *Quillette*, has suggested that this is a gross overestimate. The fact remains, a Canadian podcaster, one Gavin McInnes, founded the Proud Boys, the violence-prone far-right group that played a large role in the storming of the US Capitol on January 6, 2021.

Canadians on the far right see Canada's culture and politics as not especially different from those of the US. Ideologically, they are already collaborating. One need only think of the so-called Freedom Convoy that besieged Ottawa, and of all the Confederate flags mixed in with the Canadian ones, not to mention the signs proclaiming 1776 (the date of the declaration of American independence) and the MAGA regalia: "Make America Great Again."

As in the 1920s, when Parisians revelled in *les années folles*, so today many Canadians appear to be unconcerned that next door, an aggressive Republican minority has contracted a lethal virus: incipient fascism. In lieu of debating the nature of modernism, as literary types did in Paris, we Canadians argue about changing street names or toppling statues. Nobody seems too worried about what happens in the US when yet another demagogue becomes president.

Waiting in the wings, however, we find Matt Gaetz, a Florida Republican in his early forties who has emerged as the personification of the MAGA wing—some call it the "Putin wing"—of the Grand Old Party. Anybody who thinks Trump is *sui generis* and so one-of-a-kind that nobody could come close should check out this acolyte. Born like

Trump with a silver spoon in his mouth, an aggressive self-promoter with savvy political instincts and strong social media skills, Gaetz has figured in scandals involving corruption, illicit sex, influence trading, and fraud. Judging from a lengthy profile that turned up in *The New Yorker* in February 2024, we are talking Trump 2.0 with bells on.

Friends tell me not to worry. They point out that with the 2020 election of Joe Biden, sanity returned to the White House. True enough. But how long will the respite last? As many Americans have eloquently argued—among them historians Timothy Snyder, Robert O. Paxton, and Anne Applebaum—the authoritarianism of far-right Republicans remains a real and present danger. Thanks to checks and balances in the American system, Donald J. Trump never gained complete control—never became quite the Putin-like dictator he so admired. And, yes, he was voted out of office. But in the Republican Party, his legacy and influence continue to thrive.

Sooner or later, the radical right wing of the Republican Party will elect as president either Trump himself or another quasi-fascist to drive their agenda. In a recent book called *Canada Alone: Navigating the Post-American World*, Canadian political scientist Kim Richard Nossal describes that agenda as anti-democratic, authoritarian, illiberal, xenophobic, and racist. Sooner or later, Trumpism will rage again, possibly in more virulent and aggressive form. What happens when that next demagogue becomes president? What then?

Mark Twain is among those who have insisted, "History never repeats itself, but it does often rhyme." What nobody wants to hear in the foreseeable future is anything that sounds like Europe in the last century, when racist madness seized the most powerful nation on the continent, which then proceeded to run amok. Alas, what we want and what we get may be two different things.

2

Expatriates in Paris

TWENTY MILLION PEOPLE, give or take. That's the number who lost their lives during the First World War (1914–18). *Britannica* goes with 8.5 million soldiers and 13 million civilians. The *Centre virtuel de la connaissance sur l'Europe* offers 9.7 million military personnel and 10 million civilians. Basically, we are looking at half the population of contemporary Canada. Dead soldiers included 59,544 members of the Canadian Expeditionary Force, 51,748 of them dying in action. In France, with a population approaching 40 million in 1914, this "Great War" killed almost 1.5 million and wounded another 3 million. The war ended with the Treaty of Versailles, signed in June 1919 after months of political wrangling.

Then came the unofficial celebration—the Roaring Twenties or, in Paris, *les années folles*. In the Left Bank neighbourhood known as Montparnasse, night life whirled to a new level of crazy. "Le jazz hot" blew the roof off traditional decorum. Women bobbed their hair and dressed like men. Revellers and *flâneurs* sampled opium and absinthe and saw that they were good. Writers, artists, and poseurs of every kind joined the party. American novelist John Dos Passos suggested that the end of the war precipitated a creative tidal wave.

The semi-permanent expatriate community of Paris exploded from 8,000 to 32,000. By 1925, encouraged by a favourable exchange rate, 400,000 Americans were visiting the city annually. Arrivals that year included nineteen-year-old Josephine Baker, a

Black American entertainer who, with her risqué costumes and erotic dancing, quickly became the toast of the town. Later, during the Nazi occupation, Baker would join the French Resistance. But now, as she danced through the 1920s, that idea was inconceivable. What? Germans invade and occupy France? Are you crazy?

Most of the revellers remained oblivious to what was happening next door. Among literary types who would shape the popular image of the era, modernism—an artistic movement bent on breaking with traditional styles and forms—became *de rigueur*. Such French authors as André Breton and Louis Aragon took to ridiculing bourgeois morality and antiquated conventions. Surrealists denounced Dadaists and vice versa. French writers turned up at public events to shout each other down while shaking rattles and clanging bells.

Among literary expatriates, the Buddha-like Gertrude Stein became a cult figure and salon host, though her reputation took a hit when the "masterpiece" she had been boasting about for years finally appeared in print. The year before that, in 1924, the American poet Ezra Pound, having sojourned in Paris for more than a decade, moved to Rapallo, Italy, from whence in the 1940s he would disgrace himself by becoming a megaphone for fascist propaganda.

James Joyce remained in Paris, a living legend, though excerpts from what he called his "Work in Progress"—the extraordinary *Finnegans Wake*—left readers scratching their heads. He had made his reputation with *Ulysses*, published in 1922 with the help of bookseller Sylvia Beach, an American expatriate who was thriving with her Left Bank shop, Shakespeare and Company. Countless writers came and went, among them Kay Boyle, Robert McAlmon, Ford Madox Ford, Jean Rhys, Janet Flanner, and the young Canadian poet John Glassco, not to forget Dos Passos, Ernest Hemingway, F. Scott Fitzgerald, and Canadian fictioneer Morley Callaghan.

Callaghan, late to the party, arrived in Paris in April 1929. Twenty-six years old, and with his writing career just taking off, this former *Toronto Star* scribe could hardly wait to join the literary expatriates of Paris. He saw himself rubbing shoulders with Hemingway and Fitzgerald and Stein and maybe meeting Joyce. Paris was going to be magical.

His dreams and fond imaginings would fall victim to the navel-gazing that made most native French and expatriate writers oblivious to the looming nightmare. The darkness was not total, of course. In the autumn of 1929, Callaghan showed signs of awakening. When Fitzgerald asked him if he had yet met Stein, the young Canadian said no—and that he had no wish to do so.

In *That Summer in Paris*, Callaghan explains that he had waded through Stein's supposed masterpiece, *The Making of Americans*, and realized that the guru had nothing to say: "As for her deluded coterie, well, I had no interest in finding one of them who would lead me shyly to her den." With that decision, Callaghan avoided anything resembling the Hemingway–Stein debacle, which would evolve into a bitter, energy-draining feud that lasted decades.

In the beginning, a bedazzled Hemingway—in his early twenties and newly arrived in the City of Light—had been happy to sit at the feet of Stein, who at age forty-eight was just two years younger than his mother. "Gertrude Stein and me are just like brothers," he wrote to novelist Sherwood Anderson, who had sent along a letter of introduction. Early in 1924, Hemingway convinced Ford Madox Ford to publish a long excerpt from *The Making of Americans* in his magazine and hand-copied more than one hundred pages of typescript to make publication possible. Not only that, but he made Stein and her partner, Alice B. Toklas, godmothers to his first-born son.

Things took a sour turn in November 1925. Hemingway blasted out a short vicious book—a parody of his friend and sponsor Sherwood Anderson—to break a publishing contract so he could sign with another house. In *The Torrents of Spring*, Hemingway also ridiculed Stein, though less ferociously. To Ezra Pound, he declared that he meant to expose Anderson, Stein, Sinclair Lewis and "all the rest of the pretentious faking bastards." Stein didn't care for Hem's new attitude and so was born that decades-long feud.

That extended fracas speaks to the self-absorbedness of expatriate Paris. Writing in the early 1960s, Callaghan could recall no discussions about economics or politics or what was happening in Germany, and noted that "no one stood up and shouted about the necessity of a social conscience." The insularity of this little universe was not airtight. Hemingway did venture outside Paris. In 1920, having written for the *Kansas City Star*, he had drawn on family connections, moved to Toronto, and begun freelancing for the *Toronto Star*. The following year, newly married and based in Paris, he had begun working as a foreign correspondent for the Toronto paper.

In June 1922, reporting for the *Star*, Hemingway went to Milan to profile Benito Mussolini, who boasted that the Fascist movement was now half a million strong—"a political party," Hemingway wrote, "organized as a military force." The young American, not yet twenty-three, perceived that the political situation was volatile and reflected that "the question is now, what does Mussolini . . . intend to do" with that force?

In a second article, Hemingway focused on the Fascists, describing them as "black-shirted, knife-carrying, club-swinging, quick-stepping, nineteen-year-old potshot patriots." Acting on orders from Mussolini, 15,000 of them had occupied Bologna on June 1, 1922, burning the telegraph and post offices and thrashing anyone who protested. Then they withdrew, threatening that next time they would bring 50,000 men who "would kill instead of beating up." Having acquired a taste for violence, the Fascists, Hemingway wrote, "kept on fighting, burning, pillaging anything resembling communism." The whole business, he concluded, had "the quiet and peaceful look of a three-year-old child playing with a live Mills bomb."

Seven months later, Hemingway again wrote about Mussolini, this time while covering an international treaty conference in Lausanne, Switzerland. The previous October, with his march on Rome, Mussolini had seized control of Italy. Yet Hemingway judged him to be "the biggest bluff in Europe." As reporters crowded into the room where Il Duce sat at his desk, Hemingway noticed that the Italian leader was pretending to read a book—a French–English dictionary he was holding upside down. That observation gave Hemingway his angle. He closed the article by speculating (wrongly) that a new opposition would arise, led by the swashbuckling literary figure Gabriele D'Annunzio, who had strongly influenced Mussolini. Instead, D'Annunzio would be badly injured when he "fell" out a window.

Early in April 1923, again writing for the *Star*, Hemingway spent ten days in Germany. He then produced his best feature articles of the decade. He wrote about the French occupation of the Ruhr Valley and "the crippling of German industries"—twin results of the Treaty of Versailles. He wrote of skyrocketing inflation and "amateur starvers" who hid their condition until they died. From Düsseldorf he began one piece, "You feel the hate in the Ruhr as an actual concrete thing." Germans would look away when they passed French sentries outside government buildings and straight ahead when they passed French soldiers in the street.

Hemingway observed that the workers "are sick of passive resistance." And he described one French-German incident after hearing at least fifteen versions of what happened to kill thirteen people. He did not think the French occupation of the Ruhr could last much longer. It had weakened Germany, revived old hatreds, and caused much suffering. But had it strengthened France?

The obvious answer was no. Indeed, it may have doomed France. The French accepted a restructuring plan in 1924 and had withdrawn from the Ruhr by August 1925. By then, the French occupation of the area had helped foster radical right-wing movements like the one that would be led by Adolf Hitler. But neither Hemingway nor the other navel-gazing *artistes* of the Left Bank took notice. Savvy politicians remained oblivious.

3 / Even Churchill Sleeping

LATE IN THE summer of 1929, when Morley Callaghan was in Paris, Winston Churchill visited Canada. Formerly secretary of state for the colonies, he was now a much-reduced parliamentary backbencher. Yet in Montreal, speaking in the ballroom of the Windsor Hotel, he drew an overflow audience of 1,400 that spilled out into the corridors and adjacent rooms. At this point, Churchill was lauding pacifism. He assured his listeners that, by gradually disarming, the British Empire was setting an example for the world. The British army was now smaller, he said, than "the little army that we had" before the First World War. The air force "is not half the strength" of that of France, and even the navy—"that vital foundation of the whole unity and life of the British Empire"—had made enormous reductions, the country agreeing that Great Britain and the United States would be "equal powers upon the sea."

This disarmament, he explained, was designed to maintain world peace as the "the first and greatest of the joint interests of the whole of the British Empire." That empire, he said, had all it needed in lands, fame, and natural resources and could absorb the whole energy of its many peoples for centuries to come. All the empire needed was a reign of peace, law, and order. Churchill noted that American president Herbert Hoover regarded the world as looking more peaceful than it had for fifty years. Hoover had told him that people faced many dangers but, happily, "a great war between the civilized powers was not among them." The British backbencher took this as a practical assurance that people could look forward to a prolonged peace.

Hence he championed disarmament for most. Britons and Americans could reproach France for maintaining a large standing army, but they might feel differently if they lived next door to a mighty nation with a military that was at least twice the size of its own and that had invaded twice within living memory. Churchill would not impugn the goodwill of their German neighbour, but if the French were to disarm completely, he was not sure that would improve the prospects for lasting peace. The way to promote universal disarmament, he added, was to develop goodwill among nations—and in this case, to encourage increasing trade between Germany and France.

This message of peace and hope appeared in the *Montreal Gazette* on August 14, 1929. Winston Churchill offered variations on it as he travelled across Canada, touring as a celebrity politician with a series of books to promote. Having held senior positions in the British cabinet, most recently as Chancellor of the Exchequer in a now defeated government, he had recently completed a masterly five-volume history of the First World War entitled *The World Crisis*.

With his brother, his nephew, and his eighteen-year-old son, Churchill, age fifty-five, had now embarked on a three-month North American ramble. From Montreal the men travelled west in a private railway car, stopping in Ottawa, Toronto, Winnipeg, Calgary, and Vancouver, with Churchill making speeches to enthusiastic crowds at every stop. From Ottawa, he travelled a dozen miles to visit Canadian prime minister William Lyon Mackenzie King at Kingsmere, his country estate in Gatineau, Quebec. The two had met briefly in 1900, when both were twenty-five. Now Churchill rehearsed his Ottawa speech and found the estate charming enough that he stayed until five o'clock. Next day, after the public luncheon, King showed him around the Parliament Buildings.

From Ottawa, Churchill wrote to his wife of being impressed with Canada's size and progress, predicting correctly that the population of 10 million would double or more in the next twenty-five years.

"The United States are stretching their tentacles out in all directions," he added, but Canada was becoming powerful enough in spirit to resist being engulfed.

In Toronto, according to local papers, Churchill highlighted the need to make business flow more easily within the British Empire and "to make the Dominions of the Crown more consciously a single economic unit." Crossing the country, he returned to this theme again and again, arguing that "the Empire belongs as much to Canada and Australia as it does to the mother country." By the time he reached Edmonton, he was predicting that, having come into its own, Canada might well evolve into a truly great nation.

Along the way, a journalist writing for the *Manitoba Free Press* had observed that British statesmen tended to hide behind a curious mask "of pleasing oddity, of simpleness, of naivete." Yet Winston Churchill himself, he added, came from a long line of adventurers, pirates, seamen, and soldiers of fortune. Churchill would draw on these traits, he predicted, while helping to shape the future of England.

Early in September, having reached British Columbia ten years to the month before the outbreak of the Second World War, Churchill declared the prospects for peace to be secure. At the Empress Hotel in Victoria, he spoke of the Locarno treaties of 1925, which secured the postwar territorial settlements in western Europe. Churchill assured his audience that as France and Germany achieved mutual understanding, all other difficulties in Europe would recede in importance.

From Victoria, Churchill went south into the US and then crossed that country from west to east. He arrived in New York City on October 24, 1929, the very day the American stock market began to crash, with its most significant losses occurring over the next five days.

That crash marked the beginning of the Great Depression, an unprecedented economic downturn that brought misery and suffering to the entire Western world. In November, when he arrived back in England, Churchill blurted out to his wife that he had lost £10,000 in the crash—the equivalent today of almost $1 million. Neither he nor anybody else imagined that things would get still worse.

A statue of Sir Winston Churchill outside of Toronto City Hall.
Ken McGoogan

4 / If It Can Happen in Germany

IN NOVEMBER 2016, when Donald Trump won the American presidential election, I could hardly believe it. Yes, I had worried that he might win. But to see it happen? This reality-show ignoramus? President of the United States? By the time Trump moved into the White House, I was reading *It Can't Happen Here* by Sinclair Lewis.

The publisher's jacket copy rang true: "A vain, outlandish, anti-immigrant, fear-mongering demagogue runs for President of the United States—and wins." The novel's anti-hero, "promises poor, angry voters that he will make America proud and prosperous once more but takes the country down a far darker path." Lewis published that book during the ascent in Germany of Adolf Hitler. After a bit of digging, I realized that Hitler's rise to power was even more mindboggling than that of Donald Trump.

The Treaty of Versailles set the stage. That treaty ended the First World War but included a controversial "War Guilt Clause" requiring Germany and its allies to make reparations for loss and damages. British economist John Maynard Keynes insisted that the harsh terms and excessive demands would prove counterproductive. Those in power, looking around at the devastation in their own countries, didn't listen. Swamped with debt, Germany suffered an economic collapse and then hyperinflation; the German mark became worthless. German citizens began starving. Widespread suffering made people susceptible to racist rabble-rousers who had long since chosen their scapegoats.

Still, Adolf Hitler? Born in a small town in Austria in 1889, the son of a customs inspector, he dropped out of high school in 1907 thinking to make his living as an artist. He moved to Vienna, convinced he had a vocation, but was twice rejected by the city's Academy of Fine Arts—to him a flabbergasting bolt from the blue. Struggling to survive as a painter, Hitler moved to Munich, where in January 1914, after being drafted into the army, he failed a military fitness exam as "unsuitable for combat . . . too weak, incapable of firing weapons."

That August, when the First World War broke out, the military became less particular and Hitler managed to enlist. He saw action at Ypres, Neuve Chapelle, and the Somme. In October 1918, while fighting in the Ypres Salient in Belgium, he was temporarily blinded by a British gas shell. He was recovering in hospital when, the following month, Germany surrendered—a capitulation that shattered him. He could not understand it: "I staggered and stumbled back to my ward and buried my aching head between the blankets and pillow." The army remained in the field, undefeated. Why this sudden surrender? Hitler embraced the incipient stab-in-the-back myth: the undefeated soldiers had been betrayed by politicians and, more especially, by Jews.

Back in Munich, physically recovered, Hitler went to work for the army's information department, gathering intelligence about small political groups meeting nightly in beer halls. In September 1919, he thrilled to the anti-Semitic ranting he heard from leaders of the German Workers' Party. He joined their number, started organizing and recruiting, and soon became the party's leading orator. By July 1920, Hitler had dramatically increased membership and transformed the organization into the National Socialist German Workers' Party, or Nazi Party. He became chairman in 1921 and quickly grew the membership to 55,000.

Hitler marvelled at the way Benito Mussolini led a coup in Italy, seizing power in October 1922 by marching on Rome with 30,000 armed men. The following November, Hitler sought to emulate that action with the so-called Beer Hall Putsch. This chaotic endeavour found him leading 2,000 men into the heart of Munich to seize power and turn the city into a base for a march on Berlin. The rebels encountered a massive police presence. The two groups exchanged shots, resulting in the deaths of sixteen Nazis, four police officers, and one bystander. In the confusion, Hitler fled in an ambulance but was arrested two days later and charged with high treason.

The ensuing trial, to Hitler's joyful surprise, drew extensive newspaper coverage and provided an international platform. He moderated his tone, railing against the Treaty of Versailles while arguing that his selfless devotion to the good of the people drove him to action on their behalf. He declaimed the stab-in-the-back myth. He denounced France and Belgium for occupying the Ruhr Valley—Germany's industrial heartland—to enforce treaty provisions.

Hitler's desk-pounding nationalist defence won widespread support among German-speaking people. The sympathetic judge found him guilty of treason but sentenced the ex-soldier as leniently as possible. He gave Hitler five years in Landsberg Prison in Bavaria, where he received country-club treatment, eating three-course meals, listening to Wagner on his gramophone, and receiving regular visits from fellow Nazis.

In December 1924, when Hitler had served slightly more than eight months of his sentence, the Bavarian Supreme Court pardoned and released him. Having failed with a coup attempt, Hitler set about seeking power through democratic means. While in jail, reasoning that the Communists had a bible in *Das Kapital* by Karl Marx, Hitler decided to write—or in fact to dictate—a book of his own, *Mein Kampf* (*My Struggle*). To type his ravings Hitler enjoyed the services of fellow prisoner Rudolf Hess, first his chauffeur and later his deputy Nazi leader. Pacing the floor with his hands behind his back, Hitler unleashed a deluge of hate-filled racial theories, asserting that the Aryan German people were a master race and the genetically inferior Jews were to blame for the depression that was destroying Germany. Jewish people were like "germs," Hitler wrote, poisoning German society. The only solution was to exterminate them.

In *Mein Kampf*, Hitler argued also that Germany needed to expand its boundaries and to start by reoccupying the lands that had been taken away under the Treaty of Versailles. Published in 1925, his book sold slowly at first. Massive loans provided by the United States had brought relative prosperity to Germany—a situation in which Hitler's message failed to resonate. But that would soon change.

Released early from prison, Hitler began drawing huge crowds to hear him speak. In March 1925, concerned by his growing popularity, the state government of Bavaria banned him from giving public speeches for two years. The following July, Hitler mounted a "Re-Founding Congress" for the Nazi Party—not in Bavaria, but in the city of Weimar, in the state of Thuringia. In August 1927, after the public-speaking ban expired in Bavaria, he staged a "Day of Awakening" in Nuremberg, the second-largest city in that state. Even so, in the election of March 1928, the Nazi Party received only 2.6 percent of the popular vote in the parliamentary, or Reichstag, election. For the Nazis, the future looked bleak.

But in November 1928, Hitler spoke for the first time at the Berlin Sportpalast and drew 12,000 people to this, the largest venue in Germany. Through the following year, 1929, as the most charismatic speaker of the day, Hitler became increasingly visible—and ever more popular. He looked forward to the national election of 1930. Then came what, for him, was a stroke of luck. Late in October 1929, the American stock market crashed.

The London Stock Exchange had plummeted after a leading British investor and his associates were jailed for fraud and forgery. That shook American optimism. On day five of the crash—Black Tuesday, October 29—investors traded 16 million shares on the New York Stock Exchange—the largest sell-off in US history. Despite brief rallies, a long, slow slide continued until July 8, 1932, by which time the Dow Jones Industrial Average had lost an extraordinary 89 percent. The effect was devastating.

Economists are still arguing about whether the crash spawned or merely signalled the arrival of the Great Depression that engulfed the US, Canada, and Europe—the worst economic crisis in history. Germany was especially hard hit. The country had borrowed heavily to stay afloat while paying war reparations. Now the United States, which was also devastated, called its loans. The German economy collapsed. Millions of workers lost their jobs and faced hunger and homelessness.

During the 1930 German election campaign, Hitler blamed this disaster on the reparations. He promised to repudiate the Treaty of Versailles, retake occupied lands, and create thousands of jobs. Germany's problems, he said, derived from an international Jewish conspiracy. This time, when the ballots were counted, the Nazis registered 6.5 million votes, or 18.3 percent of the total. The party rocketed from 12 to 107 seats, winning just 36 fewer than the Social Democrats and becoming the second-largest party in the Reichstag. The Nazis celebrated with an extravagant rally in Nuremberg. Brass bands led thousands of paramilitary troops (SA Brownshirts) goose-stepping through the streets.

Two years later, Adolf Hitler ran for the German presidency against an iconic figure, eighty-five-year-old Paul von Hindenburg, a decorated First World War hero who had held office since 1925. Propaganda genius Joseph Goebbels had the inflammatory Hitler giving as many as twenty speeches a week, flying around the country in a small airplane, using the slogan "Hitler over Germany." Hitler lost the election but garnered more than 35 percent of the popular vote, compared with just over 50 percent for Hindenburg.

That same year, 1932, brought two more elections as political parties battled for enough seats to command a stable majority in the Reichstag. In July the Nazi party won 37.3 percent of the popular vote and so became the largest political party in the country. In November, with the Communists gaining votes, the party slipped to 33.1 percent but still retained the most seats. With political chaos threatening, Hitler rejected an offer to become vice-chancellor, forcing a reluctant Hindenburg, on January 30, 1933, to appoint him chancellor—a post akin to British or Canadian prime minister.

Then, on February 27, 1933, fire broke out in Berlin—at the Reichstag. Firefighters received a call just after 9 p.m. They reacted quickly but found on arrival that the Chamber of Deputies had already been lost to flames. Hitler had been chancellor since January 30 but had yet to become the country's all-powerful Führer. The Reichstag fire, quickly recognized as an arson attack, would prove to be a crucial turning point in the rise of the world's most notorious demagogue.

Historians debate the origin of that fire, most insisting that the blaze was a "false flag operation" deliberately orchestrated by Hitler and the Nazis. At the time, a police investigation identified the arsonist as Marinus van der Lubbe, an uneducated Communist Party member. He was arrested in the Reichstag building shortly after the blaze began. He confessed and claimed he had acted alone, though most historians suggest that he was a simpleton goaded into action by the Nazis. Van der Lubbe was tried, convicted, and guillotined days before he turned twenty-five.

The day after the fire, the Nazi Party passed the Reichstag Fire Decree, charging that Communists were plotting to overthrow the government. Hitler convinced President Hindenburg to issue an emergency decree suspending civil liberties. The Nazis ordered the arrest of scores of Communists. By removing all opposition members from the House, they gained a parliamentary majority. In March, they passed the *Enabling Act*, expanding Hitler's authority, freeing him from all restraint, and allowing him to exercise the powers of a dictator.

In June, Hitler visited Mussolini with a view to strengthening diplomatic ties between their two countries. Both leaders wanted to halt the spread of communism in Europe and saw cooperation as a way of accomplishing this. The *tête-à-tête* also laid the groundwork for the creation in 1936 of the Rome–Berlin Axis, also known as the Axis Powers. Back in Germany, the newly appointed chancellor had recently begun advancing the idea of replacing the democratic Weimar Republic with a totalitarian "thousand-year Reich" that would restore a mythical past greatness and rule a racially pure German state for a thousand years.

Hitler meant to establish a New World Order with himself as supreme leader and, not incidentally, to drive all Jews out of Germany. Never mind that a census conducted in June 1933 determined that, out of a German population of 67 million, Jews numbered 505,000— less than 1 percent. For Hitler, that was too many. He passed laws banning Jews from the civil service and from working as teachers or professors. He then barred Jews from acquiring a university education and from practising medicine or dentistry. He disbarred one third of Jewish lawyers and, in 1934, forbade Jews from working as stage or screen actors. Meanwhile, sales of his hate-filled *Mein Kampf* skyrocketed. In 1933 alone, the book had sold one million copies—most of them in Germany, though the book was soon translated into multiple languages.

To erase the Jewish presence from civic life in Germany, Hitler removed statues and changed street names. Tens of thousands of Jews fled Germany, among them twenty who would win Nobel Prizes (including Albert Einstein). Hitler also bought armaments, built roads and highways, and gained the backing of the armed forces by rebuilding their strength. He suppressed labour unions and jailed political opponents.

The still popular but ailing President Hindenburg became concerned about the erosion of civil liberties and democratic institutions and also about the Nazi regime's growing control over the German military. But by June 1934 he was eighty-six years old and slowly dying of cancer. He complained that Nazi storm troopers were running amok and approved a speech by Vice-Chancellor Franz von Papen calling for an end to state terror and the restoration of freedoms. Hitler's propaganda minister, Joseph Goebbels, got wind of this, cancelled Papen's broadcast, and suppressed newspaper reports.

By this time, Hitler's cabinet had passed a law stipulating that upon the death of Hindenburg, the office of president would be abolished and its powers merged with those of the chancellor. On the brink of becoming dictator, Hitler grew paranoid about internal threats to his leadership. He created an inner circle of three men. Joseph Goebbels, minister of propaganda and national enlightenment, created the cult of personality around Hitler while advancing Nazi ideology. Heinrich Himmler served as leader of the SS, an elite paramilitary organization that evolved into a powerful police force. He also played a key role in implementing the systematic extermination of Jewish people and other crimes against humanity. Hermann Göring held various senior positions, including commander-in-chief of the Luftwaffe (the German air force).

In June 1934, Hitler charged Göring with undertaking a murderous purge of possible competitors in the Nazi party. The ensuing "Night of the Long Knives" ran from June 30 to July 2, 1934. Hitler was especially concerned about his long-time ally Ernst Röhm, who had turned the *Sturmabteilung* (SA), also known as the "Brownshirts," into a paramilitary force of more than three million men. Röhm had been seeking to merge the SA and the army under his own leadership.

Enraged by this initiative, Hitler dispatched execution squads made up of Göring's personal police, Himmler's SS, and the Gestapo, or secret police, led by Reinhard Heydrich. They kicked down doors, rounded up unsuspecting party members, and murdered them in cold blood. They assassinated at least 85 people, with most historians putting the total at between 150 and 400.

On July 13, 1934, in a speech to the Reichstag, Hitler justified the murderous rampage by denouncing treacherous, undisciplined, and "diseased" elements—Röhm was gay—and declared himself Germany's supreme administrator of justice. And on August 2, 1934, two hours after President Hindenburg died, Adolf Hitler became both head of state and head of government. At age forty-five, this racist psychopath had become an all-powerful dictator—*Der Führer*.

5
Halton in Wonderland

ON MARCH 4, 1933, fifteen months before Hitler became Führer, Canadian correspondent Matthew Halton checked into the five-star Hotel Adlon in the heart of Berlin. For journalists working in Europe, east or west, this was the place to be—complete with marble lobby, cathedral ceiling, bronze statues, and any number of colleagues drinking at the bar.

From his room overlooking the Brandenburg Gate, the twenty-eight-year-old Halton, having just arrived and with evening falling, heard the approach of bagpipes and drums. He stepped out onto his balcony. As the London-based correspondent for the *Toronto Star*, Halton had come here to cover the next day's parliamentary election, and to catch up on Hitler's Nazis now that the Reichstag fire had given them an excuse to suspend civil liberties. Brownshirts and the ss had spread terror across Germany, and auxiliary police would monitor the voting. Now thousands of Berliners lined the splendid avenue below, Unter den Linden, as the torchlight parade drew nearer. Steel-helmeted veterans of the First World War led the way, followed by goose-stepping Brownshirts and then black-uniformed members of the ss, most terrifying of all. "*Heil!*" the watchers cried, throwing up their right arms in Nazi salute: "*Heil! Heil! Heil!*"

Halton made his way downstairs and out the front door. He watched as ss troops passed the French embassy, where they began to sing a Nazi anthem whose title translates as "Victoriously We Must Smash France." He followed along and saw women who, having lost loved ones in the First World War, were now howling for revenge. At a central square, urged on by a Nazi with a megaphone, storm troopers hurled their torches into a bonfire, symbolically feeding the flames of a German resurgence. Later, back at his typewriter, Halton wrote that Germany was turning back time—dragging Europe back to the start of another world war.

Next day, the Nazis won the election, gaining 44 percent of the total vote. The party needed a couple of weeks to pass an *Enabling Act* that gave Hitler dictatorial powers and allowed him quickly to turn the Reichstag into a rubberstamp legislature. Hitler was preparing the country for a war of revenge, Halton wrote, one that would unite all the German-speaking people of Europe into a single nightmare nation-state.

The insight here is bold and surprising, especially given that Halton was not yet thirty years old and that his rags-to-riches story began in Pincher Creek, Alberta, a tiny town (population 1,200) in the foothills of the Canadian Rockies. That this young journalist should end up leading so many foreign correspondents in reporting on what would become the most important story of the twentieth century— surely, that is remarkable.

Matthew Henry Halton was born in September 1904 to working-class parents recently immigrated from England. In Pincher Creek they struggled to put food on the table, though they instilled in their son a passion for British literature, values, and culture. Matthew's mother became the local correspondent for the *Lethbridge Herald*, and at fifteen Halton himself began writing occasionally for the paper. He later credited *Herald* publisher W.A. Buchanan, a former Ontario newspaperman, with teaching him the basics of reporting and editing.

Halton graduated from high school in 1922 but, though he had displayed a remarkable memory and a special flair for language, he could not afford to go on to university. By working in construction and as a cowboy—Pincher Creek is in ranch country—he saved enough to attend teachers' college. In September 1923, when Ernest Hemingway was in Paris, sitting at the feet of Gertrude Stein, Halton was teaching in a one-room schoolhouse in the Porcupine Hills, some 90 kilometres from home.

In September 1925, when at twenty-one he entered the University of Alberta, he wrote for the student newspaper, the *Gateway*, and showed that he could recite from memory *The Rubaiyat of Omar Khayyam*—all 96 four-line verses. That year as well, he met Jean Campbell, the well-to-do young woman who would become his wife. Having exhausted his funds by the end of first year, Halton spent some months saving money while teaching in another one-room school, this one in the forested wilds almost 500 kilometres northwest of Edmonton.

Back at university in 1927, Halton received a life-changing scholarship from the Imperial Order Daughters of the Empire, which was active in Pincher Creek. It funded a year of postgraduate studies in Britain at a university of his choice. Halton studied journalism at King's College, University of London, and then, after gaining a one-year extension, moved to the London School of Economics. There, while writing a weekly column for the *Lethbridge Herald*, he studied with left-leaning political theorist Harold Laski.

In the summer of 1930, Halton convinced a fellow student to go backpacking on the European continent. The two young men crossed the channel to Belgium, and then Halton led the way through the battlefields of Flanders to Ypres and Passchendaele, where during the First World War so many Canadians had died. Onward the two went into Germany and the Rhine Valley, where they stayed in a youth hostel near the ruins of an old castle.

For four days, the two hiked and drank beer with young Germans, who were given to singing patriotic songs and creating a new world order. They were still angry about the 1919 Treaty of Versailles, which had taken German territory and imposed those harsh reparations. At this point Halton felt sympathetic: Who could blame Germans for hating a treaty that punished one people for a war that was the fault of many nations?

A great many Germans wanted revenge and would set out to get it, whatever the consequences. Realizing this, and that he wanted to report on what happened next, Halton reached out to his mentor, W.A. Buchanan. After a brief exchange of letters, that veteran journalist forwarded some of the young man's best columns to his friend Harry Hindmarsh at the *Toronto Star*—the same editor who had clashed with Ernest Hemingway and, while trying to cut him down to size, had driven him to quit the paper. Not only that, but twice Hindmarsh had threatened to fire the mild and unassuming Morley Callaghan. Yet this hard-driving editor was impressed with the columns he received from his friend in the west. He assured Buchanan that, on returning to Canada, Matt Halton could have a job at the *Star*.

Then as now, that paper—which dropped "Daily" from its name in 1971—was the most left-leaning major newspaper in Canada. Matthew Halton, his worldview influenced by Laski, felt right at home. He had to travel the same route that had tested both Hemingway and Callaghan, but somehow he blew through every stop sign. Hindmarsh loved Halton's audacity and flair. Assigned to write about a spring fashion show, the young man produced a whimsical series that incorporated imaginary interviews—a palpable hit.

After a few more minor successes, Halton made a breakthrough when he interviewed eighty-year-old Alice Hargreaves, the real-life inspiration for Lewis Carroll's *Alice's Adventures in Wonderland* and *Through the Looking-Glass*. As it happened, Halton knew those works by heart and wrote an extravagant yarn mixing contemporary quotes with bits from the original works. Readers clamoured for more.

In July 1932, Halton followed up with a series of imaginative parodies lampooning an imperial economic conference, casting major players as figures from *Alice in Wonderland*. Hindmarsh applauded. Even so, Halton was astonished when, one month later, that editor called him into his office and offered him a posting as the *Star*'s London correspondent. Hindmarsh was unhappy with the incumbent and wanted not just news and analysis but eye-catching features.

In mid-December 1932, accompanied by Jean Campbell, now his wife, Matthew Halton sailed east out of Quebec City on the *Duchess of York*. So it happened that three months later, in March 1933, Halton found himself in London writing about what he had just seen in Berlin—the cheering throngs hailing a torchlight parade of brown-shirted storm troopers marching along the city's main thoroughfare.

Halton became a man possessed. He learned to speak German, befriended an anti-Nazi German journalist he had met in Berlin, and interviewed Jewish refugees as they arrived in London. One of them was Albert Einstein, who had sought refuge after the Nazis targeted him and put a price on his head. In September 1933, Halton quoted Einstein warning that Hitler was determined to start a war and urging the civilized world to unite and eradicate Nazism.

Days later, with that prognosis ringing in his ears, Halton went back to Berlin and again checked into the Hotel Adlon. This time, he had secured carte blanche from his *Toronto Star* editors to explore Germany for two months and report on what he learned—a situation almost unheard of among working journalists. Halton responded by producing the newspaper series of a lifetime: thirty articles, later known as his "Berlin Series," in which he analyzed Nazism in damning detail.

In May, the legendary American reporter and political commentator Walter Lippmann had turned up in Germany, consulted a few Nazi officials, and returned home praising Hitler as "the authentic voice of a genuinely civilized people." Then there were correspondents like Canadian freelancer Erland Echlin, who would later be interned in Britain as a suspected German agent. Starting in late July 1933, in the *Montreal Gazette* and Toronto's *Globe*, he published a thirteen-part series celebrating the "order, peace and hope" restored to Germany by Hitler's Third Reich. He dismissed reported outrages against Jews as "imaginative lies" and wrote that Hitler was fearless and modest, and stood for peace.

By September 1933, when he again reached Berlin, Halton was fired up. Soon after he checked into the Adlon, he heard Hitler speak at a rally. He described him as "unprepossessing, even absurd" with his grand gestures and Charlie Chaplin moustache. Yet when this "little Austrian house painter" thundered about the degradation of Germany, he turned his audience into howling fanatics.

In a long article, Halton described how the Führer, his voice ranging from high-pitched and hysterical to "whispering solemnity," insisted that during the First World War, Germany had been stabbed in the back. That was when the shrieking began. Who did the stabbing? Hitler clenched his fists, made a face, and asked again: Do you know who did it? Of course you do! The Jews! The crowd went berserk. Halton felt sick with horror. But Hitler was not done. Why was the face of Germany scarred by the iron fist of France? Why, why, why? Because of the Jews!

This article served as an overture to the Berlin Series. Halton sent more pieces home almost daily, but his editors held off publishing the rest of them—probably at the writer's request, so that he could continue reporting truthfully. His days in Germany were winding down when, late in October, the *Star* published a pivotal article in the series. A banner headline across the top of the front page summarized succinctly: GERMAN CITIZENRY WAR MAD, SAYS HALTON.

The young correspondent was astonished at how quickly the totalitarian dictatorship of Adolf Hitler had replaced the civilized Weimar Republic. Where were the 19 million Germans who had voted against Hitler a few months before? In Berlin, Halton interviewed numerous Jewish shop owners and found most of them struggling to hang on in the face of a systematic attempt to eradicate them from Germany. Halton had read the unadulterated German version of *Mein Kampf* and understood that anti-Semitism was at the heart of Nazi ideology. He ridiculed Hitler's "tribal mumbo-jumbo" but warned that one day, the whole Western world would come face to face with this aggressive racism.

Before this series began appearing, and after considerable negotiation, Halton got clearance to visit a Nazi concentration camp. Early in October 1934, he rode a train 25 kilometres northwest from Munich to Dachau, which already housed three thousand prisoners. Halton estimated that two-thirds of them were former Communists, Socialists, Social Democrats, union leaders, and clergymen. The other third were Jews. Accompanied always by several guards, he could visit only certain barracks and workshops and later described his visit as "a prearranged farce"—though he did get the SS commander to admit that the camp was designed to harden the four hundred young guards and make them impervious to the suffering of others.

Halton also reported that, although the Versailles Treaty stipulated that the German army could not exceed 100,000 men, the country could quickly mobilize more than ten times that number. Early in November, when he was back in Berlin at the Hotel Adlon, a

Nazi official warned him that he should get out of Germany. Back in Toronto, the *Star* had begun publishing his series. From Canada, Nazi diplomats had complained. At first Halton shrugged off the warning. But then someone told him that he was being followed. Next morning, he went straight to the aerodrome and, without incident, flew off light-hearted to the freedoms of England and Canada.

Back in Toronto, as his articles appeared in the *Star,* Halton evoked strong reactions. A small southern Ontario newspaper, the *St. Thomas Times-Journal,* hailed his series as the clearest, most damning exposure of Hitlerism yet to appear. But fervent Christians, in particular, tended to attack him as a sensationalist and a warmonger. The Roman Catholic archbishop of Toronto, who clung to the idea that Hitler was stopping the spread of godless communism, urged his congregation to stop buying the *Star*. And in a letter to the *Lethbridge Herald*, which picked up the series, the Reverend C.H. Phillips denounced Halton's work as irresponsible. A prominent figure in the African American community, Phillips insisted that the journalist had no business making people worry that war might be on the horizon.

Wide recognition of Halton's achievement would wait until the 1970s, when Pulitzer Prize–winning journalist Leland Stowe remembered Halton for his moral courage in denouncing the threat of totalitarian dictatorship. And University of Toronto professor Harold Troper would laud his foresight in warning that Nazi anti-Semitism threatened the entire world with catastrophe.

6 / Enter Stalin Stage Left

THE MENACE OF totalitarian dictatorship is with us still, certainly in the opinion of American journalist Sarah Kendzior. In her book *Hiding in Plain Sight*, she argues that as president, Donald Trump was not just a racist demagogue but the leading spokesperson for a transnational crime syndicate linked to Vladimir Putin and the Kremlin. As early as 1984, Trump was quoted in the *Washington Post* as wanting to build an alliance with Russia. Counselled at that time by Roy Cohn—infamous adviser to the red-baiting senator Joseph McCarthy—Trump surrounded himself with men who had worked closely with Russian oligarchs.

Once in power, he treated Canada, Mexico, and the European Union as enemies while praising the authoritarians running Saudi Arabia, Turkey, North Korea, and Russia. As early as 2014, when Vladimir Putin took Crimea from Ukraine, Trump gushed on Fox News about how the Russian had "done an amazing job of taking the mantle . . . And so smart. When you see the riots in a country because they're hurting the Russians, OK, 'We'll go and take it over.' And he really goes step by step by step, and you have to give him a lot of credit."

But wait. Donald Trump is an exploitive capitalist. How could he so admire a communist autocrat working in the tradition of Joseph Stalin? The most convincing answer comes from New York University historian Ruth Ben-Ghiat, who argues that the Republican Party has "fomented a personality cult around Trump, similar to those found in authoritarian regimes." Writing in the *New York Times* in March 2021, Ben-Ghiat noted that early in 2016, ten months before he became president, Trump famously boasted that he could stand in the middle of Fifth Avenue and shoot somebody and he wouldn't lose voters.

Steven Hassan, a mental health counsellor and author of a book called *The Cult of Trump*, warns that cult leaders are delusional. Because of faulty wiring in their brains, they lack respect for others and have no aptitude for reality testing. As "malignant narcissists," they lack empathy, believe they are above the law, think nothing of making threats or committing violence, and trust nobody.

In *Twilight of Democracy: The Seductive Lure of Authoritarianism*, historian Anne Applebaum writes that people living in truly dictatorial regimes, like those of Hitler or Stalin, were afraid to speak out because doing so might cost them their lives. In twenty-first-century America, she says, people are afraid of losing their Senate seats or becoming social pariahs.

The case of Joseph Stalin is especially instructive because, like Trump, he recognized the crucial significance of being the focus of a personality cult. Applebaum explains that in the 1920s, as an undistinguished Communist apparatchik, Stalin realized that he lacked celebrity status. What to do? He commandeered and exploited another man's personality cult. That cult had evolved organically around the charismatic Vladimir Lenin, the revolutionary founder, in 1922, of the Union of Soviet Socialist Republics. An activist ideologue, the well-educated Lenin developed a variant of Marxism to accommodate a delay in the anticipated world revolution, and instead focused on the one-party Communist USSR.

Never mind that Lenin had declared that Stalin lacked the polish and sophistication to succeed him as leader and urged the Communist Party to choose someone "more patient, more loyal, more polite." Ignoring this repudiation, Stalin served as a pallbearer at Lenin's funeral. He then had 500,000 copies of a photograph distributed around the country—an image of himself and Lenin sitting together on a bench, suggesting a close personal friendship that never existed.

Exuding false modesty, Stalin identified himself as one of Lenin's students. In speeches to grieving Russians, he celebrated Lenin as "the great teacher of the proletarians of all nations." He changed the name of Saint Petersburg (then called Petrograd) to Leningrad. Through the latter 1920s, Soviet propaganda posters showed the two men together, thus merging the two political figures in the public mind.

In December 1929, Joseph Stalin turned fifty-one. He lopped off a year and, during nationwide celebrations of his "fiftieth birthday," began edging Lenin from the centre of the personality cult. He had a granite mausoleum built to hold Lenin's mummified body, but he himself would stand on a platform and salute as parades marched past. Statues and portraits of Stalin started springing up everywhere. At his public speeches, which were more like rallies, people would applaud for fifteen minutes or more, everyone afraid to be the first to show any lack of enthusiasm for the Vozhd, the "great leader."

To the Soviet press, Stalin was variously "great," "beloved," "bold," "wise," "inspirational," and a "genius." He took to exchanging gifts with children, who would chant a slogan that had begun to appear as an inscription over the doorways of schools and orphanages: "Thank You Dear Comrade Stalin for a Happy Childhood." The press incorporated religious imagery into the cult of personality, and processions formerly Christian in nature featured icons and images of Stalin. By 1936, Stalin had become the "Father of Nations."

This progression seems extraordinary given Stalin's peasant-class roots in a small town in Georgia, near the Turkish border. Abandoned by his drunken shoemaker father, young Ioseb Besarionis dze Jughashvili attended an Orthodox Christian seminary in Tbilisi until 1899, when he was expelled for disruptive behaviour and spouting Marxist ideology incompatible with religious teachings. As a youth he joined the Labour Party and began editing the party's newspaper, *Pravda*. In 1903, he gravitated to the Lenin-led Bolshevik faction of the party and began "expropriating" money for that cause by robbing banks and running a protection racket.

From 1912, operating as "Stalin," or the man of steel, he was arrested several times and exiled to Siberia, where he gained a reputation for raw manners and cruelty. After the October Revolution of 1917, when the Bolsheviks seized power, Stalin joined the governing politburo of the united Communist Party. He became general party secretary thanks to his organizational skills, which also earned him the nickname Comrade Index Card.

Seeing the adulation building around Lenin, he craved a personality cult of his own. Stalin faced long odds. He was short, just five foot four. His face was scarred by smallpox. He had a squeaky voice and spoke not like a well-educated Russian but with a strong Georgian accent. Neither a theorist nor a riveting speaker, Stalin had played a negligible role in the storied October Revolution of 1917.

By 1920, the well-published Lenin was welcoming eminent intellectuals to Moscow, among them H.G. Wells, Bertrand Russell, and Emma Goldman. But after burying his wife, the grief-stricken leader himself grew increasingly ill—possibly from undiagnosed syphilis. Toward the end of 1921, though still in his early fifties, Lenin was contemplating suicide and asked Stalin and others to acquire potassium cyanide for him.

On January 4, 1923, knowing that he would not live much longer, Lenin dictated an addendum to a wide-ranging political testament. In it, he repudiated Stalin and urged his comrades to remove the man from his job as General Secretary. Stalin was "too crude" for such a public position, he declared, and called on his fellow travellers to appoint someone more tolerant, polite, and attentive—and also "less capricious." This availed nothing as by then Stalin was too well ensconced.

Two months later, despite the efforts of more than two dozen physicians, many of them brought in from abroad, Vladimir Lenin suffered a third stroke and for a time lost the power of speech. He lingered for months, and when he passed away on January 21, 1924, officially of an incurable disease of the blood vessels, his intimidating successor stood waiting in the wings.

Stalin suppressed any indication that Lenin wanted him gone and launched a campaign showcasing himself as the close companion of the great leader. Whenever he praised Lenin, which was often, he contrived to bask in the reflected glory. He had photos retouched.

He commissioned paintings of fabricated scenes depicting himself alongside Lenin at crucial moments. He also began purging the party of potential leadership rivals among the "Old Bolsheviks."

The most formidable of these was Leon Trotsky, a Communist theorist and orator who put his own spin on Marxism. Trotskyism emphasized the need for continuous revolution, the vanguard role of the working class, opposition to Stalin's authoritarianism, and a democratic centralism that combined internal democracy and open debate. Unlike Stalin, Trotsky had played a key role in the October Revolution of 1917 and in the Bolshevik victory in the Russian Civil War (1917–22). From 1918 to 1925, Trotsky had headed the Red Army while serving as one of the seven members of the first Bolshevik politburo.

After Lenin's death, Stalin pushed Trotsky out of government by leveraging an alliance with two other Bolshevik leaders. This "Troika" isolated Trotsky, appointed loyalists to key positions, and then, in 1929, expelled him from the Soviet Union. From exile in France, Trotsky wrote prolifically, denouncing Stalin and his authoritarianism.

In the early 1930s, when Stalin looked westward from the Soviet Union, he saw fascism on the rise—and that Mussolini and Hitler were aggressively anti-Communist. To battle this rising right-wing tide, Stalin encouraged the formation of left-leaning coalitions and "popular front" parties throughout Europe. In May 1936, an election in Spain brought one of these parties to power.

Spanish army officers, among them General Francisco Franco, reacted by organizing to overthrow the newly elected government. This led to the outbreak, on July 17, 1936, of the Spanish Civil War. Franco's Nationalists had the backing of Spain's staunch Roman Catholics, landowners, businessmen, and most of the military, including the fascist Falange. Against them stood the popular-front Republicans, comprising farmers, urban workers, and the educated middle class. In Spain, Stalin saw a chance to extend the Communist Revolution beyond Russia.

France and Britain, fearing that the Spanish Civil War might spread across Europe, led the signing by twenty-seven countries of a non-intervention agreement. Despite having signed, Mussolini continued to aid Franco and his Nationalist forces, sending more than 220 aircraft, 2,500 tons of bombs, and 12,000 machine guns, among other materiel. Hitler, another signatory, also assisted Franco with men, planes, tanks, and munitions. Adhering to the agreement, Britain and France remained on the sidelines. From the Soviet Union, Stalin could see that if Franco achieved victory, the USSR would face three far-right governments in western Europe—Italy, Germany, and Spain. Four if he counted France. He felt threatened by that concentration of ideological hostility.

By this time, Stalin had begun fashioning a totalitarian society—one over which he had total control. This involved mobilizing the masses, getting regular people involved in political action, and using police terror to stifle dissent. By removing various Old Bolsheviks from government positions, Stalin had created openings for new party members who owed him their careers. He regarded competence as less important than loyalty to the leader. As the focus of a fabricated personality cult, Stalin was receiving seven thousand letters a month from ordinary Russians, most of them offering thanks and hailing his achievements.

In 1928, Stalin had launched his first Five-Year Plan, a program of declared goals to achieve development. He set out to collectivize agriculture, replacing independent farms with large, state-owned agricultural enterprises on which peasants toiled like factory workers. The following year, he decreed the elimination of the *kulaks*, a class of more prosperous peasants. He deported objectors by the hundreds of thousands. Stalin instituted the death penalty for the theft of food, which was now considered state property. In neighbouring Ukraine, these policies induced the so-called Terror Famine, as Russian troops seized grain and closed off territories marked by resistance. Anywhere from five to seven million Ukrainians starved to death, though the government denied this ever happened.

Stalin also emphasized heavy industry and the building of new plants and mines and even a showcase city, Magnitogorsk, organized around iron and steel works. Bent on transforming an agricultural country overnight into an industrial powerhouse, he introduced targets and quotas and punished those who failed to meet them, sometimes blaming non-existent spies and sabotage. A massive terror campaign ensured that both the first and the second Five-Year Plan (1933–37) were completed early.

December 1934 brought the mysterious murder of a leading rival, the Bolshevik revolutionary Sergei Kirov. Stalin massively expanded the secret police, the NKVD (later the KGB). He instituted the Great Purge of 1936–38, which killed 600,000 citizens, among them party officials, Old Bolsheviks, and ordinary citizens. He was bent on eliminating perceived opponents and resorted to mass arrests, show trials, executions, and repression. This period, also called the Great Terror, saw three public trials in which prominent Communists were accused of espionage, sabotage, and plotting against the state. After making implausible confessions, they were executed.

By 1938, Leon Trotsky had retreated to Mexico. From there, he played a key role in founding the Fourth International, established as an alternative to the Comintern (Third International), which was guided by Stalinism. Trotsky survived several attempts on his life, but in August 1940, one of Stalin's secret agents tracked him to his home in Mexico and killed him. By then, the Communist Party controlled not just the present and the future but also the past. It eradicated "non-persons" from the historical record and destroyed even articles *critical* of Trotsky, erasing all evidence that the man ever existed. This rewriting of historical truth would figure in more than one classic work of twentieth-century dystopian fiction.

Meanwhile, with civil war raging in Spain, Stalin worried that the Nationalists would win. Like Hitler and Mussolini, he continued publicly to support the non-intervention agreement. Also like them, he started sending military equipment to his preferred side. As the main supporter of the Spanish Republican Army, Stalin's Soviet Union supplied 1,000 aircraft, 900 tanks, 1,500 artillery pieces, 15,000 machine guns, and 500,000 rifles. For this the Republicans paid $500 million worth of gold, or two-thirds of the country's reserves.

Stalin encouraged the creation of diverse International Brigades, which comprised groups of volunteers from around the world, many of them ideologically motivated to battle fascism. He also sent organizers to mount large-scale guerrilla operations. As the war raged, political differences emerged. On occasion, Russian agents arrested and executed left-leaning allies who failed to support the Communist Party with sufficient enthusiasm. This included leaders of the Workers' Party (POUM), which welcomed an obscure English writer who arrived to join the fight: George Orwell.

7 / The Seer and the Novelist

ON THE EVENING of March 4, 1933, when Matthew Halton stepped out onto one balcony at the Hotel Adlon, a second journalist—a syndicated American columnist—emerged onto another. She, too, heard the cries—"*Heil! Heil! Heil!*" She, too, saw the torchlight parade and the marchers singing Nazi anthems. In that moment, watching, she realized that Europe had moved from one period to another—from postwar to pre-war.

Dorothy Thompson seems an unlikely prophet. She was born July 9, 1893, in Lancaster, New York, a small town near Syracuse. Her father was a Methodist minister originally from northern England who moved from one small upstate parish to another while struggling to put food on the table. Her loving mother died when she was seven and, when her father remarried in 1903, she went to war with her stepmother.

Eventually her father sent her to Chicago to live with two of his sisters, one unmarried, the other a widow. They were both interested in the arts—theatre, ballet, music, painting. In this richer environment, Thompson flourished. In 1908, she became a student at the Lewis Institute, a low-cost prep school, where she shone. The only young woman in the debating society, she also became a favourite pupil of a supportive and encouraging English teacher. In the spring of 1912, disappointed at being unable to afford tuition at any of the top women's colleges, she enrolled at Syracuse University, drawing on a scholarship available to children of the Methodist clergy. She completed her degree in two years and graduated cum laude.

At twenty-one, Thompson went to work in Buffalo for the New York State Woman Suffrage Party. She began by stuffing envelopes but soon became an organizer and a leading speaker. Late in 1917, the campaign having failed to gain traction, she moved briefly to New York City and then to Cincinnati, where she directed publicity for the National Social Unit Organization, which advocated preventive medicine.

She dreamed of becoming a writer and followed the international news. Thompson wept when, in 1919, she learned the details of the Versailles Treaty, immediately seeing them as a betrayal of freedom, justice, and tolerance. While working with the Social Unit and advocating for the right of women to vote, she published articles in three New York newspapers—the *Times*, the *Sun*, and the *Tribune*. In July 1920, with a close female friend, Thompson travelled to Europe, determined to become a foreign correspondent.

She wrote several articles after interviewing Zionist leaders who chanced to share her Atlantic crossing. Then, by a second stroke of journalistic good luck, she became the last person to interview the Irish Sinn Fein leader Terence MacSwiney before he starved to death in a Unionist prison cell following a seventy-three-day hunger strike.

From Paris, Thompson placed stories with the *New York Evening Post*, the *Christian Science Monitor*, and the Hearst chain of newspapers. She spoke rudimentary German and, on the advice of a veteran journalist, moved early in 1921 to Vienna, where her language skills would give her more opportunity to shine. She did publicity work for the Red Cross and then, after getting interviews with several eastern European leaders, landed a salaried position with the *Philadelphia Public Ledger*.

Thompson perfected her German and outhustled her rivals. She covered an abortive coup in Hungary, gained access to Empress Zita of Parma by disguising herself as a Red Cross nurse, and reported on a Polish rebellion in evening clothes and silk slippers. In 1925, she moved to Berlin and became the first woman to head an important foreign news bureau.

In 1923, she had married a strikingly handsome but philandering would-be writer who talked a good game but published nothing. She divorced him in 1927. On the day before she finalized her divorce, at a weekly afternoon tea for the foreign press, Thompson met Sinclair Lewis, the bestselling American novelist. She admired his works, many of which—*Main Street, Babbitt, Elmer Gantry*—presented a satirical view of capitalism. On a whim, she invited him to a dinner party she was hosting on July 9 to celebrate her thirty-fourth birthday.

She found Lewis—eight years her senior—wonderfully witty and entertaining and did not need any special gift to perceive that he was compensating for the startling ugliness of his red and pockmarked face. Thompson's heart went out to this unhappy man. She found him fascinating. To a friend she revealed that as the party wound down, Sinclair Lewis—who had been sullen and morose—suddenly came to life. He simply would not leave but stayed and stayed until, at three o'clock in the morning, he asked Thompson to marry him. Recounting this to her friend, she took a beat and wondered, perplexed, whether she should say yes.

A few months later, on May 14, 1928, Dorothy Thompson married Sinclair Lewis. According to one writer friend, she was entranced with his "violent loquacity." But soon enough, she realized that he had an alcohol problem. In those distant days, before the creation of Alcoholics Anonymous, nobody but family members grasped the destructive power of alcohol addiction. Thompson set out to save Lewis from himself. After marrying in London and taking a "caravan honeymoon" around the British Isles, the two Americans went house-hunting in the US. They bought a glorious two-mansion homestead on a three-hundred-acre estate in rural Vermont.

With the novelist at her elbow, Thompson improved her writing style. But if Lewis expected her to become an intellectual trophy wife to the great man, he was soon disappointed. As early as February 1929, Thompson writes in her diary of agreeing reluctantly to travel to Florida with Lewis because he had been drinking again and only some such holiday would make him stop.

Thompson missed the dinner parties of Europe, the evenings out, contact and conversation with others. She had told herself that she was married to a man of genius and that, through sacrifice, she could make him happy. Turned out she could do nothing for him. She likened him to a vampire who absorbed all her vitality and energy and then came slavering back for more. She did become a loving mother to a stepson and in 1930 gave birth to a son of her own. But soon afterward she left the baby with a nurse, went back to Europe, and resumed working.

This was an era when high-profile journalists would weave opinions into whatever they wrote. At this Thompson excelled. She emerged as an American leader in the crusade against fascism. And she talked, she talked endlessly, sharing her insights and observations with well-informed others. Lewis complained that if he heard anything more about political conditions and situations, he would shoot himself. And again: "If I ever divorce Dorothy, I'll name Adolf Hitler as correspondent."

Yet Lewis must have been listening carefully because Thompson's views pervade his anti-fascist novel *It Can't Happen Here*, which he wrote in three months and saw published in October 1935. The novel tracks the election of a fascist rabble-rouser who becomes a dictator after promising to rid the United States of crime, welfare cheats, immigrants, and a lying liberal press. The fictional fascist is Berzelius "Buzz" Windrip, who exploits fear and mindless patriotism while promising pie-in-the-sky reforms and a return to traditional values.

Much of the novel follows the reaction of Doremus Jessup, a "mild, rather indolent" editor of a small-town Vermont newspaper who begins to fear that he is witnessing the rise of a fascist dictatorship in the land of the free. Once in the White House, Buzz Windrip renders the United States Congress powerless, declaring it an "advisory" body. When members of Congress resist, he throws them in jail. He outlaws dissent and creates a paramilitary force called the Minute Men. They attack political dissidents with bayonets, round them up, and haul them off to concentration camps, where the recalcitrant end up in torture chambers.

Windrip curtails minority and women's rights. His supporters see these harsh measures as difficult but necessary to restore the US to greatness. Jessup, who opposes both fascism and communism, creates a newspaper called the *Vermont Vigilance*. Writing anonymously, he denounces Windrip's abuse of power. Betrayed and arrested, he ends up in a concentration camp. Six months into his sentence, he escapes and joins the resistance emerging in Canada— often the destination of last resort for fictional Americans fleeing a. nightmare. Over time, as Windrip's vaunted new age of prosperity fails to materialize, more and more of his fellow citizens become disillusioned. At this point, the novel moves from political dystopia into thriller territory as an army general stages a bloody coup, taking power by leading his militia into the White House.

In the 1930s, reviewers of *It Can't Happen Here* highlighted the resemblance between the fictional Buzz Windrip and two real-life figures. The first was the fast-talking politician Huey Long, the Louisiana governor and pipe-dreamer who set out to build a national "Share Our Wealth" movement with a view to running for president in the 1936 election. He was shot to death by a lone assassin in September 1935, one month prior to the publication of Lewis's novel. The second was Father Charles Coughlin, aka "the Radio Priest," a Canadian-American Roman Catholic clergyman based in Detroit. During the 1930s, as one of the first to use radio to reach a mass audience, Coughlin drew 30 million listeners to his weekly broadcasts. But as his rhetoric became increasingly anti-Semitic, he lost both audience and sponsors, and in 1939, his superiors in the Catholic Church cancelled his program.

By that time, the marriage of Dorothy Thompson and Sinclair Lewis was history. The two had ceased cohabiting in 1932, separated in 1937, and would divorce in 1942. Professionally, meanwhile, Thompson had come into her own as a journalist—queen of the foreign correspondents. Early in 1931, while stationed at the Hotel Adlon in Berlin, she had reported joining a crowd of 15,000 at the Sportpalast and listening amidst flags and banners and portraits of Hitler while the frenetic Joseph Goebbels spouted hateful Nazi propaganda.

Thompson was stunned by how much Germany had changed in the past couple of years. The country had flourished through the late 1920s thanks to American loans, but the 1929 stock market crash had ended that idyll. By 1931, six million Germans were out of work.

Banks failed and industries collapsed. This happened throughout the Western world, but Thompson found many Germans obsessed with laying blame, mainly on communists and Jews.

She described the curious experience of leaving a vast hall where the speaker had depicted the contemporary world as a ruin into which they had been plunged, only to drive along a brilliant thoroughfare lined with cafés, theatres, and super-cinemas, or else to enter the newly completed subway, bright and sparkling, with station walls boasting colourful murals.

Thompson's piece appeared in the *Saturday Evening Post* under the headline POVERTY DE LUXE—the first of a dozen long articles that would turn Thompson from a well-known journalist into a celebrity. She asked how this ruined nation had built the world's most luxurious ships, most modern hospitals, and most numerous swimming pools and sports arenas, not to mention the most lavish theatres. She contrasted the shabby, demoralized Germany of 1920 with the wealthy state she encountered in 1931. When she advanced this view in conversation, a German responded glumly, "Yes, we are the best outfitted poorhouse on earth."

In December 1931, Thompson secured an interview with Hitler himself. She had tried to reach him in 1923, immediately after the Munich Beer Hall Putsch, but he had gone into hiding. Then, after his stint in jail, he had disdained to speak with foreign journalists. Now, however, with the Nazis heading for power, someone among them—almost certainly Goebbels, the chief propogandist—got the idea of making an impression internationally. Thompson was the first journalist he contacted. Things did not go as intended.

On her way to meet Hitler at the Hotel Kaiserhof, his Berlin headquarters, Thompson was certain she was about to meet Germany's future dictator. But in less than a minute, while face to face with his "startling insignificance," she thought otherwise. She described Hitler as formless, inconsequential, ill poised, insecure—the prototypical Little Man.

This she wrote in an article, which she quickly expanded into a short book called *I Saw Hitler*, published in 1932. The man spoke, she reported, as though he were addressing a mass meeting. In answering any question he would look off into the distance, choose a theme, and then go into a trance, speaking almost hysterically, screaming once in a while, and sometimes banging the table. He was going to create a state, he told her, with authority above, discipline and obedience below.

At this point, like most analysts, Dorothy Thompson simply could not believe that Germany would let this confused little man take power. But before 1933 was out, she would describe Hitler's rise to power as a mass flight from reality. She denounced Nazism as a repudiation of the reason, humanism, and Christian ethics on which liberalism and democracy had been built.

To Thompson, as to Matthew Halton, the 1933 elections proved especially alarming. Hitler's private army broke up opposition meetings, terrorized people in the streets, muzzled journalists, and even assaulted leading Catholics. The Jews, of course, came in for special mistreatment. Thompson was in Berlin on February 27 of that year when the Reichstag burned. To Sinclair Lewis, she wrote that German Nazism made Italian fascism look like a kindergarten.

8 / Zamyatin Anticipates 1984

IN NOVEMBER 1931, a few weeks before Dorothy Thompson interviewed Adolf Hitler, Yevgeny Zamyatin left the Soviet Union of Joseph Stalin and settled in Paris. Few had ever heard of the man until Margaret Atwood spoke of him in connection with *The Handmaid's Tale*. She mentioned that this Old Bolshevik had influenced both her and George Orwell. In his novel *We*, she said, written in the 1920s, Zamyatin had laid out precisely where Stalin was taking the Soviet Union.

Born in 1884, the son of a Russian Orthodox priest, Yevgeny Zamyatin lost his Christian faith as a youth and became a Marxist. In 1902, he began training as an engineer with the Imperial Russian Navy in Saint Petersburg. He joined the Communist Party's pre-revolutionary underground and was jailed, beaten, and temporarily exiled for his pains. After the October Revolution of 1917, back in Russia, he became disenchanted with the Party's enforced conformity. He began publishing stories and essays while working as an engineer, both at home and abroad in Germany and England, where he spent two years supervising the building of icebreakers. He also read the dystopian works of H.G. Wells. In the early 1920s, he would translate several of Wells's novels into Russian and publish an essay on the English writer's scientific romances.

But first, in 1920, he began writing *We*, the dystopian novel that would influence not just Orwell but writers as different as Vladimir

Nabokov, Ayn Rand, and Kurt Vonnegut. One century later, writing in *The Telegraph* in November 2020, Margaret Atwood marvelled that not until the 1990s did she discover the novel—"one of the most important dystopias of the twentieth century, and one that was a direct influence on George Orwell's *Nineteen Eighty-Four*—which was a direct influence on me."

We unfolds in the twenty-sixth century following a two-hundred-year war that has wiped out all but an infinitesimal fraction of Earth's population. It takes place in the oppressively urban OneState, which is ruled not by Big Brother but by the Benefactor. People wear uniforms and have no names but only letters and numbers. The narrator, D-503, is a chief engineer leading the building of a spaceship designed to invade distant planets. Like all other citizens, he lives in a glass-walled apartment building under constant surveillance. The state controls even his sex life, ordaining that he meet and have impersonal, pink-ticketed sex twice a week with his assigned female, whom he shares with another man.

Our hero, D-503, meets a rebellious woman, I-330, who smokes, drinks, flirts with him, and even suggests a clandestine meeting. He flees, determined to report her to the Bureau of Guardians, but finds he cannot. Instead, infatuated, he begins an illegal affair with I-330, who reveals that she is a leader of the Mephi, an underground resistance movement. She takes him through tunnels and outside the Green Wall that surrounds the brutalist OneState, where he discovers a natural world peopled by wild human creatures bent on liberating the citizen numbers of OneState.

D-503's misbehaviour leads to his capture. In the end he reports, dispassionately, that he has been tied to a table and subjected to the Great Operation, a lobotomy that removes emotions and imagination and causes him to betray I-330 and tell the Benefactor everything he knows about the Mephi. He is surprised to have learned that I-330 and her comrades have survived torture, betrayed nothing, and been sentenced to death. Zamyatin does offer a final hopeful note in that the Mephi have destroyed parts of the Green Wall and citizen numbers are showing signs of rebelling.

Zamyatin's novel, like *It Can't Happen Here*, takes issue with the work of Frederick Winslow Taylor, a mechanical engineer who, in the name of efficiency, pioneered time-and-motion studies to control the lives of workers with mathematical precision. In the Soviet Union, both Lenin and Stalin sought to implement just such a dehumanizing system. In 1920, Lenin established the Central Institute of Labour to train workers to function like robots, believing this to be an improvement.

The following year, the Soviet censorship bureau became active and banned Zamyatin's clearly subversive novel even before it was published. The author responded by smuggling his work to the United States, where it appeared in English translation in 1924. Eventually, the book made its way into the hands of George Orwell, where it would help shape his anti-totalitarian masterpiece.

In 1927, Zamyatin sent the book to the editor of an anti-communist magazine based in Prague, which published the work in Czech. This translation incensed the Soviet authorities. Communist Party writers and critics launched a campaign against Zamyatin, attacking him as a bourgeois intellectual. Soviet magazines and book publishers closed their doors to him. Theatres refused to stage his plays. Former colleagues turned their backs. Once a leading member of the Russian Association of Proletarian Writers, Zamyatin resigned in September 1929, explaining that he could not remain part of a literary organization that persecuted, even indirectly, some of its members.

Early in 1931, Zamyatin decided: Enough! He wrote Joseph Stalin asking for permission to leave the Soviet Union. The reason was "the death sentence that has been pronounced upon me as a writer here at home." Receiving no answer from Stalin, Zamyatin appealed to his influential friend, the writer Maxim Gorky, who had remained on good terms with the Russian dictator.

Gorky invited Zamyatin to attend a twenty-guest literary dinner at his country home. In a book of essays called *A Soviet Heretic*, Zamyatin described how partway through the dinner, he wandered out onto the large stone terrace. Gorky followed and told him that his passport was ready: "But if you wish, you can return the passport and stay. I said I would go." Gorky's expression turned sad, and then he returned to the dinner.

That November, Zamyatin moved with his wife to Paris. There they lived poor and lonely until March 1937, when the author died of a heart attack. In the Soviet Union and elsewhere, his death went unremarked. Even George Orwell, obsessed by then with the Spanish Civil War, did not learn of his passing until later.

9 / Mackenzie King
Judges Hitler a Saint

IN THE SPRING of 1937, Canada's prime minister was still clinging to the view, originally espoused by British prime minister Winston Churchill, that the greatest guarantee of world peace was a strong British Empire working in concert with the United States. By then, the media baron Lord Beaverbrook, a Canadian expatriate, had become furiously anti-Hitler. And Churchill himself was churning out syndicated political articles warning that the Nazis were rearming for war.

That William Lyon Mackenzie King did not perceive Hitler as a threat to the Empire presents a puzzle. What was wrong with the man? Certainly, he lived in a world of his own. Born in 1874 in Berlin, Ontario—now Kitchener, two hours west of Toronto—young William had grown up worshipping his mother far beyond what might be considered typical of a son, regarding her as a kind of saint. She was the daughter of William Lyon Mackenzie, leader of a failed Canadian rebellion in 1837. The grandson did not lack intelligence. He earned a scholarship to the University of Toronto, where he studied law, politics, and economics. Then he earned a doctorate at Harvard University before returning home to Canada and entering public service. He became a trusted adviser and confidant to Prime Minister Wilfrid Laurier and, after his death in 1919, became Liberal Party leader.

King would become the longest-serving prime minister in Canadian history—twenty-two years over three non-consecutive terms. Having held the office from 1921 to 1930, he regained it in 1935.

Two years later, King sailed to London, where at an Imperial Conference he met German ambassador Joachim von Ribbentrop. This man would serve as Hitler's minister of foreign affairs from 1938 to 1945 and would play such a vital role in creating the death camps that, after the Nuremberg trials, he would become the first war criminal to be executed by hanging.

But now, at the Imperial Conference of 1937, King judged Ribbentrop to be friendly, pleasant, and "a man I could get along with quite easily." While the two men talked, Churchill happened by and, as King noted in his diary, the German cooled, "indicating, I thought, a sort of feeling that Churchill did not fully understand Germany." In fact, the British politician was beginning to understand it all too well.

Confident that he himself knew better than Churchill, King accepted an invitation from Ribbentrop to add a four-day visit to Berlin to his foray abroad—one that would include a meeting with Hitler. The German ambassador drew up a schedule, and on Sunday, June 27, King arrived in Berlin and checked into the Hotel Adlon. From here, journalists like Matthew Halton and Dorothy Thompson had worked tirelessly to tell the world that the Nazis were building a war machine to wreak havoc on the rest of the Western world.

King wasn't listening. Since the death of his mother in 1917, he had sought solace and direction in spiritualism, the belief that the living could communicate with the spirits of the dead. He engaged in seances and tried to contact his mother through mediums. He believed that he received guidance from the spirit world, though he knew better than to let this become widely known. King's intense belief in spiritualism, rooted in his veneration for his mother, probably made him less discerning than he might have been. But King saw himself as a man of destiny. Not only was he smarter than any mere journalist, but some higher power was guiding him to this meeting with Hitler. He would be the man, almost certainly, to establish a lasting peace with Hitler. All the signs and symbols said so. When he glanced at a clock and saw that the hands were perfectly aligned, that conjunction was indicative. He was on the right track.

In Berlin, therefore, on Sunday and Monday, he happily visited the touristic highlights of the city and met a few officials. Then at last the day came: Tuesday, June 29, 1937. That morning, as he wrote later in his dairy, while leaving the Adlon, the Canadian prime minister sensed "the presence of God in all this," guiding his every step toward this meeting on "the day for which I was born." Clearly, he was destined to bring peace to Europe.

After speaking privately with the Nazi leader, King concluded that the Führer was a fellow mystic who spoke the truth when he insisted "that there would be no war as far as Germany was concerned." Hitler's face, the King wrote in his diary, was "not that of a fiery, overstrained nature, but of a calm, passive man, deeply and thoughtfully in earnest . . . As I talked with him I could not but think of Joan of Arc."

Before he left Berlin, King wrote a note thanking Hitler for the gift of a silver-framed photo of the Führer—"a gift of which I am very proud." By this time, Hitler had already dispatched more than four thousand innocents to concentration camps and created laws turning German Jews into targeted second-class citizens.

In his book *Mackenzie King in the Age of the Dictators*, former diplomat and high commissioner Roy MacLaren delivers an exhaustively detailed, tightly controlled, yet merciless takedown of King's responses to both Mussolini and Hitler. If with Hitler we were not confronting the most obscene tragedy of the twentieth century—the industrialized slaughter of more than six million Jews—King's meeting with the Führer could be staged as a farce in which a delusional country bumpkin encounters the worst tyrant of the age and mistakes him for a female saint.

In March 1938, nine months after he met Hitler, and following the Nazi annexation of Austria, an unperturbed King wrote in his diary, "I am convinced he [Hitler] is a spiritualist—that he has a vision to which he is being true . . . that [his] Mother's spirit is . . . his guide and no one who does not understand this relationship—the worship of a highest purity in a mother—can understand the power to be derived therefrom or the guidance . . . the world will yet come to see a very great man—a mystic, in Hitler."

Here King was projecting what historian Charlotte Gray has described as his "pathological obsession with his mother's memory" onto Hitler and fusing it with his ludicrously inflated fantasies of his own significance. As MacLaren writes, King himself felt "he had played a central, even divinely ordained role in keeping peace in Europe."

Any number of Canadians saw Hitler more clearly. Around the time King was confiding to his diary that he was "being made the instrument of God," Canadian journalist Matthew Halton described Hitler at a Berlin rally as a demonic orator who "turned his hearers into maddening, moaning fanatics." Over the course of a month in Germany, Halton had "seen and studied the most fanatical, thorough-going and savage philosophy of war ever imposed on any nation."

When in 1938 King hailed the Munich Agreement, which ceded to Hitler an important part of Czechoslovakia (the Sudetenland), Winnipeg journalist J.W. Dafoe—who had repeatedly warned against Hitler's hate-filled rhetoric—wrote a scathing editorial in which he denounced the appeasers for validating "the doctrine that Germany can intervene for racial reasons for the 'protection' of Germans on such grounds as she thinks proper in any country in the world." And Ian Kershaw, the British biographer of Hitler, suggested with the advantage of hindsight that only the naïvely optimistic or "irredeemably stupid" could imagine that Hitler's ambitions ended with the taking of the Sudetenland.

Enter Prime Minister William Lyon Mackenzie King. Early on, Canadian diplomat Vincent Massey had deplored King's "ostrich-like policy of not even wanting to know what is going on." He concluded that King combined an anti-British bias with an extreme egotism. Then came *Kristallnacht*, when on November 9 and 10, 1938, Nazi thugs went on a racist rampage throughout Germany, destroying shops and homes, beating Jews and incarcerating 30,000 of them in concentration camps. On November 15, from London, Massey wrote to King that "the anti-Jewish orgy in Germany is not making [British prime minister Neville] Chamberlain's policy of 'appeasement' any easier." Chamberlain would not be deflected by disappointment, he added, and remained determined to stabilize Europe.

On December 3, King responded that "the post-Munich developments have made appeasement difficult and positive friendship [with Hitler] for the moment out of the question. That is no reason,

however, why the effort should be abandoned." If that is not suffi-
ciently disillusioning, worse can be found in the response of the King
government to the idea of accepting Jews into the country during the
Nazi persecution.

In one infamous incident, on June 7, 1939, Canada denied entry
to 907 Jewish refugees aboard the MS *St. Louis*, which had sailed
from Hamburg with 937 passengers. The ship found safe harbour
for the refugees in four European countries, but several of them fell
under Nazi control and 254 later died in the Holocaust. During the
twelve years of the Nazi regime, when Jews were being systematically
slaughtered and some Allied countries were admitting tens of thousands of refugees, the King government judged them impossible to
assimilate and accepted only five thousand.

To those of us living in the twenty-first century, the King story
offers countless lessons. One of them, surely, is to wake up to what is
happening around the world. Those who remain unconcerned about
the rise of fascism and neo-Nazism in other countries and who say
these "isms" could never take root here might do well to remember
that Mackenzie King—elected time and again to the highest office in
the land—once mistook Adolf Hitler for Joan of Arc.

10 / Churchill Calls for an Air Force

ON SEPTEMBER 30, 1938, British prime minister Neville Chamberlain emerged from an airplane in London, waved a piece of paper in the air, and announced that both he and Adolf Hitler had signed it. This Munich Agreement, he declared, signalled a mutual commitment. Never again would Germany and England go to war against each other. He had negotiated "peace in our time."

The British public erupted in jubilation. Across the pond, in the heart of Toronto, dozens of young men and women stopped where they were and stood motionless, digesting the news. Then, according to the *Star*, "their eyes alight, their faces gleaming, they danced happily off to celebrate the lifting of the curtain of death which hung like a black heart-stopping pall over their lives during the last week and more."

In Ottawa, the Canadian prime minister rejoiced. Two weeks before, when Chamberlain had announced that he intended to reduce escalating tensions by meeting Hitler face to face, King had issued a press release describing that decision as the right one and a truly noble act. In his diary, he wrote that Chamberlain would go down in history "as one of the greatest men that ever lived—a great conciliator."

Chamberlain had flown to visit Hitler in the Bavarian Alps. He assured the Führer that Britain would not seek to prevent the annexation of the Sudetenland, a border area of Czechoslovakia over which

Germany asserted a specious claim. Not only that, but Chamberlain had secured the backing of French prime minister Édouard Daladier, even though France—like Britain—had signed a treaty to defend the Czechs.

The previous March, neither England nor France—indeed, none of the world powers—had actively opposed the Anschluss, Hitler's annexation of Austria into the Third Reich. After all, the people of both countries spoke German as their native language. Czechoslovakia presented a different case, but British and French leaders wanted to avoid war at any cost. And in Munich, late in September, Chamberlain and Daladier abandoned efforts to defend the territorial integrity of Czechoslovakia and signed a pact that allowed Germany to annex the Sudetenland without opposition. The Munich Agreement told the world that the Czechs were on their own.

When Chamberlain arrived back in London proclaiming this agreement a great victory, one parliamentary backbencher recognized this delusion for what it was: "You were given the choice between war and dishonour," Winston Churchill told Chamberlain in the House of Commons. "You chose dishonour and you will have war."

On October 5, Churchill gave a passionate 45-minute speech to the House of Commons that is widely recognized as one of his most significant—and prescient. After opening with pleasantries, Churchill declared flatly "that we have sustained a total and unmitigated defeat, and that France has suffered even more than we have."

All of Czechoslovakia was doomed, he said. "Not only are they [the Czechs] politically mutilated, but, economically and financially, they are in complete confusion." The Czechoslovak state, he sorrowfully predicted, would soon "be engulfed in the Nazi regime." This would be "the most grievous consequence of what we have done and of what we have left undone in the last five years—five years of futile good intentions, five years of eager search for the line of least resistance, five years of uninterrupted retreat of British power, five years of neglect of our air defences."

Churchill recognized that "this great matter of Czechoslovakia, and of British and French duty there, has passed into history." It was "settled beyond recall." Turning therefore to the future, he regretted that "the system of alliances in Central Europe upon which France has relied for her safety has been swept away, and I can see no means by which it can be reconstituted." In recent years, Churchill had argued that "the maintenance of peace depends upon the accumulation of deterrents against the aggressor, coupled with a sincere effort to redress grievances." But while the Nazis had built up a formidable army, Britain had devoted itself to disarmament—a folly he had long since put behind him. Already the German army was larger than that of France, and next year it would be larger still.

Relieved from "all anxiety in the East" as a result of the Munich Agreement, the Nazis would be able to look in any direction: "If the Nazi dictator should choose to look westward, as he may, bitterly will France and England regret the loss of that fine army of ancient Bohemia which was estimated last week to require not fewer than thirty German divisions for its destruction."

Diplomatic relations might be possible, he added, "but there can never be friendship between the British democracy and the Nazi power, that power which spurns Christian ethics, which cheers its onward course by a barbarous paganism, which vaunts the spirit of aggression and conquest, which derives strength and perverted pleasure from persecution, and uses, as we have seen, with pitiless brutality the threat of murderous force. That power cannot ever be the trusted friend of the British democracy."

Britain's priority, Churchill insisted, must be "the timely creation of an Air Force superior to anything within striking distance of our shores." Above all, "we do not want to be led upon the high road to becoming a satellite of the German Nazi system of European domination."

The only way forward, Churchill added, would be to acquire "that supremacy in the air which we were promised, that security in our air defences which we were assured we had, and thus to make ourselves an island once again. That, in all this grim outlook, shines out as the overwhelming fact." He called for immediate rearmament, noting that "all the resources of this country and all its united strength should be bent to that task."

People should know, Churchill said, "that there has been gross neglect and deficiency in our defences; they should know that we have sustained a defeat without a war, the consequences of which will travel far with us along our road; they should know that we have passed an awful milestone in our history, when the whole equilibrium of Europe has been deranged."

People should "not suppose that this is the end," he said. "This is only the beginning of the reckoning. This is only the first sip, the first sour taste of a bitter cup which will be proffered to us year by year unless by a supreme recovery of moral health and martial vigour, we rise again and take our stand for freedom as in the olden time."

Six months later, on March 15, 1939, Nazi troops marched into Prague and occupied the whole of Czechoslovakia, so turning Churchill into a kind of prophet. Yet even then, William Lyon Mackenzie King clung to his belief that appeasement was the best response to Hitler's aggression. On April 27, he worried in his diary that bringing Churchill into the British cabinet, as many in Britain were now advocating, might be regarded in Germany as a threat which would provoke action. On July 1, when he learned that Chamberlain was making that very move, he told his diary, "there will be war without doubt, and London will be bombed [within] 24 hours . . . [I]f that report be true, war is inevitable." As if Hitler's aggression were contingent upon anything but his own insatiable lust for power.

11 / American Oracle Disrupts Nazi Rally

DOROTHY THOMPSON INSISTED on making a detour. As an internationally celebrated journalist and broadcaster, the forty-five-year-old public figure was supposed to be heading to the Hotel Astor (then at Times Square) to give a speech to the prestigious Phi Beta Kappa Society. She climbed into the limousine that collected her from her home on Central Park West and directed her driver to take her first to Madison Square Garden—or as near as he could get.

The streets were closed for two blocks around the site to prevent an estimated 100,000 protesters from storming the place. The date was February 20, 1939. On the pretense of celebrating the birthday of George Washington (February 22), the pro-Nazi German American Bund had organized a shocking festival of bigotry and racism. More than 20,000 American Nazi sympathizers took over the Garden to roar approval and offer straight-armed salutes as speakers denounced "International Jewry" and the socialist plots of "President Franklin D. Rosenfeld."

Thompson turned up to register her outrage. As a European correspondent for American newspapers, she had been denouncing Hitler and the Nazis since the early 1930s. And when she set out on that Monday evening to cause an uproar, she knew she would be plunging into a sea of Hitler portraits and Nazi paraphernalia.

April 26, 1939: Foreign correspondent Dorothy Thompson advocates repeal of
the American Neutrality Act before a foreign affairs committee. *Alamy*

She knew because in 1934, bored with living quietly in New York
and Vermont, she had returned to Berlin to report on the rise of the
Nazis—arguably the story of the century. On the morning of August
25, Thompson was finishing her breakfast in her room at the Hotel
Adlon when a Gestapo agent came calling. He presented an official
letter that referred to her "numerous anti-German publications" and
advised her that "the German authorities, for reasons of national self-
respect," could not offer her "a further right of hospitality." She had
twenty-four hours to leave the country—"in anticipation of formal
expulsion."

More than one American commentator described this as unprecedented. In fact, Canadian Matthew Halton had been told to get out of
the country the previous November. Shortly before that, Edgar Ansel
Mowrer of the *Chicago News* had departed under threat, questioned
even as he boarded a train. And British journalist Noel Pantar of the
London Daily Telegraph had been arrested and jailed before he was
thrown out of Germany. Still, Dorothy Thompson was the most prominent of these foreign journalists. And as the *New York Times* reported,

her departure brought most British and American correspondents "to the railway station to see her off and wish her good luck."

Thompson's expulsion from Nazi Germany made her an American heroine. She arrived in New York in mid-September 1934, disembarking from the *Leviathan* as a human symbol of the war against fascism. Thompson predicted a future of tyranny, murder, blackmail, and war. And the following month, in a speech to the Foreign Policy Association, she declared, "Germany has gone to war already and the rest of the world does not believe it."

Dorothy Thompson became an oracle. Like Matthew Halton, though on the larger American stage, she reached more people as a broadcaster and a speaker than as a print journalist. During the winter of 1935–36, she gave talks in forty cities throughout the United States. She started writing a thrice-weekly column called "On the Record" for the *New York Herald Tribune*. Syndicated through 150 newspapers, her column reached 7.5 million readers. Later, she would move to the Bell Syndicate: 200 newspapers and 9 million readers. Thompson had vision and she had reach. In 1937, she received honorary degrees from six colleges and universities—grateful recognition of her influence on public opinion. And she got her own weekly radio show on NBC—thirteen minutes every Monday night.

The following year, Thompson wrote 132 columns of 1,000 words each, plus twelve long analytical articles, more than fifty speeches, scores of radio broadcasts, and a book entitled *Refugees: Anarchy or Organization*, which treated anti-Semitism and statelessness. A book-length collection of her columns, *Let the Record Speak*, became a bestseller and, according to the *New York Times*, should have been called *Let the Record Shout*. *The New Yorker* estimated that between 1938 and 1940, Thompson published "On the Record" columns totalling 250,000 words—150,000 of them attacking Hitler's Third Reich. Case in point: when Germany annexed Austria in 1938, Thompson described the event as cataclysmic, predicting that as a result, either Germany would dominate Europe or millions of lives would be lost in another war.

So it was that in Manhattan on the evening of February 20, 1939, when the elegantly dressed Dorothy Thompson set out for the Hotel

Astor to speak to the Phi Beta Kappa Society, she well knew that she would call first at Madison Square Garden. As her car neared that destination, she could see that the streets were blocked off to prevent protesters from storming the Garden. She piled out of the car and walked the last couple of blocks. She elbowed her way to the entrance, held up her press pass, and cried, "Press! Press! *Herald Tribune!*"

One of the guards squinted at the pass, admired her splendiferous evening gown, and waved her through. The event was billed as the largest pro-Nazi rally ever held in the United States and, sure enough, Thompson found 20,000 wannabe Nazis crowded into the Garden. She took a seat in the front row of the press gallery, and as speakers took turns at the podium, she interrupted them with gales of laughter. When the leader of the German American Bund, Fritz Kuhn, began speaking, spewing the old familiar anti-Semitic hatred, Thompson increased the volume of her raucous laughter.

After ten minutes of this, the Bundists began shouting, "Throw her out!" Kuhn's security goons arrived, hauled her out of her seat, and muscled her toward the door. "Bunk!" she shouted. "Bunk! Bunk! Bunk! Nothing but *Mein Kampf*, word for word!" Fellow columnist Heywood Broun followed her out the door and tried to persuade her to fight her way back inside. But now a line of New York City police blocked her way. Thompson brushed herself off and then, still laughing, set out to find her car and carry on to the Hotel Astor.

By laughing out loud, *Newsweek* reported, Thompson had violated "one of journalism's oldest traditions of courtesy" and dramatized her contempt for bloviating American Nazis. *The New Yorker* judged Thompson's agitation "more damaging to the composure of Herr Kuhn and his mob than all the angry clamor in the streets."

PART TWO

The Spanish Dress Rehearsal

12 / Orwell
Boards a Train

IN 2016, WHEN mainstream media outlets reported the total atten-
dance numbers for the inauguration of Donald Trump, the newly
elected president dismissed the stories as "fake news." He and his
public relations staff insisted that the crowd was the largest ever to
attend such an event. Never mind that newspapers like the *New York
Times* and the *Washington Post* produced photographic evidence to the
contrary. In truth, the Trump event attracted about 250,000 people,
while in 2009, the inauguration of Barack Obama had drawn an overflow audience of 1.5 million.

So began the era of "alternative facts" and the forty-fifth president's war on truth, reality, and the mainstream media. If this was not
Orwellian, nothing ever has been. Like tens of thousands of others, I
dug out a dog-eared copy of *Nineteen Eighty-Four*, a nearly seventy-
year-old novel that now rocketed onto bestseller lists. I reread that
work and then turned to reading everything else George Orwell had
written.

In his 1943 essay, "Looking Back on the Spanish War," Orwell
wrote: "I remember saying once to [Hungarian journalist and novel-
ist] Arthur Koestler, 'History stopped in 1936,' at which he nodded
in immediate understanding. We were both thinking of totalitarianism in general, but more particularly of the Spanish civil war." Orwell

Novelist George Orwell in 1944, around the time he was struggling to find a publisher for *Animal Farm*. Alamy

also complained of "newspaper reports which did not bear any relation to the facts, not even the relationship which is implied in an ordinary lie."

To another friend, Orwell wrote: "When the fighting broke out on 18 July, it is probable that every anti-Fascist in Europe felt a thrill of hope." The fascists had been winning victory after victory. The previous October, Mussolini had taken Abyssinia (now Ethiopia). In March, thumbing his nose at the Treaty of Versailles, Hitler had reoccupied the German Rhineland. England and France had done nothing. But now, at last, a democratically elected government—that of Spain—was resisting a fascist assault, an attempted coup led by General Franco.

In England, the thirty-three-year-old Orwell—happily married and immersed in writing a book about the hardships of the British working class—resolved immediately to go to Spain, either to work as a newspaper correspondent or else to join the fighting. While finishing *The Road to Wigan Pier* as quickly as he could, Orwell went searching around London for newspapers that would hire him as a correspondent and so enable him to join the struggle.

His byline in those papers would identify him not as "George Orwell"—the pen name under which he would become famous—but as Eric Arthur Blair, who had come into the world on June 25, 1903. His father, Richard Blair, was by then forty-six and working in Bengal, British India, in a branch of special services. His mother, born Ida Limouzin in London in 1875, had grown up sporadically wealthy in colonial Burma. She married Richard in 1896 and they had two children. In 1904, she took Eric and his older sister back to England. For the next seven years, with a single brief interlude, her husband continued working in India to qualify for a pension.

Ida Blair set up house in Henley-on-Thames, a lively market town 40 kilometres southeast of Oxford. She encouraged Eric in reading and writing, and when he was eight, she managed through her brother to place him in a preparatory school with a good reputation. Young Eric hated St. Cyprian's, located south of London, but shone in literature and history. He managed to move on, as a subsidized King's Scholar, to the prestigious Eton College, where, among boys mostly from the upper middle class, he felt an outsider. A gangly youth, six foot three, he failed to win the scholarship he needed to attend Oxford or Cambridge.

His father, now finally retired and back in England, declined to pay for Eric's further education. His mother encouraged him to join the colonial service and go to Burma, where she still had relatives. In 1922, as he turned nineteen, Eric Blair took a week-long competitive exam to join the Indian Imperial Police. He landed a posting and, in October, sailed for Burma (now Myanmar). He spent the next five years with the police, earning good money. He trained at a main hill station (Maymyo) before moving through a series of increasingly responsible postings around the country.

Blair did a lot of reading, meanwhile, learned to speak fluent Burmese, and grew a pencil moustache. He spent a few months in Moulmein—now called Mawlamyine—where he visited his grandmother. But then, in Upper Burma in 1927, he contracted dengue fever. As a result, he took a scheduled leave a few months early. Back in England, to the consternation of his parents, the young man resigned from the Police to embark on a career as a writer—a boyhood dream long set aside.

After living with his parents for a few months, he moved into a cheap flat in working-class London. He had been much taken with Jack London's memoir *The People of the Abyss*—an early example of what today we would call "immersion reporting." In that book, the American writer describes his turn-of-the-century experience of living for weeks in the slums of London while disguised as a hobo.

Three decades after the publication of London's memoir, Eric Blair donned ragged old clothes and emulated this example. He wanted "to get right down among the oppressed," he explained later, "to be one of them and on their side against their tyrants." Blair drew on this experience for his first published essay ("The Spike") and for the London half of his first book, *Down and Out in Paris and London* (1933).

As for the Paris half, Blair had moved, early in 1928, to the French capital, where a supportive aunt, Nellie Limouzin, encouraged his writing. He wrote a first version of a novel that would become *Burmese Days*, put it in a drawer, and began publishing journalistic articles, many arising out of his preoccupation with the destructiveness of poverty. In February 1929 he fell seriously ill and was hospitalized—the first manifestation of lung problems that would eventually kill him. On regaining his health, he worked at a series of menial jobs, among them washing dishes in an upscale hotel on the fashionable Rue de Rivoli. Meanwhile, he wrote.

His first version of *Down and Out*, called *A Scullion's Diary*, drew rejections from two major publishers. Disappointed, Blair left the typed pages with an encouraging friend, Mabel Fierz. "Throw them away," he told her, "but keep the paperclips." She read the second draft of the book, *Days in London and Paris*, and in April 1932 took it to an agent friend, Leonard Moore. He tried to brush her off but finally read the work and saw possibilities. Eric Blair responded happily but told Moore, "If by any chance you do get it accepted, will you please see that it is published pseudonymously, as I am not proud of it."

Reduced to near penury, Orwell landed a job teaching at a small day school on the outskirts of London. He was there when Moore placed *Down and Out* with the relatively new (four-year-old) publishing house of Victor Gollancz. On holiday that summer, while staying with his retired parents in Southwold, East Anglia, Orwell courted Eleanor Jaques, a well-educated woman a few years younger. One afternoon, during a walk in the woods, they stopped and made love—an event that, suitably fictionalized, would make its way into both *Keep the Aspidistra Flying* and *Nineteen Eighty-Four*.

In the fall, while teaching again and losing touch with Eleanor, Blair edited his page proofs and considered four pseudonyms:

P.S. Burton, Kenneth Miles, H. Lewis Always, and George Orwell. One speculation is that with the name George, he was invoking St. George, patron saint of England. And the surname may have come from the River Orwell, which flows through East Anglia.

The following Christmas, while staying with his parents, he received a parcel containing the first copies of *Down and Out* by George Orwell. Blair continued to write articles under his real name until 1934. But when, in January 1933, positive reviews of the book started surfacing—despite the fragmentary, uneven nature of the work—he began to settle into his new identity: writer, George Orwell.

By December 1933, while teaching French at a high school on the outskirts of London, Orwell had finished rewriting a novel that drew on the five years he spent in Burma. Again he was less than thrilled with the finished product: too heavily influenced, he thought, by the romantic fatalism of A.E. Housman and Somerset Maugham. He had discovered James Joyce and decided that *Ulysses*, as he wrote to a friend, "sums up better than any book I know the fearful despair that is almost normal in modern times." He admired Joyce's stylistic and structural innovations, and his ability to enter the mind of "an ordinary uncultivated man" and track him from both within and without. Joyce, the quintessential apolitical artist, would be the last inappropriate model for the political Orwell.

A couple of weeks before Christmas, while riding on his motorcycle from west of London to the East End, Orwell got caught in a snowstorm. Back at the school, soaking wet and chilled to the bone, he came down with his fourth bout of pneumonia—the worst yet. Desperately ill, he became delirious. But by the time his mother arrived, having been summoned from Southwold, he was recovering. This incident would inspire an essay called "How the Poor Die," in which he reflected on social inequality and health care. His mother convinced him to quit teaching and return to Southwold, where he could devote all his time to writing.

Publisher Victor Gollancz rejected *Burmese Days* because he feared it might attract libel suits. A visiting American editor at Harper & Brothers saw less risk, suggested a few changes, and agreed to publish the book. Orwell began working on another novel, *A Clergy-man's Daughter*, but when he compared his artistry with that of Joyce, "it gives me an inferiority complex. . . . I feel like a eunuch who has taken a course in voice production and can pass himself off fairly well as a bass or baritone, but if you listen closely you can hear the old squeak just the same as ever." He finished the novel and sent it to his agent early in October 1934.

Later that month, Harper published *Burmese Days* in the US. By then, thanks to a recommendation from his aunt Nellie, Orwell had started working part-time at a London bookshop in upscale Hampstead. *A Clergyman's Daughter* appeared in March 1935. It drew qualified praise, and Orwell himself would later dismiss it as a "silly potboiler."

At a party co-hosted by his landlady, a university professor named Rosalind Obermeyer, Orwell met a graduate student—Eileen Maud O'Shaughnessy. The two spent the evening talking. Orwell walked her to the bus stop and, back at the house, told Rosalind that Eileen was "the sort of girl I'd like to marry."

Eileen had won a scholarship to Oxford and earned a degree in English Letters. She had taught school for a while and had then done social work and run a small secretarial agency before returning to university to pursue a graduate degree in educational psychology. Orwell courted Eileen for more than a year and married her in June 1936—one month before that history-stopping moment in Spain, when great hordes of people stood up to fight fascism.

Knowing that Communist Russia was actively supporting the democratically elected Republican government in Spain, Orwell had applied to the British Communist Party for a reference that would enable him to join the struggle. That party rejected his request, judging him to be "politically unreliable." He persevered and the Independent Labour Party gave him a letter of introduction.

With fighting escalating in Spain, Orwell worked furiously to finish his non-fiction book *The Road to Wigan Pier*. On December 23, 1936, eight days after submitting his final edits—and with his wife, Eileen, promising to join him—Orwell boarded a train heading south out of

London. He didn't see that he had much choice. He felt driven to join the battle against fascism. For his generation, this was it: do or die. He saw the moment and seized it.

13 / Malraux Takes to the Air

IN EUROPE OF the early twentieth century, anti-Semitism was shockingly pervasive. Books published in the 1920s and 1930s, even by visiting American, Canadian, and British writers, contain a steady stream of derogatory asides about Jews. And the French themselves were still dealing with the fallout from the Dreyfus affair, an infamous example of anti-Semitism that culminated in polarizing the country.

In 1894, a Jewish-French artillery officer, Captain Alfred Dreyfus, had been wrongly convicted of treason. He had spent nearly five years imprisoned in an island hellhole. Eventually, an open letter by the revered French novelist Émile Zola led to another tumultuous trial and exoneration. But the division in French society remained, embittering politics and engendering a right-wing Catholic movement called *Action française*.

That movement was still attracting adherents in the 1930s, despite the furious opposition of celebrated figures like French novelist André Malraux. On the evening of Saturday, July 18, 1936—the same date Orwell viewed as inspiring every anti-fascist in Europe—Malraux went to the theatre with his wife and a few politician friends. One of them—Pierre Cot, France's Air Minister—relayed the big news: the democratically elected government of Spain had started fighting back.

Until now, General Franco had been leading the military in a slow-motion coup against precious little resistance. Now, at last, the elected Popular Front government was taking a stand. Like Orwell, who was two years younger, Malraux thrilled to hear this news. But where the English writer was still unknown, Malraux was already legendary as both novelist and adventurer—the most celebrated writer in France.

Born in 1901, he grew up mostly in Bondy, a suburban town commuting distance from Paris. His parents separated, and André was raised by his mother and aunts. He had Tourette syndrome, a then little-known condition that induced involuntary motor tics and vocalizations. Doctors said he would grow out of it, but he never did.

During the First World War, as a high school student who commuted to Paris, young Malraux spent countless afternoons viewing movies, including propaganda films. He left school without graduating and, wanting to become a writer, set about educating himself, reading voraciously: Hugo, Baudelaire, Verlaine, Rimbaud, Stendahl, Voltaire. He haunted the kiosks along the Seine, figured out how the book trade worked, and began scratching out a living by buying and selling rare books. From age eighteen, as Symbolists, Dadaists, and Surrealists moved across centre stage, the autodidact Malraux entered the literary world by publishing articles in little magazines—for example, on the origins of cubist poetry. He joined forces with a publisher of limited editions, dabbled in reprinting pornography (the Marquis de Sade), but then withdrew to concentrate on writing. To obtain a deferment from military service, Malraux cited his motor tics and added a few imaginary ailments. Like certain others who came later, he had developed a theory of truth as being flexible, and as consisting of whatever suited him.

Malraux met the multilingual Clara Goldschmidt, a fiercely intelligent Jewish woman three years older, at a literary review where she worked. He charmed her with his eloquence, took her rowing, to art exhibitions, and to the theatre. The two slipped away to enjoy a romantic whirl around Italy, scandalizing Clara's wealthy family. Finally, in October 1921, with Malraux disguising the fact that he was just twenty, the two married. As a result, Clara came into a dowry that, in contemporary terms, would be worth more than $1 million. With that, the young couple went travelling—Prague, Vienna, Brittany, first class all the way. Magdeburg, Berlin, Tunisia, Italy, Greece.

Meanwhile, Malraux had invested almost everything that remained in Mexican mining stocks and—boom—the bottom fell out. The young couple was broke.

Meanwhile, Malraux had become obsessed with the swashbuckling T.E. Lawrence, a.k.a. Lawrence of Arabia, who had begun his writing career by co-authoring a book—*The Wilderness of Zin* (1914)—about excavating the ruins of an ancient city in what is now Syria. Lawrence created literature out of exploration and adventure. He was a writer but also a man of action—the perfect model for the young Frenchman. And after reading an unrelated article about Cambodian art, Malraux did some research and proposed to go to Cambodia with Clara and his oldest friend, Louis Chevasson, a lesser-known writer who published in literary magazines.

In Cambodia, Malraux had learned, where the predominant religion was Theravada Buddhism, many Buddhist temples, pagodas, and stupas stood abandoned, isolated, and filled—almost certainly—with valuable artifacts. In the late nineteenth century, along with Laos and Vietnam, the country had become part of French Indochina. It would remain under French colonial control until the mid-twentieth century.

By now, based in Paris, Malraux had advanced from buying and selling rare books to dealing in paintings and sculptures. With his enthusiasm, he swept up Clara and Chevasson and the three sailed from Marseille to Saigon, arriving early in November 1923. They made their way up the Mekong River beyond Phnom Penh and laid their hands on art objects deriving from the Khmer civilization, cutting out tenth-century bas-reliefs and sculptures from the Angkor Wat and Angkor Thom temple complexes.

Malraux loaded the stolen pieces, which he valued at about $100,000, onto a steamer in boxes labelled "chemical products" and sent them ahead to Saigon. But a suspicious French detective, who in disguise had shadowed the three from France, intercepted the cargo and arrested the art thieves at their hotel just before midnight. Although French archaeologists had been removing large numbers of artworks, even the fast-talking Malraux could not get away with this barefaced caper.

The French miscreants, benefiting from "colonial justice," were placed under house arrest at a hotel in Phnom Penh. After faking a suicide attempt, Clara gained her freedom and sailed to France, where she organized a petition to free Malraux. Signed by such literary luminaries as André Gide, François Mauriac, Max Jacob, Louis Aragon, and André Breton, it attested to "the intelligence and true literary value of this personality, whose youth and already-accomplished work authorize the highest hopes." Eventually, Malraux and Chevasson were convicted of theft but given suspended sentences and released. They sailed for Marseille on November 3, 1924—the day Malraux turned twenty-three.

Four years later, André Malraux published his first novel, *The Conquerers*, set in China during a tumultuous period in 1925. A politically engaged work, it made Malraux a leading spokesman for the younger generation of writers. As such, he was rivalled only by Pierre Drieu La Rochelle, who was eight years older, friendly with the accomplished Louis Aragon, and as yet politically uncommitted. Malraux's novel gained momentum after it was banned in Russia and Italy. Two years later came *The Royal Way*, a novel that recounts the exploits of two Europeans who travel into the Cambodian jungle to steal sculptures from Buddhist ruins. The work was marketed as an adventure but was really an existentialist novel drawing on the God-is-dead philosophy of Friedrich Nietzsche and suggesting that European progress was finished.

In France, intellectuals were held in high esteem—not least by themselves. By the early 1930s, left-leaning writers like Malraux were becoming uneasy about the rise of the Nazi party in Germany. They were so worried about the rise of Adolf Hitler that they ignored or made allowances for the ruthless purges of Joseph Stalin.

In March 1933, when the Nazis arrested Communist leader Georgi Dimitrov, Malraux went to Berlin with the equally famous André Gide, now in his sixties, who represented an older generation of writers. Thinking they might secure the release Dimitrov, they sought an audience with Hitler but met neither him nor any other Nazi of consequence. Dimitrov, accused of orchestrating the Reichstag fire, mounted his own defence and was acquitted and expelled to the USSR. Later, he was elected prime minister of Bulgaria.

That March, the Nazis also created their first concentration camp—not yet an extermination camp—at Dachau. Malraux had been visiting Germany since the early 1920s. Recently, he had seen posters—DO NOT BUY FROM THE JEWS—and learned that the Nazis were burning books in public squares. Drawn to anti-fascist associations emerging in France, he resisted becoming a card-carrying member of any organization. In 1933, at a Paris meeting of the Association of Revolutionary Writers and Artists chaired by Gide, Malraux made a short speech "against Hitlerism." Like many other writers, he felt uneasy about the emerging totalitarianism of the USSR but regarded that as a lesser threat.

French essayist Jean Guéhenno asserted that artists and writers had a duty to declare which side they were on. And Malraux raised his fist to shout that if war were to come, writers belonged in the ranks of the Red Army. In September 1933, Malraux wrote that authoritarianism alone "does not entail anti-Semitism." Answering a questionnaire in *Le droit de vivre*, a left-leaning French newspaper, he made a crucial distinction: Hitler was an anti-Semite, Lenin was not.

That same year, Malraux published his breakout novel, *Man's Fate*. Set in Shanghai, it treats the failed Communist rebellion of 1927. Some critics have argued, decades later, that the book exemplifies stereotypical Orientalism. The fact remains that the first printing was massive—more than 25,000 copies. And they sold out rapidly.

Publisher Gaston Gallimard campaigned furiously, and in December the novel won the Prix Goncourt, France's most prestigious literary prize. At thirty-three, André Malraux became a literary celebrity on the scale of Ernest Hemingway or, today, Margaret Atwood. In March 1934, Malraux overcame his reluctance to commit publicly and joined France's Anti-Fascist Intellectuals' Vigilance Committee—a decision that would lead directly to his engaging in the Spanish Civil War.

On July 19, 1936, the day after he learned that the battle had begun in Spain, Malraux and other prominent French writers sent a telegram "to the Spanish people struggling heroically for the cause of humanity as a whole." Known as the Telegram of the 400—"*Le Télé-gramme des 400*"—its signatories included Jean-Paul Sartre, Albert Camus, Louis Aragon, and Paul Éluard. France had also elected a Popular Front government, and Madrid was calling for military assistance. French prime minister Léon Blum, fearing that armed revolt might spread to his own country, refused to send aid.

Behind the scenes, after meeting with Air Minister Cot and his right-hand man, Jean Moulin—later to become a French Resistance leader—Malraux called a meeting at his upscale apartment on the Rue du Bac, inviting German refugees and other foreign nationals. The main problem, Malraux explained, was that the Spanish Republicans were short of airplanes and pilots. Taking the hint, Cot and Moulin asked Malraux, well respected as a literary man of action, to go to Spain and assess the situation.

The writer flew out of Paris three days later. Near the Spanish border, during a stop to refuel, Malraux heard rumours that Madrid had fallen to the fascist rebels. On arriving in Spain, he quickly determined that these rumours were false. He sent a telegram to Cot reporting that the Republican democrats retained control of Madrid. In Paris, right-wing newspapers denounced Malraux as a puppet to the French Communist newspaper, *L'humanité*. They described him as a thief who had stolen statues in Cambodia and a "Bolshevik" supporter of Communist Russia. Malraux was no Bolshevik puppet, but the rest was not entirely false.

Back in Paris after a week in Spain, Malraux immediately told prominent politicians that he would be joining the fight in that country, where he would help build an air force. Never had the man fired a gun, let alone piloted an airplane, yet few on the left doubted that he would put his plan into action. He turned his Paris apartment into a Republican hub.

Malraux managed to acquire 129 aircraft for the Spanish government, including 83 equipped for military use. French reserve pilots secretly flew these planes to Spain. They transferred 59 of them before the international embargo kicked in. On August 1, 1936, Prime Minister Blum committed France to non-intervention. Five days later, a defiant Malraux left again for Spain, bent on creating that air force.

Toward the end of the month, he did not comment when, in Moscow, Stalin had two political leaders, formerly his closest allies, shot to death: Lev Kamenev and Grigory Zinoviev.

Obsessively focused, Malraux just kept shuttling between Paris, Barcelona, and Madrid. In Spain, the aviation minister made him a lieutenant-colonel. He commanded the planes he imported as part of a Spanish squadron. Many of the aircraft were obsolete, and others were not properly armed. Between August and November 1936, with the French government refusing to be seen as breaking the non-intervention agreement, Malraux dedicated thirty-two men to the air defence of Madrid. These included seventeen pilots, one bombardier, three gunners, and five mechanics.

As the war unfolded, the squadron moved from Madrid to Valencia and La Serena and took part in at least twenty-three missions. Biographers differ as to how many missions Malraux himself flew on, usually as a gunner, and about how he got slightly wounded. At the Gran Hotel La Florida in Barcelona, he crossed paths with Ernest Hemingway, but the two famous writers scarcely nodded to each other. Shuttling through Paris and Geneva, Malraux drew attention to how Germany and Italy were providing arms to the fascists and called on democratic governments to end their policy of non-intervention. No response.

In November, the Spanish war ministry moved to centralize the air force, and Malraux had to relinquish his command. Yet many from his squadron, now renamed the André Malraux, fought on. In February 1937, back in Paris, Malraux learned that two Potez bombers from his squadron flew out to protect refugees fleeing from the coastal city of Málaga. Attacked by superior aircraft—German and Italian airplanes—one of the bombers made a forced landing and the other crashed into the water near a beach at Castell de Ferro—a disaster witnessed by Canadian doctor Norman Bethune.

Late in February 1937, to raise money and increase support for the cause, Malraux sailed from France and undertook an extensive lecture tour in the United States and Canada. Except in Montreal, where he did not have to work through a translator, he proved only marginally effective. But speaking to a *Toronto Star* journalist, he predicted that a world war would erupt within two years. He was off by six months.

Before undertaking this lecture tour, Malraux had roughed out a novel about the Spanish Civil War. He had worked on it while travelling and, once back in France, rented a chalet near Perpignan in the south of France and finished the book. Called *Man's Hope*, the novel takes place over eight months and ends in March 1937 with a Republican victory at Guadalajara. The good guys have hope.

Man's Hope arrived in bookstores just before Christmas 1937. It rocketed onto bestseller lists and stayed there. Its overtly communist themes drew mixed reactions from critics. Right-wing reviewers attacked the novel, although one of them, Henry de Montherlant, admitted that he would have liked to have both lived and written the book. A British historian, Antony Beevor, denigrated Malraux as a myth-maker who exploited the story of the Spanish Republic.

Olivier Todd, an avowed anti-communist who in 2001 published an unsympathetic biography of Malraux, compared *Man's Hope* and Hemingway's novel about the war, *For Whom the Bell Tolls*, and concluded that George Orwell's personal non-fiction account, *Homage to Catalonia*, transcended both. The English writer, he insisted, had fought in the trenches, not in the air, and demonstrated a more sympathetic view of the enlisted workers and peasants. Orwell even noticed such things as their "pathetic reverence" for those who could read.

The fact remains that in Spain, André Malraux put his life on the line to battle fascism. And he would do so again in France when, in 1939, the conflagration he had predicted exploded into the world.

14 / Bethune Reports from Madrid

IN JULY 1936, like George Orwell, like André Malraux, Canadian surgeon Norman Bethune became obsessed with the Spanish Civil War. From his home in Montreal, he followed newspaper and radio accounts of how General Franco was leading an armed uprising against the democratically elected government of Spain. For the past three years, he had been working as head of thoracic surgery at the Hôpital du Sacré-Cœur-de-Montréal while crusading to introduce a national medicare program in Canada.

Discouraged by his lack of success, he remained bent on accomplishing something major with his life. When he read that Franco was advancing toward Madrid, the forty-six-year-old physician contacted the Canadian Red Cross and offered to go to Spain. That organization responded that it did not intend to get involved in the Spanish war. Late in September, Bethune read a front-page story in a Toronto newspaper published by the socialist Co-operative Commonwealth Federation (CCF), which later became the New Democratic Party. Editor Graham Spry wrote in the *New Commonwealth* that an organization had been established to send a medical unit to Spain.

Bethune sent an advisory telegram and, next day, jumped in his car and drove 540 kilometres to Toronto, only to learn that the activist-editor had fabricated the story in a bid to kickstart just such a venture. Over the next few days, Bethune and the well-connected Spry put their heads together and set up a Committee to Aid Spanish

Norman Bethune in Montreal in 1928, soon after he started working at the Royal Victoria Hospital. *Library and Archives Canada/PA-160590*

Democracy (CASD). It would raise funds to buy medical supplies that Bethune would take to Spain to fight fascism.

By mid-October 1936, Bethune had quit his well-paying job. CASD announced his mission at a Toronto rally built around a visit by Spanish dignitaries. A similar rally slated for Montreal on October 23 was quashed by the Roman Catholic diocese, which supported Franco's insurrection, and by several hundred chanting students from the Université de Montréal. Next day, undaunted, Bethune drove 270 kilometres to Quebec City, bringing surgical instruments, blood transfusion equipment, antitoxins, and serums. He then sailed to Paris on the *Empress of Britain.*

Bethune visited the Spanish ambassador, handed him money orders for medical supplies—worth roughly $20,000 today—and in return received a safe-conduct pass allowing him to enter Spain. He flew to Madrid, took a room in the Hotel Gran Via, opposite the

Gran Hotel La Florida, and met up with thirty-five-year-old Henning Sorensen, a multilingual Danish Canadian who had agreed to act as his interpreter.

Over the next three days, with Franco's forces nearing Madrid, Bethune went from one hospital to another, offering to set up a blood transfusion unit using Canadian funds. None of them wanted to work with anyone who did not speak Spanish. Bethune applied to the International Brigades, those groups of foreign volunteers who had come to battle Franco, but the chief of medical services declined to bring him aboard. With war casualties imminent, nobody in Madrid wanted him to set up a unit.

But Norman Bethune was not one to take no for an answer. Born in Gravenhurst, Ontario, in 1890, the son of a Presbyterian minister and his missionary wife, young Norman moved with his family seven times within Ontario before he turned fourteen. Religion proved the only constant in his early life. In the 1890s, devout Presbyterians would say grace at the beginning of each meal, read the Bible for an hour each day, and go to church twice on Sunday.

After graduating from high school in Owen Sound, Bethune worked as a lumberjack in northern Ontario and then taught school in a one-room schoolhouse. He was studying medicine at the University of Toronto when the First World War broke out. Bethune joined the Army Medical Corps as a stretcher bearer. The following year, after training in England and while serving at the second battle of Ypres, he was wounded—took a piece of shrapnel in the leg. After spending three months in an English hospital, Bethune received a medical discharge.

He returned to Toronto, completed his medical degree in an accelerated program, and re-enlisted, serving this time as a navy doctor aboard a patrol ship in the North Sea. When the fighting ended in 1918, Bethune took a six-month internship in London, where he worked at the Great Ormond Street Hospital for Sick Children. Then, back in Ontario, he served in the Canadian Air Force. After a failed marriage and travels around Europe, he settled in Detroit, set up in private practice, and, his missionary side surfacing, began treating the poor. This meant working long hours in difficult conditions, and in 1926, Bethune contracted tuberculosis. While being treated at an advanced sanatorium in upstate New York, he told a fellow patient, "I'm going to find something I can do for the human race, something great, and I am going to do it before I die."

While analyzing the literature on tuberculosis, Bethune found an article on "compression therapy," an experimental technique that involved opening up the chest and collapsing the worst-affected lung. He insisted that the procedure be tried on him—and it worked. Discharged from hospital in December 1927, he moved to Montreal to practise thoracic surgery at the Royal Victoria Hospital.

In 1930, when the Great Depression rolled across Canada, Bethune saw that his patients were battling not just illness but unsanitary living conditions and a lack of continuing heath care. He opened a free clinic for the unemployed and began lobbying his fellow surgeons to reform the health care system. By 1933, tired of the lack of response among his colleagues at the Royal Victoria, he moved to the Sacré-Cœur Hospital in Cartierville, a Montreal suburb, to become head of thoracic surgery.

In August 1935, Bethune attended an international physiological conference in the Soviet Union. He inspected hospitals and sanatoriums and came away impressed by the Soviet system of free universal health care. Back in Canada, while trying to introduce something similar, he told the Montreal Medico-Chirurgical Society that Canadian medicine was a luxury trade, and that half the population could not afford decent health care. He was right, but the Society expelled him.

In November 1935, a disillusioned Bethune joined the Communist Party of Canada. The following July, when Franco led the anti-democratic coup in Spain, he turned immediately to that struggle. More than 40,000 volunteers from fifty-two countries would flock to Spain during the next three years. Norman Bethune went with the first wave, arriving in Madrid on November 2. By then, Italian and German planes (the Condor Legion) had bombed Oviedo and Gijón in northern Spain, and also Barcelona in Catalonia.

In mid-November, when bombing began in Madrid, Bethune saw men dying from loss of blood as they lay on stretchers. He wanted desperately to set up a blood transfusion service, but when even the International Brigades declined to back him, he decided to go independent. Using Canadian funds, he would create a mobile medical unit specializing in bringing blood transfusions to the wounded within a twenty-five-mile radius. For this he eventually gained the support of skeptical doctors with the Communist-backed *Socorro Rojo Internacional* (SRI), which looked after "the wounded, the orphans and the widows."

He wired home to the Committee to Aid Spanish Democracy, requesting enough money to buy a station wagon and fit it out. On November 21, bringing his interpreter, Bethune flew to Paris and then proceeded to London, where he examined the latest papers on hematology and bought a wood-panelled Ford station wagon. He installed a fridge, a sterilizer, an incubator, a water distiller, and shelving to hold bottles.

Bethune proposed to use the latest methods of collecting blood, storing it in vacuum bottles, and transporting it as needed from Madrid. Every day a regiment would turn up from which he would collect voluntary donations—one or two gallons of blood. He outlined his plan in a cable to the CASD, and the Toronto-based *Daily Clarion* published his appeal for funding to do this work. On December 14, Bethune set up the unit in a fifteen-room flat just below SRI headquarters in the Salamanca district.

Through newspaper stories and radio broadcasts in Canada, he appealed for blood donors, and soon people were lining the streets to give blood to the *Instituto Canadiense de Transfusión de Sangre*. Besides Bethune and Sorensen, the Canadian unit included a driver and utility man, two Spanish medical students, a Spanish biologist, an American technician, plus four servants (a cook, two maids, and a laundry man), all protected by a military armed guard.

By December 17, he wrote of Madrid that "about one quarter of the city is badly damaged and abandoned except by troops." Some 300,000 people had been evacuated, mostly women, children, and the elderly. Between seven and eight thousand civilians had "been killed by bombardment in the last month and many more thousands wounded." Yet he insisted that morale was excellent: "Madrid won't fall but will be the tomb of Fascism."

The previous day, three bombers had flown over the city, along with twenty-four pursuit planes, and dropped several tons of bombs. They made "an awful mess," but the water remained potable and no epidemics had broken out. The electricity was still functioning. Gas and coal were practically gone, meat was scarce, and the city lacked milk, butter, and sugar, though vegetables, oranges, and apples could be found.

Long a secret writer of poetry, Bethune came into his own as a war correspondent and speaker. He made a Christmas Eve radio broadcast beamed throughout North America, and he sent an open "Letter to All Canadian Doctors" inviting them to join him in Spain. He did another radio broadcast on December 29, in which he summarized the situation in Madrid. The city had fifty-seven hospitals of various sizes and more than 10,000 beds.

He brought listeners into a military hospital installed in the landmark Palace Hotel (Palacio de Cibeles), located in a prominent square in the heart of Madrid. There he set up an operating room in the splendiferous dining room. In one of his pleas, Bethune described some of the wounded: "Here they lie—row on row—Spaniards, English, German, Italians, French, Belgian, Scotch, Irish, American. The wounded soldiers of the greatest anti-Fascist army the world has yet seen. They represent the United Front of International anti-Fascism. They have fought this war for you and for me. They need your help."

On New Year's Day, in yet another broadcast, Bethune spoke of heavy fighting and how "the staccato tick-tack-tack of machine guns came through the windows, as if they were firing at the end of the street." Worse were the fascist bombers. Bethune described how five fighter jets attacked one solitary Spanish government pursuit plane. They set the plane on fire, but the pilot, as he went down, "charged full-out, head-on into one of Franco's planes. They fell together, in flames, crashing into a vine-covered hill one hundred yards apart. Both pilots were killed instantly."

Again and again, Bethune demonstrated that he could write as well as any professional journalist. On January 2, 1937, he recounted how a dozen "huge Italian tri-motored bombers" arrived and targeted a poor quarter of the city. "The massacred victims were mainly women, children and old people . . . No one can realize what utter helplessness one feels when these huge death-ships are overhead." No point going into a building: "The bombs tear through the roof, through every floor in the building and explode in the basement, bringing down concrete buildings as if they were made of matchwood."

Bethune wrote that after the bombs fell, clouds of dust and explosive fumes filled the air and the sides of houses tumbled into the street. "From heaps of huddled clothes on the cobblestones blood begins to flow—these were once live women and children. Many are buried alive in the ruins. One hears their cries—they cannot be reached."

Bethune was working eighteen-hour days with his blood transfusion unit. Hoping to expand its range, he travelled back and forth between Madrid, Barcelona, Paris, and Valencia. At one point, he flew from Paris to Valencia in one of the planes acquired by André Malraux. In Valencia, he got wind of trouble ahead. The Republican government was planning to centralize military health services, which threatened his unit's independence. Bethune remained optimistic. His unit now had a staff of twenty-five, including a hematologist, a bacteriologist, five Spanish doctors, and six nurses. Surely, the government would think twice before disbanding such a well-established operation.

15 / Gellhorn Heads for Spain

IN DECEMBER 1936, with war raging in Spain, twenty-eight-year-old Martha Gellhorn visited "Hemingway country." Her father had died early that year and, with her mother and younger brother, the ambitious young writer took a Christmas holiday in Key West, Florida. Born in St. Louis, Missouri, in 1908, Gellhorn had grown up in upper-middle-class comfort—her father a leading gynecologist and obstetrician, her mother an activist who had led the St. Louis campaign for women's suffrage. Both parents were half-Jewish, though this hardly registered in the early life of the family's only daughter.

After graduating from high school, Gellhorn enrolled at her mother's alma mater, Bryn Mawr, a notable women's college in Pennsylvania. Wickedly smart and stylish, bent on becoming a writer, she hung a picture of Ernest Hemingway in her room. Her favourite quote came from French novelist François Mauriac, though she first read it in the work of André Malraux, another writer-adventurer: "*Travail—opium unique.*" For Gellhorn, too, work was the greatest high.

At twenty-one, after finishing her junior year, she left Bryn Mawr. She was determined to find work that would help her land a writing job in Europe. "Oh Gosh! How I ache to get over there. It's a real malady." She published two articles in *The New Republic*—one a parody of crooner Rudy Vallee and the other about a train journey out of New York City's Grand Central Station. She landed a job as a cub reporter for the *Albany Times Union*. The only woman on staff in a typically raucous, heavy-drinking newsroom, she held her own as "the blonde peril," a nickname given to her by a male beat reporter.

After six months, convinced by a family friend that she was wasting her time "hobnobbing with odd persons who wore loud checked suits," she went home to regroup. She rented a modest office and began working on what would become her first novel, *What Mad Pursuit*. But she soon got fed up with parochial St. Louis. She needed to get away to France, centre of the literary universe. Her mother lent her train fare to New York, and both parents travelled that far with her. She visited a shipping line and, by promising to write a promotional article, gained a berth in what was called College Steerage.

In the spring of 1930, Gellhorn arrived in Paris with two suitcases, a typewriter, and $75 in cash—the equivalent today of $1,200. Hemingway and F. Scott Fitzgerald had come and gone, but Sylvia Beach was thriving at Shakespeare and Company, Josephine Baker was going strong with her risqué shows, and young Americans were dancing nightly at *bals musettes* on the Left Bank. Gellhorn tried and failed to land work as a European correspondent with the *New York Times*.

She worked in a beauty shop and then as a glorified clerk for the United Press news agency, where she got fired after complaining about unwanted sexual advances from her boss. Having taken a room in a house on the outskirts of Paris, she was visiting the office of an older journalist she admired when she experienced a life-changing moment. She met the patrician Bertrand de Jouvenel—a strikingly handsome philosopher and political economist just five years her senior. His father was both a politician and the influential editor of *Le Matin* newspaper, while his mother hosted a salon on Boulevard Saint-Germain where she entertained leading thinkers.

At the age of sixteen, Bertrand de Jouvenel had been seduced by the famous writer Colette, who, at the time, was his father's wife. But that was ancient history. Now he was married to a woman twelve years older than he was. Never mind. In July 1930, Martha Gellhorn took a fancy to the elegant Frenchman and with him plunged into a passionate affair. Meanwhile, she convinced her hometown newspaper, the *St. Louis Post-Dispatch*, to send her to Geneva, where she could report on a conference from a woman's point of view. She had twice visited the city with her parents, and now she renewed old friendships.

Over the next four years, Gellhorn bounced back and forth between France and the US, building her portfolio as a journalist, mastering French and German, and making connections, through Jouvenel, with French intellectuals—many of whom were finally wrestling with how to respond to the rise of Nazism next door. In Paris, Jouvenel was editing and writing for a left-wing journal called *La Lutte des jeunes* and was much in demand for commentary on current events. By 1934, he was predicting war: "Yes, and before five years."

Jouvenel's wife refused to grant him a divorce. He set up accommodations for Gellhorn in a family home in the south of France, the Villa Noria, and there her mother, Edna, came for an extended visit. In the autumn of that year, dissatisfied with her role as mistress, Gellhorn broke off the affair and returned to the US, determined to write about the effects of the Great Depression on American society. A journalist friend introduced her to Harry Hopkins, a key figure in Franklin Roosevelt's Federal Emergency Relief Administration (FERA). With 17 million people out of work, Hopkins was coordinating a fleet of investigators, getting them to report on what was happening at street level. He brought Gellhorn aboard, introduced her to Eleanor Roosevelt, and sent her to the Carolinas and New England to gather stories about the devastation caused by growing poverty and unemployment. Gellhorn excelled at this, her tone one of controlled fury and outrage. Then, late in 1934, she published *What Mad Pursuit*. The novel tells the story of three college girls who go chasing experience and end up in all kinds of trouble. Some reviewers recognized a talent in embryo, but most panned the book as juvenile.

Meanwhile, Gellhorn got fired from FERA. In Coeur d'Alene, Idaho, she had learned that a corrupt contractor was exploiting some impoverished farmers. She urged the men to do something dramatic, like breaking the windows of the local FERA office, and so they did. The contractor was arrested for fraud, but Gellhorn was recalled and fired. As she was cleaning out her desk, she heard from Eleanor Roosevelt. The First Lady had been friends with her mother at Bryn Mawr.

She had taken a shine to Gellhorn at first meeting and invited her now to move into the White House.

Gellhorn did so and stayed for a while, helping the First Lady respond to correspondence and charming such visitors as H.G. Wells, who in his late sixties indulged himself in a fantasy of having an affair with Gellhorn, not yet thirty years old. She was living large but had no time to write. When she fretted about this in a letter to her father, he responded with a tough-love note, urging her to pull herself together. She wanted to write? Then why the devil didn't she do it?

Gellhorn went to stay with a family friend in New Hartford, Connecticut. Soon enough she finished a non-fiction book, *The Trouble I've Seen*, about her experiences working for FERA. Published in 1936, the work tells four stories of the Great Depression, and reviewers hailed it as riveting and devastating. She would continue to write novels, but with this book Gellhorn had harnessed her gift for close observation and emotional reportage.

Now came that Christmas holiday in Florida. One afternoon in December 1936, out strolling with her mother and younger brother, Gellhorn spotted a bar called Sloppy Joe's. She knew that name. Sure enough, there at a corner table sat a muscular, dark-haired man wearing an old T-shirt and dirty white shorts, shuffling through a pile of mail. Gellhorn recognized him instantly. She walked over and stuck out her hand: "Ernest Hemingway? My name is Martha Gellhorn. I'm a writer, too, and I've been a fan of yours forever."

Hemingway was thirty-seven, married to his second wife, and the father of three children. Gellhorn had admired him for a decade—ever since she had read *The Sun Also Rises*. From Hemingway's perspective, here stood a beauty in a tight black dress: bright, sassy, blonde, legs to her shoulders. His first thought was: How do I get rid of this inconvenient young husband? But wait: The man was her brother? The coast was clear.

So began the famous affair that had its joyful moments but broke hearts and busted homes before devolving into misunderstanding, hurt feelings, emotional abuse, jealousy, spite, and recrimination. As always, Hemingway would emerge as the more vicious battler. But all that would come later. In December 1936, the celebrated novelist was weighing a generous offer from the North American Newspaper Alliance—sixty newspapers, $1,000 per article—to go to Europe and cover the Spanish Civil War.

Martha Gellhorn, who had recently spent months rambling around France, Germany, and Italy, was soon casting about to do that same thing for whatever publication she could find. She convinced a friend at *Collier's* magazine to give her not an assignment, exactly, but a letter identifying her as a special correspondent. To pay for her Atlantic crossing, she agreed to write an article for *Vogue* on the "beauty problems of the middle-aged woman." This involved undergoing an experimental treatment that peeled away a layer of skin to expose a fresh layer underneath—risky, but Gellhorn would stop at nothing. Before boarding the ship, exultant, she wrote to a family friend: "Me, I am going to Spain with the boys, I don't know who the boys are, but I am going with them."

16 / Orwell Gets Shot in the Throat

WHILE MARTHA GELLHORN was getting to know Hemingway in Florida, George Orwell set out from England for Spain. He stopped briefly in Paris and went to dinner with one of his literary heroes— American writer Henry Miller. Orwell was thirty-three, Miller forty-four. In the older writer's *Tropic of Cancer* (1934), Orwell had heard a voice "with no humbug in it, no moral purpose . . . [one that carried readers away] from the lies and the simplifications, the stylized marionette-like quality of ordinary fiction." Through the early 1930s, Orwell had paid less attention to social or political concerns and more to literary artistry. So he had looked to original stylists like Miller and James Joyce.

But in 1935, with fascism on the rise in Germany and Italy, he had turned increasingly to European politics. Long before most, he predicted that "the capitalist-imperialist governments" of England and France would seek to appease Hitler and Mussolini. And in 1937, writing to a friend, he would articulate a view that he held for the rest of his life: "Fascism after all is only a development of capitalism and the mildest democracy, so-called, is liable to turn into Fascism when the pinch comes."

In his 1946 essay "Why I Write," Orwell would look back and see that he had spent the past decade trying to turn political writing into an art. His starting point was always a felt need to expose some injustice. And this is where he parted ways with Henry Miller. Over dinner in Paris, Orwell wrote later, the anarchistic older writer argued that Western civilization would soon be swept away, and that these ideas about fighting fascism and defending democracy "were all baloney." In subsequent essays, Orwell would describe Miller's attitude as defeatist and irresponsible, and would argue that to survive one sometimes has to fight.

In Paris, the two men agreed to disagree. Before parting, Miller insisted on giving the business-suited Englishman the sturdy corduroy jacket off his own back—far more suitable for heading off to fight fascism. Orwell caught the night train south. Travelling with men and teenage boys bent on joining the Spanish war, he realized that his years serving with the imperial police in Burma had prepared him well: "I saw that I had relatively a lot of training as a soldier and decided to join the militia." He surmised that when he tried to enlist, he would be rejected because of his chronically weak lungs. But on reaching Barcelona, he learned that the Republicans were desperate for fighting men and conducted no medical exams.

He made his way to the headquarters of POUM, the socialist workers' party. John McNair, the working-class Briton in charge, did not at first like the looks of this "great, big, tall chap who spoke with a very pronounced Etonian accent." Decades later, McNair told an editor (Ian Angus) working on a volume of Orwell's *Collected Essays* that he welcomed the newcomer only when he realized that this great lunk had written *Down and Out in Paris and London*, one of his favourite books. Orwell would have to wait a few days in a former calvary barracks, a vast complex that served as POUM's military headquarters. But when enough recruits arrived to form a *centuria*, a company of one hundred soldiers, they would all head out to fight the fascists on the Aragon front, some 270 kilometres northwest of Barcelona.

By early January 1937, Orwell was part of a contingent holding a hilltop at the Aragon front. As he wrote later in *Homage to Catalonia*, he was "indescribably disappointed" to see that the Fascist trenches were not, as he had anticipated, fifty or a hundred yards away, but at least seven hundred. He resolved to make the best of this and, thanks to his gift for languages, became a *cabo*, or corporal, almost immediately. His wife, Eileen, told his literary agent that this "distresses him because he has to get up early to turn out the guard."

At the front Orwell found not well-trained soldiers but a motley crew of ill-equipped volunteers. He saw five of these men wounded in shooting accidents before the Fascists had even scored a hit. He was troubled more by the "unspeakable cold" than anything else. Freezing rains, stiff winds, and a dearth of firewood made things worse. Together with the Russian-born commander Georges Kopp, Orwell and another Englishman, Bob Edwards, undertook several daring raids. Edwards described Orwell as "a fine type of Englishman, 6 ft. 3 in. in height, a good shot, a cool customer, completely without fear. I know this because we have on numerous occasions crept over the parapet and have managed to get very close to the Fascist lines."

Another volunteer, John "Paddy" Donovan, viewed Orwell as almost reckless. "Orwell always wanted to be in action, he never wanted to lie down and take things easy but wanted always to carry on." When he wasn't rushing forward, "Eric was always writing. In the daytime he used to sit outside the dugout writing, and in the evenings he used to write by candlelight." Despite the condition of his lungs, Orwell smoked incessantly. He filled the dugout with stinking smoke and, Donovan wrote later, "nearly killed me with his black tobacco."

Orwell regarded the occasional shelling from the Fascists as a "mild diversion." Many of the shells failed to explode. In mid-February, Kopp moved the unit to a hill overlooking Huesca, a city in the Pyrenees in northeastern Spain. Edwards reported daily bombardments with high explosive shells, many of them "whizzing over our parapet" and some "causing considerable alarm in the cook-house, at which they seemed to be directed." Orwell described this as receiving "a little shell-fire."

Back in Barcelona, Eileen arrived to work as a volunteer in the office of John McNair. In mid-March, wanting to visit Orwell, she talked Commander Georges Kopp into taking her to the Huesca front in his staff car. Orwell thrilled to see his wife. Eileen spent a day in the dugouts and experienced "a small bombardment and quite a lot of machine-gun fire." She found Orwell looking "very tired" but healthy. A couple of weeks later, while taking part in a daring night raid, Orwell got caught in crossfire and narrowly escaped getting killed.

In April 1937, after 115 days at the front—almost four months— Orwell returned to Barcelona on leave. Eileen described him as "completely ragged, a little lousy, dark brown, and looking really very well." He wanted to see more continuous action and so sought to leave POUM and join the International Brigade, which was fighting on the Madrid front. But now he discovered that various anti-Fascist groups had started wrangling among themselves. The Russia-backed Communists even claimed that POUM was a fifth column secretly supporting Franco's Fascists.

Orwell decided to stick with the devils he knew. He was still in Barcelona when, on May 3, factional fighting erupted in the streets. Orwell spent the next three days on the roof of a cinema with a machine gun, guarding the entrance to POUM headquarters. On May 10, after the street fighting petered out, Orwell returned to the siege of Huesca. At first light on May 20, he awoke and went to relieve an American standing watch from behind a wall of sandbags. When he poked his head over the parapet to look around, an enemy sniper fired and hit him in the throat.

His companions thought he might be finished but put him on a stretcher and carried him a mile or so to a small hospital at Monflo-rite. He was then transported to a larger hospital at Siétamo, where doctors told him the bullet had nearly killed him but had missed his carotid artery by a millimetre. Within forty-eight hours, Orwell was in a modern hospital at Lerida—known to the Catalans as Lleida—where with Kopp's help, Eileen was able to visit. Over the next few weeks, Orwell began slowly to regain his voice.

In a letter to her brother, a leading British expert on tuberculo-sis, Eileen described Orwell as "violently depressed, which I think is encouraging." His medical discharge included the words "declared useless." He now had "an overwhelming desire to get away from it all; away from the horrible atmosphere of political suspicion and hatred, from streets thronged by armed men, from air-raids, trenches, machine-guns."

Get away he eventually would—but not as easily as he had hoped. In Barcelona, the sectarian infighting had resumed. While he was away for a few days getting exit papers, Communist soldiers arrested Georges Kopp and searched Eileen's hotel room. Orwell spent several nights sleeping rough in the streets of Barcelona. But he managed to visit Kopp in jail and ran around town trying to secure a letter that would exonerate him. The Communists would continue to hold Kopp for a year and a half.

But on June 23, 1937, Orwell and Eileen caught a train out of Barcelona. They crossed the border into France, spent a few days in a seaside town, and then made their way home to England. That August, in a letter answering an admirer, George Orwell wrote, "If Fascism means suppression of political liberty and free speech, then the present [elected] regime in Spain is Fascist." Compared with what Franco would set up, "it is only different in degree, not in kind." Sickened by the infighting he had witnessed in Barcelona, Orwell was developing the perspective that would inform and inspire his two classic novels, *Animal Farm* and *Nineteen Eighty-Four*.

He had started by writing an article called "Eye-witness in Barcelona," which outlined how Communist pressure drove the Republic to accept the brutal suppression of the merely socialist POUM. He argued that the Spanish government "has more points of resemblance to Fascism than points of difference" and could not achieve socialist ends by adopting fascist methods.

The left-leaning newsmagazine *The New Statesman* rejected the article because it might "cause trouble" with England's Russian allies. The editor assigned but then spiked a book review Orwell wrote because it reiterated his opinions and implied "that our Spanish Correspondents are all wrong." Orwell published the review in the British weekly *Time and Tide*, where he asserted that "so far from pushing the Spanish Government further towards the Left, the Communist influence has pulled it violently towards the right."

Orwell was working on *Homage to Catalonia*, a memoir of his Spanish experience in which he traced the evolution of these ideas. He and Eileen had returned to the village of Wallington, where they had established a ramshackle retreat 20 kilometres south of London.

Orwell completed *Catalonia* and in April 1938, saw it published by Frederick Warburg to a lukewarm response.

Meanwhile, in early March, he had caught a cold and found himself coughing up blood. Eileen's doctor-brother sent him to a sanatorium near Aylesford, southeast of London. He and other doctors suspected tuberculosis and tried to make Orwell rest. A wealthy admirer of Orwell, and a novelist himself, L.H. Myers, visited the sick man. On learning that doctors were urging Orwell to sojourn in a warmer climate, Myers insisted on making an anonymous gift to facilitate this.

From September 1938, with Eileen, Orwell spent six and a half months in Morocco. There he wrote his seventh book, *Coming Up for Air*, a nostalgia-laced novel that laments the disappearance of pastoral England and features a scene that anticipates the daily frenzy of rage, the "Two Minutes Hate," that appears in *Nineteen Eighty-Four*. A nondescript middle-aged man in a suit mounts a podium and stirs up hatred by spouting slogans. The narrator calls it "a ghastly thing, really, to have a sort of human barrel-organ shooting propaganda at you by the hour . . . Hate, hate, hate. Let's all get together and have a good hate . . . I saw the vison that he was seeing . . . It's a picture of himself smashing people's faces in with a spanner."

17 / Bethune Witnesses
a War Crime

ON THE EVENING of February 7, 1937, while George Orwell sat wet and shivering in a trench northwest of Barcelona, Norman Bethune set out driving southwest from Valencia. With two utility men, Hazen Size and Thomas Worsley, he was heading for the coastal city of Málaga, a distance of 620 kilometres, bent on expanding his blood transfusion service. After the three had travelled about a third of the way, a sandstorm forced them to stop at a small hotel in Alicante. Next morning, Bethune heard a rumour that the Fascists had taken Málaga, population 100,000. He carried on, stopping next in Murcia to visit local hospitals. Here he left one of two vehicles, the Ford, in which he and his men had been travelling, and pushed on in the larger Renault truck.

On February 10, the trio reached Almería. There Bethune learned that early on the morning of the seventh, three warships had shelled Málaga while airplanes dropped leaflets warning militiamen to vacate the city. Late that afternoon, the leaders of the Republican Army of the South had decamped without notice. Málagans feared that Franco's North African troops were almost upon them: "The Moors are coming, the Moors are coming!" On Monday, people took to the highway that twisted east along the coast toward Almería. With the country to the southwest already in Nationalist hands, this was the only possible direction in which to escape.

Having taken Málaga unopposed, Italian troops began harassing the fleeing refugees. Fighter planes strafed the masses, and two warships pounded them with shells. The slaughter would continue for three days. From Almería, Bethune and his men drove on toward the carnage. They began seeing scattered groups of people coming toward them, sometimes with mules carrying their possessions. These were the first groups of refugees. Separated groups became a steady stream.

At the crest of a hill, Bethune and his men stopped, stood, and looked ahead at the winding road, which was just an undulating black line of refugees. Cut into the rocky coast along the edge of the Sierra Nevada mountains, this road was now the only way out of Málaga. Defeated militiamen shuffled along, maybe three thousand in all, their uniforms dusty and torn. Civilians followed, some shoeless or with bloody rags wrapped around their feet. Mothers swaddled babies, and fathers carried larger children on their backs or shoulders.

The three men stood debating what to do. They carried no weapons. What if they encountered Italian soldiers? Bethune pointed to Spanish lettering on the side of the truck: "See that, boys? Service at the front. To the front we go." They saw older men and women who had collapsed at the side of the road. But Bethune was still more troubled by the sight of children, hundreds of them, some without shoes, struggling forward. With night coming on, Bethune pulled over and stopped. He had decided to turn the Renault around, fill it with children and perhaps a few mothers, and shuttle them back to Almería.

The moment he opened the doors, people gathered around. He crammed three dozen children and women into the truck, slammed the door shut, and sent Size to Almería, telling him to return as soon as he could. With Worsley, Bethune fell to tramping along with the refugees. Around midnight, he spotted a stable not far from the road and found enough straw to make a rough bed. Back on the road before dawn, he saw the headlights of the Renault returning from Almería.

Bethune sent both Worsley and Size to Almería with a second load of children and women while he walked on along the coastal road. Approaching Castell de Ferro, about 90 kilometres from Almería, he heard airplanes, looked up, and saw three Italian Fiats attacking two small Republican bombers. One of the latter got hit and, with black smoke trailing, came down into the water. Later he would learn it was a Potez from a squadron André Malraux had formed the year before. Bethune scrambled down a steep embankment and joined a small crowd on the shore, where militiamen helped crewmen ashore—two unharmed, five seriously injured.

Bethune took charge, wading out to the plane and ripping out wires to serve as tourniquets. Somehow he commandeered a truck and got in with the wounded. He did what he could without instruments, but the co-pilot died on the way to Almería. At the hospital there, surgeons amputated the arm of one man while Bethune performed necessary transfusions on the others, all of whom died despite his best efforts.

Around 7 p.m., the city went dark and a siren sounded. The ground shook amidst thunderous explosions. When the shaking stopped, Bethune heard screams. He stepped into the street and saw buildings engulfed in flames. He ran toward the burning buildings hollering, "*Medico! Medico!*" People were trapped beneath broken walls and timbers and electrical wires. The German Condor Legion had carried out a savage attack on defenceless civilians. Two months later, this same squadron would destroy the town of Guernica.

Bethune and his men went out, collected one more load of refugees, and got back to Almería around midnight. Bethune was sickened and enraged by the attack on the defenceless refugees, especially the children. Unable to sleep, he wrote a furious account of the past three days and later published it as a pamphlet—*The Crime on the Road: Malaga-Almeria.* This forced march, he wrote, was "the largest, most terrible evacuation of a city in modern times."

After describing the horror on the highway, the slaughter of unarmed peasants, he turned to the saturation bombing of Almería by German and Italian airplanes. These did not try to hit the government battleship in the harbour or the soldiers' barracks but "deliberately dropped ten great bombs in the very center of the town where on the main street were sleeping huddled together on the pavement . . . the exhausted refugees." Bethune carried three dead children from "where they had been standing in a great queue waiting for a cupful of preserved milk and a handful of dry bread, the only food some of them had for days."

At the bank, Bethune arranged to have money sent from his account in Madrid to pay his staff, then checked into the Valencia headquarters of the Military Health Service, the *Sanidad Militar* (SM). To those in charge, he described the war crime he had just witnessed and learned that the SM had not yet approved his expansion plans. Things did not look good. But Bethune began thinking that if the SM started paying for the blood transfusion unit, maybe he could direct the CASD funds to creating a "Children's City" in the foothills of the Pyrenees to accommodate the thousands of orphans now emerging from the provinces of Valencia and Catalonia.

But in Valencia on March 1, Bethune learned that the SM had refused to put him in charge of an expanded blood transfusion service. Not only that, but two Spanish doctors already working at his Madrid unit would now share command with him. And the SM expected that Canadians would not only continue to finance the Madrid operations but would also finance a planned expansion into Valencia.

For Bethune, this repudiation marked the beginning of the end. Shameless bureaucrats had gained control of what he had seen as a revolutionary movement. Feeling betrayed, angry, and resentful, he resumed working in Madrid, where demands for blood escalated in the face of 10,000 casualties. Gone now was the camaraderie of former days, replaced by infighting and recriminations.

Even so, Bethune would not walk away from a struggle in which he believed passionately. The Russian-supported Communists found him far too independent. He had begun an affair with Kajsa Ryen von Rothman, his Swedish interpreter, and that gave the Communists an excuse to go on the offensive. They claimed she was a Fascist spy and used that accusation to drive both her and Bethune out of Spain. Von Rothman fled to France along with 600,000 others and eventually went with a large group of Spaniards to Mexico, where she lived for thirty years.

On April 12, 1937, Bethune cabled his Canadian sponsors explaining that the SM had taken control of the Canadian blood transfusion unit. He sought clearance to withdraw Canadian personnel and donate the equipment to the Spanish government: "Our work as Canadians here is finished." He would return to Canada to complete and promote a film for anti-Fascist propaganda.

A few days later, he submitted his resignation to the SM. On May 4, after his closest colleagues expressed dismay, Bethune cabled the CASD again, urging them to continue supporting the unit, now under Spanish control, and reiterating that, back in Canada, he would use the propaganda film, *The Heart of Spain*, to raise money. He also advocated sending Canadian funds to support war orphans.

Bethune left Madrid for Paris. Early in June, with two young filmmakers, he sailed aboard the *Queen Mary* for New York City. After disembarking on June 7, he gave an interview to a reporter from the *Montreal Gazette*. "What's the matter with England, France, the United States, Canada?" Bethune asked. "Are they afraid that by supplying arms to the Loyalist forces they'll start a world war? Why, the world war has started. In fact, it's in its third stage—Manchuria, Ethiopia, and now Spain. It's democracy against Fascism."

Pulling no punches, Bethune said that "we in Madrid cannot understand such timidity, such poltroonery on the part of the democratic nations. Supplied with the proper arms, the Loyalists would throw the Franco forces into the sea in one month. The war would be over, the danger gone. But as long as Italy and Germany are openly waging war against the Spanish people, the war will go on indefinitely. And . . . the lingering Spanish war will surely spread all over the world."

From early July through mid-September of 1937, Bethune toured Canada showing the half-hour-long *Heart of Spain* and often giving two or three speeches at each stop. In Winnipeg on July 20, he "came out" as a proud Communist—this at a time when Joseph Stalin was yet to be recognized in the West as a murderous tyrant.

Throughout his tour, while hailing the work of the Canadian medical unit, Bethune also praised the heroism of the Mackenzie-Papineau battalion, "composed of Canadian anti-Fascist volunteers." At one point, according to the *Winnipeg Free Press*, he noted that "the Canadians in the international brigade stayed in the trenches for 90 days on end—a longer period than any brigade had known during the World War."

Bethune proposed to return to Spain to set up "a little Canada" that would remove children from the war and make them safe from German and Italian bombing. He had raised tens of thousands of dollars for the Spanish Republican cause and, not incidentally, put his life on the line. But the Russians in Spain did not want him around. Bethune at last said, enough. He turned his attention to China, which was under attack from the imperialist forces of Japan. On January 8, 1938, Bethune left Canada for the last time, sailing from Vancouver for China, eventually to do the work that would make him world famous as a humanitarian.

18 / Garner Hits the Trenches

IN FEBRUARY 1937, soon after Norman Bethune saw civilians get bombed in Almería, Hugh Garner took a series of trains south from France into Spain. With some three hundred other raw recruits, the twenty-three-year-old Canadian had come to battle Fascists. In Barcelona, while the train waited on a siding, he witnessed the arrival of refugee survivors from the recent atrocities committed on the road from Málaga—"frightened little people" he would later write, "seemingly stunned."

When they cleared the track, the war train resumed its journey to Valencia, and then inland to the International Brigade depot at Albacete. Garner, an aspiring writer from Toronto, fiercely working class, was exactly where he wanted to be. More than twenty years later, in a 1960 magazine series, he would echo Orwell and Malraux when he wrote that the outbreak of the Spanish Civil War affected him more than anything else in his life, before or since. He described how, in 1936, reading about the losses suffered by the Loyalist forces, he grew sick inside and began to hate everything about the Fascists, the army generals, and the Spanish Catholic hierarchy.

Garner vowed to join the struggle. In his essays and especially his fiction, which would grow to include a dozen novels and more than one hundred short stories, he would provide a singular perspective on Canadian participation in the Spanish Civil War. He was a roistering, working-class anti-hero who showed a deep concern for those marginalized by race, class, ethnicity, gender, age, or whatever else.

Born in Yorkshire, England, in 1913, Hugh Garner moved to Toronto with his mother at age six. His parents separated and he grew up mostly in the Cabbagetown neighbourhood—now a chic, middle-class enclave but then widely regarded as a working-class slum. As a small boy in a broken home, Hugh was left to his own devices by a mother who had to work all day.

During his first seven years in Toronto, he attended eight different schools. As a teenager, he became a voracious reader. In 1926, he entered Riverdale Technical School, where he resisted efforts to steer him toward a trade, and instead took to writing poetry. The two things he hated most during his childhood, he wrote later, were bedbugs and social workers.

In 1929, on the day he turned sixteen and could legally do so, Garner dropped out of Riverdale Tech. The next day, he became the youngest copy boy at the *Toronto Star*. He was learning the journalistic ropes when he refused to act as a tour guide for a group of "giggling teenagers"—read *middle-class*—and was fired on the spot.

Over the next few years, as the Great Depression brought misery to millions throughout the Western world, Garner laboured at a series of low-paying jobs. He and his mother, working as a waitress, had trouble paying the rent and had to go "on relief," collecting groceries at the equivalent of today's food banks. Through most of 1930, he worked as a bicycle messenger. The following year, Garner joined the thousands of men riding freights, heading west to Saskatchewan to work the wheat harvest. He spent most of that winter working on a section of the Trans-Canada Highway near Kamloops.

Back in Toronto, he packed boxes in a soap factory where workers wore masks to reduce the respiratory impact of soap dust. Then came another wheat harvest and more semi-hazardous factory jobs. While working as a pattern cutter in a button factory, he cut his finger and had to get stitches. He was fired before he returned. The Ontario Workmen's Compensation Board refused to help him get his job back and threatened to have him arrested if he kept complaining.

Garner became increasingly angry about the way society treated workers, yet he remained suspicious of Canadian socialists and communists, many of whom had university degrees. So he remained a loner. In the summer of 1933, now twenty, Garner ventured south instead of west. He spent the next two years hitch-hiking, riding the rails, and doing odd jobs around the United States: Jackson, Mississippi; Shreveport, Louisiana; Gladewater, Texas; Yuma, Arizona; Fresno, California; and then Los Angeles.

In the public library there, he perused works on psychology and philosophy, reading everyone from Freud, Jung, and Adler to Spinoza, Descartes, and Nietzsche. In San Francisco, he lived in a YMCA and, to support himself, stole shirts from a department store and sold them to fellow residents. Starting in late spring 1934, he spent a year and a half in New York City, where in Union Square he listened to scores of political speeches. He worked as a dishwasher, a busboy, and a door-to-door salesman. After leading a failed strike against a shoe store that was exploiting handbill distributors, he was kicked out of his YMCA room as a troublemaker.

He moved to the Hotel Majestic, where "rooms" were cubicles covered with chicken wire. Here, influenced by a convicted safecracker from Utah, he began reading Marxist thinkers—though it was George Bernard Shaw, whom he read in Toronto the following year, who turned him into "a social radical." While at the Majestic, Garner also started reading literary quarterlies that carried stories about the poor. Here he discovered a sense of direction. He bought paper and pencils and began writing out of his own experience.

Back in Toronto in the fall of 1935, he became active with the youth wing of the socialist Co-operative Commonwealth Federation. After a few months, he was elected president. The following spring, he attended the first Canadian Youth Congress in Ottawa, where he publicly advocated a revolutionary uprising. Meanwhile, he worked full-time selling men's clothes and part-time shelving books at a public library. There he read everything he could find on left-wing politics while also powering through fiction by Hemingway, John Dos Passos, and H.G. Wells.

That spring, Garner published his first piece—an essay called "Toronto's Cabbagetown." A detailed evocation of the eponymous place and its people, it appeared in the well-respected literary and political magazine *Canadian Forum*. But now came the news from Spain. Under General Franco, the military had risen in revolt against the country's democratically elected Popular Front government. In Toronto, Garner attended political meetings. He saw the Spanish Civil War as a battle between workers and fascists. Like Orwell, like Malraux, Garner knew immediately that he had to join the struggle.

The Canadian government maintained an official neutrality—though in truth it sided with the anti-democratic Nationalists, who had the backing of the Roman Catholic Church. For Prime Minister William Lyon Mackenzie King—always concerned with retaining the support of Catholic Quebec—that was sufficient reason to repudiate the Loyalists. Soon his bureaucratic underlings would be stamping passports as "invalid for travel in Spain." Canadians who left to join the International Brigades were warned that when they returned home, they would be jailed.

Like many others, Garner would not be dissuaded. He advertised in the *Toronto Star*'s personal classified ads: "Young socialist, aged 23, wants fare to Spain to fight in Loyalist militia." This produced nothing, but soon enough, through an acquaintance he found himself talking with local Communist Party members. He was not converted but he needed to get to Spain and they agreed to fund him.

In early February 1937, the young socialist took a bus south into the US, claiming at the border that he was a student going to study in Paris. In New York City, supplied with an old American army uniform, he boarded a ship and, with eight fellow volunteers, sailed third class to Cherbourg, France. He travelled by train to Paris, enrolled in the International Brigades, and then carried on to Barcelona, where he saw the refugees from Málaga.

At Albacete, after spending one night sleeping on the ground in a bullfight arena, Garner became a soldier in the Spanish Republican Army. He surrendered his passport and received "a Loyalist woolen uniform with trousers that folded over the tops of my boots." The

Canadian Mackenzie-Papineau Battalion had yet to be created, so he was posted to the xvth Brigade, the Lincoln Battalion, which comprised Yugoslavian, French, English, and American volunteers.

Garner spent a week cleaning up old army telephones and then joined a detachment of trainees heading for an artillery school at Almansa. After trying and failing to obtain a transfer to where the action was, he left and made his own way to the Lincoln Battalion's position on the Jarama front. Issued a French tin helmet, a Russian rifle, and some ammunition, he spent his first night on sentry duty, huddling behind two sandbags while a sniper kept firing over his head, bent on picking him off.

Next morning he transferred to a machine-gun company that included many Canadians and a number of radical students from New York. With three men he had met on the train south from Paris, he took charge of a heavy Russian Maxim machine gun. One evening in April 1937, when rain was pelting down and Garner was crouching in his dugout with a blanket over his head, a Fascist patrol began strafing the Lincolns with gunfire.

With his fellows, Garner rushed out into the downpour to man the machine gun. When the fighting stopped, he returned to his dugout, soaked to the skin. He slept the night away but next morning awoke, shivering with cold, to find himself caked with yellow clay.

As spring turned to summer, tensions arose between the anti-authoritarian enlisted men and the army officers, most of whom were communist ideologues—"Red Rotarians," as Garner called them. This led to desertions, insubordination, and increasingly harsh penalties meted out by those officers. Several deserters were executed. In mid-June, the fractious Garner and his friends were assigned to what was essentially a punishment battalion. When night fell, they were sent out with picks and shovels to dig a new trench line. This noisy action attracted gunfire, and Garner became so jumpy that, with shots cracking, he would pat himself down, checking for wounds.

At the end of the month, in secrecy, most of the Lincolns withdrew from the line, leaving Garner and his friends behind. The next day, with no idea where the battalion had gone, they set out for Madrid to report to headquarters. The men decided to enjoy a bit of a drinking binge before reporting for duty. When the secret police began asking questions, Garner reported to brigade headquarters. A Red Rotarian officer threatened to have him shot for desertion, and Garner bolted from the office, escaping cleanly.

Later that day, he learned that the Lincolns had moved to a village twenty miles east, Alcalá de Henares. When he reported there, another officer threatened to charge him with desertion, but a more lenient third one changed that to "absent without leave" and restored him to the battalion. While rambling around that village, Garner introduced himself to a fellow Canadian, Dr. Norman Bethune, who was operating a mobile blood transfusion unit in the area.

Early in July, Loyalist leaders decided to mount a major offensive to relieve the siege of Madrid, using Garner's unit as shock troops. They were to punch a hole in the Nationalist lines by seizing three small villages, one of which was called Villaneuva de la Cañada. Reserves would then pour through the hole to take the town of Brunete. On July 6, Garner joined the nighttime march of singing men, picking out the accents: Cockney, Scots, Welsh, Lancashire, West Country. Later, in a story called "How I Became an Englishman," he would describe an epiphany, when he realized that the men were singing not of revolution but of England: most were communists, but they were Englishmen first.

Resuming work with his machine-gun crew, Garner found himself lugging an 80-pound mount and other gear uphill and down. Next day, when the gun was knocked out of service, Garner's section joined the attacking infantry, stumbling over rough terrain with bullets whizzing past, occasionally killing a comrade. For the first time, Garner felt afraid.

When a pause came, he made his way to the rear and volunteered to carry wounded men, an experience he would describe in his story "The Stretcher Bearers." At a first-aid station, he witnessed Spanish soldiers tormenting a wounded man and then heard them murder him. At that he lost faith in the brotherhood of man and thought the whole stinking war was "all balls."

After ferocious hand-to-hand combat, the Loyalists took Villan-
ueva de la Cañada. They also seized Brunete but soon relinquished
it to enemy reinforcements. Final tally: a tiny gain in territory cost
the lives of 25,000 Loyalists and 10,000 Nationalists. This situation
gave rise to insubordination. One brigade mutinied and had to be
withdrawn. Officers promised not to use the English Battalion, now
fewer than ninety men, in any frontal attacks. Faced with the bloody
futility of the entire action, Garner found he could no longer function as a soldier. Along with several others, he was sent to hospital in
Albacete, suffering from "shell shock"—now clinically regarded as
post-traumatic stress disorder.

After a month in hospital and several weeks in Albacete, he
received new orders: he would return to Canada and, as a journalist,
write propaganda for the Republican cause. Still just twenty-four, and
initially lacking a valid passport, the resourceful young man made his
way home roughly along the route by which he had arrived: Valencia,
Barcelona, Perpignan, Paris, adding only London before sailing to
Canada. In Toronto, he wrote articles for the *New Advance* and the
Canadian Forum while also working as a janitor and furnace tender.

Early in 1939, he was doing odd jobs and residing with his mother
when the Royal Tour of King George VI and Queen Elizabeth,
escorted by Prime Minister William Lyon Mackenzie King, visited
Riverdale Park. Later, recalling his ties to England, Garner wrote of
suddenly feeling himself to be "a bigger royalist than Beaverbrook,"
the London-based Canadian media baron whose newspapers were
famous for lauding the monarchy.

In July, Garner hitch-hiked to Simcoe in southwestern Ontario and
took work picking tobacco. On September 3, he was enjoying a lei-
surely breakfast when, via radio, he learned that Britain had declared
war on Germany. Seven days later, Canada did the same. Back in
Toronto on September 11, and despite his previous experience with
shell shock, Garner enlisted in the Royal Canadian Artillery.

Before long, because the RCA would not send him abroad, dis-
trusting his socialist past, he moved over to the Royal Canadian Navy.
After completing basic training in Halifax, Garner spent three years

seeing action, and plenty of it, while fighting the Nazis aboard a series of corvettes. In 1945, soon after Germany surrendered, Garner left the navy. At age thirty-two, he set out to forge a career as a writer. That career would encompass eleven novels and seven collections of short stories, one of which (*Hugh Garner's Best Stories*) won the 1963 Governor General's Award for fiction.

19 / Gellhorn Angry to the Bone

IN MARCH 1937, while waiting for the papers she needed for Spain, Martha Gellhorn spent a few days in Paris, which was crowded with volunteers doing the same. They came from around the world to fight for democracy, roughly 35,000 of them, according to the History Channel. Other estimates, like that of the *Holocaust Encyclopedia*, run as high as 40,000, including 2,800 Americans and 1,700 Canadians.

Most French citizens were still hoping that the Spanish conflagration would quickly resolve itself and they could cut a deal with Hitler. André Malraux, however, Gellhorn's sometime hero, had looked around Europe and seen authoritarian regimes or dictatorships emerging not just in Germany and Italy but in Poland, Portugal, Lithuania, Greece, and Romania. "Fascism," he wrote, "has spread its great black wings over Europe."

Gellhorn wandered in and out of the cafés on the Left Bank, talking with volunteers setting out to serve in Spain as soldiers, nurses, ambulance drivers, and translators. Hugh Garner had just passed through. Later Gellhorn would tell an Australian journalist, "We knew, we just *knew* that Spain was the place to stop Fascism. It was one of those moments in history when there was no doubt." Finally, papers in hand, Gellhorn pulled on a windbreaker and a knapsack and left Paris on the "Red Express," so-called because it referred to the Republican faction, often associated with socialist or communist ideals.

Because France and Spain used different track gauges, Gellhorn changed trains at the Spanish border. At twenty-eight, attractive and vividly American, she found the border guards baffled by her arrival, complete with duffle bag, canned goods, and American passport. What was she doing here?

At villages along the way to Barcelona, she reported in her diary, young men clambered aboard to join the fighting, looking like boys heading back to boarding school after Christmas. On reaching Barcelona, she found it thick with soldiers and militiamen carrying rifles in the streets. She found a room, fell into bed, and slept through a bombardment.

Gellhorn talked a trucker into taking her down the coast to Valencia, at the time a day-long drive. There she ran into Sidney Franklin, a young American who had come to Spain as Hemingway's assistant. In the car assigned to Hemingway as a celebrity correspondent, Franklin had driven to Valencia to collect supplies. The vehicle was piled high with Spanish hams, kilos of coffee, and a basket filled with oranges, grapefruits, and lemons, but he made room and gave her a lift to Madrid.

Gellhorn found Hemingway eating and drinking among a throng of journalists, all of them hot with recent events. She took a room in the Hotel Florida, where Hemingway had two rooms—one for himself, another for his assistant—and set about exploring the city. Madrid had been under bombardment for five months. The front line was two miles from the main shopping district, and to get there, journalists often took a tram. The shelling usually came three times a day—before breakfast and then on both sides of the lunch hour. Food was hard to find.

During her first weeks in Madrid, Gellhorn wrote only in her diary—mainly notes of what she observed. Near the edge of town, she climbed in and out of Republican trenches and visited makeshift hospitals smelling of cabbage and ether, where she found untrained volunteer nurses doing the best they could.

The Fascist forces were well within shooting range of the city, and on March 29, while she was brushing her teeth, Gellhorn heard a shell fall just down the street. She looked out and saw that it had decapitated one man and wounded two others. With Hemingway and another correspondent, Gellhorn drove to the nearby town of Morata, where American volunteers manned the trenches. The battalion commander, a schoolteacher from Alabama, told her that some of his men did not know how to load a gun so he had to offer on-the-spot instruction.

At the military hospital in the Palace Hotel, she met a twenty-three-year-old aviator who, with a badly burned face and hands wrapped in sacks, remained determined to rejoin the fight against fascism. Madrid was a city of contrasts. From the Hotel Florida, she took a short walk to the Plaza de España, where the booming of the guns made it hard to think. From the ruined houses around the square, people watched and waited and then scrambled out to resume desperately searching for food. Not far away, at the most expensive shoe store in town, Gellhorn saw a well-dressed woman trying on fancy high-heeled slippers.

The next day, jittery with a lack of cigarettes, worried that she was not writing, not finding an angle, Gellhorn jumped at the chance to visit a field hospital near the Jarama front. Interpreter Kajsa von Rothman had introduced her to Norman Bethune. Some men had been injured in an infantry attack and he was setting out to bring them blood transfusions. Did she want to come and see for herself?

The trip to the Jarama front with Bethune proved to be the catalyst she was seeking. Jolting along a rutted road for 25 or 30 kilometres, Gellhorn felt she was finally seeing action. The field hospital, filthy and disorganized, was housed in the farmhouse section of an old mill. Gellhorn was sobered by the sights and sounds of wounded men. Bethune treated one young soldier by putting peroxide on the wound where a chunk of flesh had been sliced from his shoulder. The man kept his mouth shut, Gellhorn observed, though his stomach shook and trembled.

Having written nothing for weeks, Gellhorn felt galvanized. Back in Madrid, she agreed to go on radio to share her impressions of the Spanish Civil War. With television still in its infancy, radio was playing an ever-increasing role in international coverage. Thanks to Hemingway's connections, Gellhorn was able to arrange for

America's National Broadcasting Company (NBC) to carry her talk internationally.

In her room at the Hotel Florida, she sat down at a borrowed type-writer and began banging away. Gellhorn would become famous for her acute, observational eye, and now, drawing on notes she had taken since leaving Paris, she let flow. When she showed the piece to Hemingway, he nodded and grinned and said, "Daughter, you're lovely."

Gellhorn felt so relieved to be writing again that she treated herself to an armful of yellow mimosa. She had found her time, her place, her voice, and her vision. In Spain in 1937, she launched her career as one of the great truth-telling witnesses of the twentieth century.

In mid-April, urged on by Hemingway, she punched out her first article for *Collier's* magazine, describing daily life in a city under siege and highlighting the courage of civilians going about their business. With Gellhorn, we hear the roaring of shells as they fall on the

Journalist Martha Gellhorn and Ernest Hemingway travelling together shortly after their 1940 marriage. *Everett Collection / Alamy*

cobblestones of a square. During a lull, an old woman starts hurrying across the plaza, holding the hand of a frightened little boy. She
is trying to get the child home, where both will feel relatively safe.
She is in mid-square when the next shell explodes. A piece of twisted
steel whirls up off the shell and catches the boy in the throat, killing
him instantly. The old woman stands stupefied, silent, holding the
hand of the dead child. Men run out to lead her away and carry off
the small body.

Collier's published the piece and then took another. Then *The
New Yorker* accepted two pieces, one on the local zoo, the other on
her trip to the front with Norman Bethune. By the end of April, the
now confident Gellhorn, her name on the masthead at *Collier's*, was
talking about writing a book about the civil war and raising funds
for the Republican cause by undertaking an American lecture tour.
Hemingway, meanwhile, had finished helping to shoot a propaganda
film, *The Spanish Earth*, and needed to assist in editing and doing a
voice-over. The two travelled separately to Paris and sailed for New
York. Disembarking in that city in May, Gellhorn told reporters who
met her ship that the Loyalists would win in Spain because they had
an endless supply of courage.

The whirl of events forced Gellhorn to postpone her lecture tour.
But she wrote to Eleanor Roosevelt asking if the US could bring over
some five hundred Basque children orphaned by the Fascist destruction of Bilbao. The First Lady, an outspoken supporter of the Spanish
Republicans, had a better fix on the mood at home and suggested
raising and sending funds to help the children in Spain.

Like Hemingway, Gellhorn was invited to address the Second
Congress of American Writers. Speaking on June 5, the second afternoon, to an audience of 3,500 at Carnegie Hall, she insisted that any
writer who has fought for the underdog has a story to tell—one that
is true and will last.

On July 8, 1937, thanks to Gellhorn's connection with Eleanor Roosevelt, Hemingway got to show *The Spanish Earth* at the White House
to both the First Lady and the president. They approved. Trying to be
discreet about their affair, Gellhorn and Hemingway sailed separately
for Paris in mid-August. By early September, they were back in Spain.

Things had taken a dark turn. The Fascists had gained control of the north, including the Basque country. Italian ships and planes controlled the Mediterranean, cutting Republican supply lines. In Madrid, every night brought out the death carts, ferrying bodies to pickup locations. One evening, out front of the bar where she and Hemingway liked to drink, Gellhorn came upon a dead horse, a dead mule, and a smear in the road—all that was left of a dead man.

With Hemingway and one other journalist, Gellhorn headed to Belchite, 335 kilometres northeast along a wending, rutted road. They slept out overnight, parked near a farmhouse, and cooked food over an open fire. Gellhorn wrote later about seeing houses slumping in on each other and soldiers digging out dead bodies, the air sometimes thick with the stink of death.

Every so often, Hemingway would throw a temper tantrum, as when Gellhorn mentioned one night that, back in the US, she hoped to undertake a lecture tour. Hemingway attacked this for money-grubbing at the expense of the Republicans, which was the opposite of what she intended. Did he feel threatened? Most of the time, even so, they were happy together—though the sex left Gellhorn either making excuses to avoid it or hoping that the activity would soon be over.

By Christmas 1937, Martha Gellhorn was back in the States, where she visited the parents of some young Americans she had met and reassured them that their sons were alive and well. In January she set off on that lecture tour, trying desperately, in a nation gone isolationist, to drum up support for the Republican cause. In St. Louis, speaking to an audience of three thousand, she called Franco "a butcher." She warned repeatedly that worse things would happen if the Fascists were allowed to overthrow the democratically elected government of Spain.

The following February, exhausted, and having lost twelve pounds while delivering twenty-two lectures in under a month, she cancelled the last few lectures and went with her mother to lie on a beach in Florida. She was tired of playing Cassandra. But then, on March 4, 1938, she learned that Franco's army was splitting the Loyalist forces in two—an action that presaged the end. With Hemingway, she boarded the *Queen Mary* to cross the Atlantic.

To Eleanor Roosevelt, from on board ship, Martha Gellhorn wrote a twelve-page letter explaining her sudden departure and predicting the eruption of an all-consuming European war. The news from Spain was so terrible that she felt she had to get back there, and to be among those who were still fighting Fascism. She felt helpless and "crazy with anger" to see another Great War on the horizon. Idealistic young men would die; powerful old ones survive to bungle the peace. The world was going to be destroyed by a man who, judging from *Mein Kampf*, could not think straight for half a page.

She wished she could see Mrs. Roosevelt, although she would not be pleasant company as she had "gone angry to the bone" because of what she saw coming. The Spanish Civil War was one thing. The next world war would be "the stupidest, lyingest, cruelest" of the century. She asked forgiveness for the miserable letter: "I can't write any other kind."

20 / Halton Sees Canadians Home

IN JANUARY 1939, while based in London for the *Toronto Star*, Matthew Halton received an urgent phone call from Paris. One Albert MacLeod was seeking help for 300 Canadian troops, members of the Mackenzie-Papineau Battalion, who were stranded in the port city of Le Havre. They were among 1,700 Canadians who had gone to Spain to fight for the democratically elected Popular Front government. Nationalist troops had killed more than 700 "Mac-Paps."

Now the French government was threatening to confine the survivors in a refugee camp unless they left the country in four days. The Canadian Pacific Railway stood ready to transport the men to Canada for $10,000—the equivalent today of roughly $200,000. A desperate MacLeod was hoping Halton might be able to help.

Three years before, when the Spanish Civil War broke out in July 1936, Halton had been disappointed to find himself on the ground in London. He had visited Madrid the previous month and seen angry demonstrations in the streets. A Spanish socialist leader told him that Catholic Church lands were being turned over to hard-working peasants. He wrote that civil war seemed inevitable—"the smell of blood was in the air."

But when war erupted, with right-wing Spanish generals calling for army officers to overthrow the elected Republican government, The *Star* had sent not Halton but its Paris-based correspondent to cover the fighting. Pierre Van Paassen soon began filing dramatic stories, including eyewitness accounts from the front lines.

But then the *Star*'s editor Harry Hindmarsh turned up in Paris, having heard that Van Paassen was not witnessing anything but was simply rewriting reports that he read in the French press. Having discovered this to be true, Hindmarsh fired the pretender on the spot and, shortly thereafter, sent Matthew Halton to cover the war. On arriving in Barcelona in November 1936, Halton encountered a city roiling with competing groups who shared only their opposition to the Nationalist generals. He spent a week securing the passes and safe conducts he needed to travel to the Aragon front near Huesca, 270 kilometres northwest of Barcelona.

He made the three-hour drive one cold rainy morning and reached the front about a month before George Orwell got there—though unlike the British writer, he was reporting for a daily newspaper and did not intend to stay and fight. A militia captain gave him a coffee and told him to take shelter behind a stone wall. Halton described ill-equipped militiamen preparing to attack Fascist positions as German bombers unloaded nearby. He heard a wounded man groaning and another man vomiting. He wished he were anywhere but here. He saw a third man, shot in the stomach, fall to the ground screaming in agony. Halton felt sick. He watched from behind the barricades as eventually the militia drove Franco's men from the ridge.

Back in Barcelona and having been in Spain for less than a month, Halton received urgent messages summoning him back to London immediately to cover the abdication of King Edward. Upset by this turn of events, Halton did as ordered but continued to write about the Spanish war, lambasting Britain and France for not intervening while Germany and Italy were using the war to train troops and test weapons. Their bombers were learning important lessons, he predicted, "for the big war when they will drop 3,000 tons of bombs a day on London instead of 30 tons a week on Madrid."

In summer 1937, Halton joined high-profile British socialists pressuring the Foreign Office to demand the release of Canadian William Krehm, a supporter of the socialist POUM party jailed in Barcelona by Stalinist agents. Having spent nine weeks in a lice-infested jail cell,

Krehm was deported. On his way to Toronto, he stopped in London to thank Halton, who then, in the *Star*, painted a grim word-picture of how members of the NKVD, the Russian secret police, were taking control of the Republican struggle. Most correspondents, Hemingway included, were whitewashing Soviet activities, not wanting to weaken Stalin's commitment to the cause.

Eighteen months later, in January 1939, Halton received that urgent phone call. In *Ten Years to Alamein*, he would write, "I sat beside the telephone, sick at heart." Three hundred of his bravest fellow Canadians were waiting "like a herd of criminals either for someone to find $10,000 or to be taken to the ghastly camps at Perpignan" in southern France. Halton called the only two men he knew with anything like the requisite funds. Former Canadian prime minister R.B. Bennett, having retired to England, told Halton he admired these young men but could not help because he was dealing with unusual expenses.

Unsurprised, Halton tried his last hope. In London, he had become friendly with Canadian businessman and philanthropist Garfield Weston. He had not finished describing the plight of the surviving Mac-Paps, some of them wounded and starving, when Weston interrupted: "I'll send you a cheque for $5,000 in the morning." Today, that equates to more than $100,000.

MacLeod managed to raise the other half of the money from other sources. When the Mac-Paps arrived at the little English port of Newhaven, Halton and two other reporters were there to greet them. Halton travelled with the vacating men by train to London, and then reported that while a few might be soldiers of fortune, most were "intelligent Canadians who saw what everyone is beginning to see now that it is too late, and who had the courage to do something about it."

PART THREE

Invaders, Collaborators, and Scapegoats

21 / An Arrival
of Aliens

ON OCTOBER 30, 1938, a sensational radio adaptation of *The War of the Worlds*, a novel by H.G. Wells, caused widespread panic in the United States. The prevailing political context set the stage, with many people speculating that war might erupt in Europe. But director Orson Welles, just twenty-three, also struck with genius. He presented the broadcast as a series of news bulletins that made an alien invasion seem all too real—and terrifying.

H.G. Wells is often called the "father of science fiction," but given the breadth of his thematic concerns, and, following Margaret Atwood, we might prefer "father of *speculative* fiction." His dystopian works include *The Time Machine* and *The Sleeper Awakes*. From the perspective of this narrative, his greatest contribution, given its treatment of a generic invasion by an overwhelming force, is *The War of the Worlds*. The novel is allegorical.

Several notable dystopian works—*The Handmaid's Tale, It Can't Happen Here, The Plot against America*—suggest that a fictionalized "Canada" might provide a safe haven for those under threat. But *The War of the Worlds* offers no sanctuary. Early in the novel the nameless narrator marvels, "It seems to me now almost incredibly wonderful that with that swift fate [an invasion] hanging over us, men could go about their petty concerns as they did." Later, in the epilogue, the storyteller reveals that he has grown more wary: "At any rate, whether we expect another invasion or not, our views of the human future must be greatly modified by these events. We have learned now that we cannot regard this planet as being fenced in and a secure abiding place for Man; we can never anticipate the unseen good or evil that may come upon us suddenly from out of space."

First serialized in 1897, *The War of the Worlds* develops a scenario along the lines of what would happen to France and other European countries during the Second World War. The prospect is one of invasion, subjugation, and occupation. Obviously, Canada is not exempt. Why would it be?

In 1933, in his novel *The Shape of Things to Come*, Wells had predicted that a world war would begin in January 1940—missing the actual date, September 1939, by four months. Also in 1933, because he had criticized what he saw happening in Germany, his books were among those burned by Nazi youth organizations. In 1934, Wells visited US president Franklin D. Roosevelt and then went to the Soviet Union and interviewed Joseph Stalin for *The New Statesman*. He had hoped to transform Stalin by force of argument but discovered lawlessness, state violence, and censorship and realized that he had been naïve: change was not about to pass this way.

Scholars have classified *The War of the Worlds* as an example of "invasion literature," a subgenre exemplified by *The Battle of Dorking: Reminiscences of a Volunteer*, an 1871 novella by George Tomkyns Chesney. Published as a pamphlet, that work describes an invasion of Britain by a German-speaking country characterized simply as "The Enemy." A realistic work, it has nothing like the imaginative power of *The War of The Worlds*, which brought the idea of invasion into mainstream literature.

Since the sensational radio drama of 1938, the novel has inspired reworkings in a variety of media, among them comic books, video games, TV series, and sequels. Of the seven film adaptations, the 2005 version stands out. Directed by Steven Spielberg, starring Tom Cruise and featuring spectacular special effects, it moves the action to the contemporary US and tinkers with the plot, yet remains clearly recognizable.

The original novel has a universal aspect. Wells explained that he developed his plot after talking with his brother Frank about how, in the early nineteenth century, Britain had wreaked havoc on the indigenous population of Van Diemen's Land, now Tasmania. He found himself wondering how the British would react if suddenly they were invaded by all-powerful enemies. Call them "Martians" and set the story in motion.

Wells's Martians are ugly, immobile, octopus-like creatures with big eyes . . . but they can build and manipulate giant tripods that transport them and their devastating weapons hither and yon. In the Spielberg adaptation, the tripods have lain buried deep in the earth for millennia, awaiting the arrival of their pilots.

But these are details. What matters is that *War of the Worlds* is allegorical. Consider the antagonists of the original story. On the one hand you have all-powerful invaders—Martians or, more broadly, *aliens*, no matter their distinguishing characteristics. On the other hand, you have their victims—easy targets, really, some more vulnerable than others.

So, in the beginning: imperial British Martians, aboriginal Tasmanians. Flash forward to the 1930s. The all-powerful invader? The Nazis, of course. You want easy targets, take your pick: Czechoslovakians, Poles, Belgians, Norwegians, Danes, the French. Some of those easy targets might choose to save themselves by identifying with the aliens. You see where this is going. We will focus mostly on France and pursue the story through individuals.

22 / Hitler
Invades France

ADOLF HITLER WANTED to avoid a two-front war. He would deal first with the west, then with the east. So in 1939 he opened negotiations with Joseph Stalin. The Russian dictator had sought an alliance with France and Britain but had been rebuffed. In the Spanish Civil War, those two countries had remained officially neutral while Germany and Russia fought on opposite sides. That war had evolved into a weapons-testing struggle, and Stalin did not like what he had seen.

Hitler had taken to pushing the idea of *Lebensraum*, which had evolved out of America's "Manifest Destiny." To fulfill Germany's destiny, he proposed to invade eastern Europe and create a vast German empire that would accommodate more people and produce more food and raw materials. That was the long-term objective. He kept that quiet. No Jews, of course.

The Nazi leader had been promising to reverse the Versailles Treaty and restore Germany to greatness. He would do this by waging war. Late in 1937, he had detailed his "last will and testament" to his generals. First, he intended to unite the German-speaking peoples by taking control of Austria and Czechoslovakia. Then he would invade eastward, taking Poland and Ukraine. He would deal with western Europe (France and England) before confronting Russia.

When he revealed this, two of his generals—Werner von Fritsch and Werner von Blomberg—told him they had serious misgivings.

Hitler turned up embarrassing material on both men and forced them to resign. Then he started acting on his plan. First came the Anschluss. On March 12, 1938, Nazi troops rolled into Austria—which was mostly ethnic German—and were welcomed by exuberant crowds. In Vienna, Hitler addressed more than 250,000 cheering people. This was going better than he had dreamed.

Hitler continued to portray himself as a man of peace—but explained to those who asked that he was now under pressure to respond to the terrible mistreatment of Germans in the Sudetenland region of Czechoslovakia, home to three million Germans. Nobody was being mistreated, of course. But Hitler concocted stories about killings and, when British prime minister Neville Chamberlain came calling, bamboozled him into believing that the Nazis would be satisfied if the Czech people could vote in a plebiscite.

Like Canadian prime minister William Lyon Mackenzie King, Chamberlain was given to wishful thinking. He gained acceptance in England and France for Hitler's plebiscite idea, but then the Führer flew into a histrionic rage and repudiated his own conciliatory offer. Back home in Britain, Chamberlain dissembled and described the situation as "a quarrel in a faraway country between people of whom we know nothing."

On September 30, 1938, along with Germany, France, and Italy, Britain signed the Munich Agreement, which permitted the annexation of the Sudetenland on condition that this would be Hitler's last territorial expansion. The Führer made that promise. But he had no intention of keeping it. He invaded and seized control of the Sudetenland. Then, on March 15, 1939, in flagrant violation of the Munich pact, Hitler occupied the Czech provinces of Bohemia and Moravia.

The western allies looked the other way. They had established a formal alliance with Poland but not Czechoslovakia. Surely this would be the end of the Nazi expansion? Wrong again. Hitler was just beginning. Britain and France had declined to sign a non-aggression treaty with Russia. But now Hitler convinced Stalin that the Nazis would win any pan-European war. Why not be on the winning side? On August 23, the two dictators signed a mutual non-aggression covenant—the Nazi–Soviet Pact.

Eight days later, a German warship anchored at Danzig harbour opened fire without warning on a Polish garrison. So it began. The Nazis were invading Poland, just as Churchill had foreseen. Hitler ignored an ultimatum to withdraw and, on September 3, honouring their treaty with Poland, Britain and France declared war on Germany. Only then, on behalf of Canada, did William Lyon Mackenzie King step up. In a radio broadcast on September 10 he announced that "the forces of evil have been loosed in the world." And he called on Canadians "to unite in a national effort to save from destruction all that makes life worth living, and to preserve for future generations those liberties and institutions which others have bequeathed us." Within days, Australia, New Zealand, and South Africa had joined the fray.

On September 17, as agreed under the Nazi–Soviet Pact, Russia invaded Poland from the east. By October 6, the annexation and division of the Second Polish Republic was complete. Stalin was happy. And so for the moment was Hitler. He now controlled all of Czechoslovakia and most of Poland. *Lebensraum* was unfolding as it should. And he could turn his attention to assaulting western Europe without worrying that Russia might attack his armies from the east.

In the spring of 1940, the Nazis invaded Denmark, Norway, Luxembourg, the Netherlands, and Belgium. In June, they focused intently on France. During the previous decade, the French had built the Maginot Line along their border with Germany—an array of armed fortresses linked by an underground railway. It ended in the hills and woods of the Ardennes region, which encompassed parts of Belgium, Luxembourg, and northeastern France. The French believed those woods, backed by the Meuse River, to be impenetrable.

They were wrong. German tanks broke through the French lines at Sedan in the Ardennes, then rolled over French and Allied forces. On June 9, Nazi troops launched a ground offensive on Paris. Next day, the French government declared Paris an open city (so that it would not be bombed) and fled south to Bordeaux. On June 14 at 7 a.m., motorcyclists led a roaring parade up the Champs Élysées. Parisians watched, horrified, as Nazi troops marched darkness into their radiant city.

The French government retreated 360 kilometres south to Vichy, a small city in the heart of France. Édouard Daladier had already resigned as leader and on June 16, 1940, eighty-four-year-old Henri-Philippe Pétain became prime minister—a man lionized for spearheading a First World War victory at Verdun. Pétain signed an armistice with Germany on June 22, and the next day, Hitler himself arrived in Paris to gloat. At the Eiffel Tower, he proclaimed himself the greatest strategic genius of all time: "No one has achieved what I have."

So began the occupation of France by its next-door neighbour. Two million refugees flooded the roads out of Paris, many of them pushing carts and wheelbarrows loaded with their possessions. Those Parisians who remained found themselves in a city under curfew from nine at night until five in the morning. French radio stations broadcast nothing but German propaganda. The Nazis began rationing food, tobacco, coal, and clothing. As supplies grew scarce and prices rose, still more Parisians fled to the provinces.

Bastille Day, 1942: General Charles de Gaulle in exile during the Second World War saluting Free French Commando Unit Troops in London. *Alamy*

The Nazis forced Jews to wear an identifier, the yellow Star of David, and banned them from certain professions and public places. The Nazis reduced the City of Light to a dark shadow of its former self. But then, slowly at first, resistance began to build. From London, where he had gone into exile, General Charles de Gaulle made rousing broadcasts via the BBC.

By November, French university students had begun staging protests. As the Nazi occupation dragged on, resistance became multifarious. Some groups answered to the French Communist Party, others to de Gaulle. Resisters published newsletters, planted bombs, attacked German officers—and frequently paid a terrible price. With the help of the collaborationist French government based in Vichy, the Nazis established four main internment camps just outside Paris. Here they kept Americans, political dissidents, resisters, and Jews, housing them according to their label. And then they began doing worse.

23 / Three Shades of Anti-Semitism

ANTI-SEMITISM WAS NOT a universal component of twentieth-century fascism, which came to prominence in Italy under Mussolini. In Spain, Franco's Fascist regime did not emphasize anti-Semitism but focused more on ultra-nationalism and anti-communism. But then Hitler's Third Reich, an extension of fascist government, infamously incorporated anti-Semitism as a key element of its political mandate. The most enthusiastic Nazis were racist, ignorant, violent, nationalistic, and blindly, stupidly supportive of an authoritarian megalomanic.

But if we take fascists in France as our case study, we see that some of them were educated, articulate, and even capable of repentance. We can also distinguish different degrees of culpability, depending on the prevalence of anti-Semitism. In 1930s France, as elsewhere in the world, the economic misery of the Great Depression sent people searching for scapegoats. Right-wing extremist groups, like *Action française*, accused Jews of undermining French national identity. They stoked fears of a "Jewish-Bolshevik" conspiracy. They claimed that Jews belonged to a capitalist elite that manipulated global finance or else, contradictions be damned, that they were Communist agents bent on overthrowing capitalism.

The Nazi occupation of France fanned the flames of anti-Semitism. The collaborationist Vichy regime introduced the *statut des Juifs* to exclude Jews from public life throughout the country. Some leading French intellectuals befriended the Nazis and became collaborators. Among them were Bertrand de Jouvenal, Pierre Drieu La Rochelle, and Louis-Ferdinand Céline. To look closely at these three will provide a sense of the range of anti-Semitism among French collaborators during this period.

1

Bertrand de Jouvenel, the sometime lover of Martha Gellhorn, was a political philosopher. He was more pragmatic than ideological, more a fascist than an anti-Semite. He was less concerned with racial purity—Gellhorn was part Jewish, after all—than with creating a powerful state capable of restoring order.

After surviving his boyhood affair with his father's wife, Jouvenel married an older woman. But then, from 1930 to 1934, he had that intense affair with Gellhorn. Had Jouvenel's wife agreed to a divorce, Gellhorn would have married the man. Instead, she decamped. With Gellhorn gone, Jouvenel joined other youngish French intellectuals in supporting the creation of the *Institut pour l'étude du fascisme*. As a contributor to the right-wing paper *Gringoire*, he provided sympathetic coverage of Hitler's 1935 Nuremberg Congress, which enacted anti-Semitic and racist laws "for the protection of German blood and German honour." Those laws forbade marriages or sexual relations between Jews and Germans and stripped Jews of German citizenship.

While moving in French nationalist circles, Jouvenel became friendly with writer Pierre Drieu La Rochelle and other collaborators. In February 1936, Jouvenel did a supportive interview with Adolf Hitler for the daily newspaper *Paris-Midi*. He joined the *Parti populaire français* and supported fascism as editor-in-chief of its journal. He quit that job when the party supported the 1938 Munich Agreement—not realizing, obviously, that Hitler had no intention of adhering to its constraints.

After the Nazis occupied Paris in 1940, Jouvenel stayed in the city and published *Après la défaite* (*After the Defeat*), a monograph urging France to join Hitler's new world order. In 1944, with the allies about to liberate Paris, Jouvenel realized that they might not look favourably on his recent writings and fled to Switzerland. Over the next two decades, he would abandon fascism and move leftward on the political spectrum. He would sympathize with the 1968 student protests in Paris, criticize the US war in Vietnam, and support François Mitterand, the first left-wing politician to assume, in 1981, the presidency of France.

That Jouvenel moved from far right to centre left is indisputable, as further evidenced by the political and economic books he wrote later, notably *The Ethics of Redistribution* (1951). Probably he could make that transition because he was always more a detached intellectual than a passionate racist driven by unreasoning, almost incomprehensible hatred.

2

Certain other French intellectuals found it impossible to escape their anti-Semitic trajectories. During the mid-1930s, Pierre Eugène Drieu La Rochelle, a novelist, political essayist, and editor, became one of the most prominent advocates of fascism in France. After embracing left-wing politics in his twenties, he moved to the right during the 1930s and, as director of *La nouvelle revue française*, became a leading figure of cultural collaboration. In 1939 he published *Gilles*, his most celebrated novel, whose eponymous hero develops a fusion of Christianity and fascism. The young man revelled in anti-Semitic stereotypes, declared that he detested the modern world, and insisted, "I am not an anti-Semite, because I have a horror of politics. But I cannot tolerate the Jews, since they are par excellence the modern world that I abhor."

Elitist and anti-bourgeois, Drieu was the son of a lawyer who squandered his wife's dowry and then abandoned the family to return to a former mistress. As a child, when Pierre had difficulty understanding the Dreyfus affair, he was strongly influenced by the woman who became his primary caregiver—his maternal grandmother. She

supported the false accusations against Jewish Captain Alfred Dreyfus and expressed such virulent anti-Semitism as could hardly fail to
scar the youth.

A brilliant student with a keen interest in writing, young Drieu
attended the prestigious *École libre des sciences politiques* in Paris,
intending to pursue a career in diplomacy. But then, in 1914, inex-
plicably, he failed his final exam. He considered suicide but instead,
with the First World War breaking out, joined the French army. During the war, he was wounded three times—something he never forgot.

In 1917, not yet given over to anti-Semitism, Drieu married Colette
Jéramec, the sister of a Jewish friend. In his student notebooks he
had written, "Two beings whom I will spend my life to discover: the
woman and the Jew." The marriage lasted four years. In the 1920s,
Drieu became part of the Dada and Surrealist movements that
emerged out of the war. Their adherents rejected the logic, rational-
ity, and bourgeois aesthetics of capitalist society, instead championing
the significance of dreams and the unconscious mind.

Drieu became friends with the left-leaning surrealist Louis Aragon, a friendship that kept him from joining *Action française* and the
emerging fascist movement until later. In 1925, the two men fell out
over a woman. While Aragon rose to prominence in the French Communist Party, Drieu took to denouncing the parliamentary system and
saying that France could stay strong only by embracing authoritarianism. He inspired Aragon to create, in one of his novels, the character
Aurélien, who exemplifies those intellectuals of the postwar generation who drifted toward fascism.

In 1922, Drieu had gained attention with a controversial essay,
"Mesure de la France," deploring the weakening of France in the wake
of the Great War. Two years later, he published a book of stories that
was nominated for a Goncourt Prize. And in 1925, he produced an
autobiographical first novel, *L'Homme couvert de femmes* (*The Man
Covered with Women*).

Drieu enjoyed relationships with a series of wealthy women while
producing a steady stream of books and essays critical of what he saw
as the increasing decadence of postwar France. By the early thirties,

established among the literati, Drieu had become friends with André Malraux. In 1931, always vacillating, he mocked racist theories and praised the left-leaning writer André Gide. With Bertrand de Jouvenel, he sought to create a party that would unite young leftists and, like Aragon and Malraux, he attended anti-fascist rallies.

But when, in 1933, Malraux sought to enlist him in denouncing Hitler, Drieu declined. He admired the way the Führer had seized power. The following year, he went to Berlin with Jouvenel, who was committed to a Franco-German alliance. He became friendly with Otto Abetz, who would become Nazi ambassador to Vichy France. Back in Paris, he tried and failed to convert his friends to "fascist socialism," his notion that socialism could be attained only through fascism.

By the mid-thirties, Drieu could see little difference between Hitlerism and Stalinism. In 1940, when the Nazis occupied France, Abetz appointed him director of *La nouvelle revue française* (NRF), France's foremost literary journal. He acted on his mandate to reduce contributions from Jews and communists, but also convinced the Vichy regime to release from prison certain writers who opposed collaboration, among them Jean-Paul Sartre. In October 1941, Drieu visited Berlin to attend a German Writers' Congress organized by Joseph Goebbels. It encouraged writers to align themselves with Nazi ideology and to celebrate nationalism, Aryan superiority, and anti-Semitism.

The elitist Drieu, swinging erratically between Marxism and fascism, embraced Nazism as a reaction against the mediocrity of parliamentary democracy. In 1943, disillusioned and still vacillating, Drieu quit the collaborationist NRF and began studying eastern religions. He rejoined the fascist *Parti populaire français*, to which he had belonged from 1936 to 1939, while writing in his secret diary of his admiration for Stalinism.

The following year, when in 1944 the Allied forces began marching on Paris, he refused to leave the city and rejected Malraux's offer of a place to hide. On August 11, realizing that he would probably be imprisoned, he tried to kill himself with a drug overdose. Friends rescued him. But the following March, newspapers announced that a warrant had been issued for his arrest on the charge of collaborating with the Nazis during the occupation. Drieu told his cook, "Now I can't get out of here." That night, he took his own life by turning on a gas oven and swallowing an overdose of barbiturates.

3

Those who admire Louis-Ferdinand Céline despite his rabid anti-Semitism insist that he revolutionized French literature in the early 1930s. They point to the working-class vernacular he used while attacking the polished "bourgeois" language of more conventional authors. Admirers included Henry Miller, whose stylistic fireworks owed much to Céline and so impressed George Orwell. More surprisingly, postwar novelist Philip Roth would write, "Céline is my Proust!" He explained, "Even if his anti-Semitism made him an abject, intolerable person—to read him, I have to suspend my Jewish conscience, but I do it because anti-Semitism isn't at the heart of his books."

Others dispute this last assertion and perceive Céline's anti-Semitism as raw, visceral, vulgar, and obsessive. This third Nazi sympathizer was not a thinker like Jouvenel or even the indecisive Drieu, but rather gave voice to a chaotic torrent of paranoia, misanthropy, and nihilism. Yes, if we momentarily look past its racism, his 1932 novel *Journey to the End of the Night* is a howling masterpiece of rebellion. The book won the Prix Renaudot. But while here we see a wildly original talent at work, we also find a viscerally rooted anti-Semitism. This would emerge more clearly after 1937, when Céline produced anti-Semitic polemics and urged France to forge a military alliance with Nazi Germany.

Born Louis Ferdinand Auguste Destouche just outside Paris, he adopted the pen name Céline when he began publishing. His father was a middle manager in an insurance company, and his mother owned a boutique in which she sold lace. After graduating from primary school at age eleven in 1905, he worked at entry-level jobs in various trades. His parents sent him to Germany and England, one year in each, to learn languages. Back in Paris, working often for jewellers, he bought schoolbooks and resolved to become a doctor.

In 1912, rebelling against his parents, he joined the French army and moved to Rambouillet, southwest of Paris. After adapting to military life, he became a sergeant. In October 1914, near the outset of the First World War, he volunteered to carry a message under heavy German fire. Wounded near Ypres, he received a medal for bravery but later wrote that his wartime experience left him disgusted with "all that is bellicose."

March 1915 found him in London, working in the French passport office while embracing a nightlife among habitués of the London underworld. Declared unfit for further military duty because of his previous injury, he was discharged. The following year, Céline went to French Cameroon, where he worked as a plantation overseer but also ran a pharmacy for locals, having his parents ship him medicines from home. In April 1917, plagued by health problems and repelled by being part of European colonialism, he returned to France, determined to make a career in medicine.

He found work with a team that, sponsored by the Rockefeller Foundation, travelled around Brittany conducting information sessions on tuberculosis and hygiene. In the small city of Rennes, he courted the daughter of a doctor on the medical faculty of the local university. He studied part-time, earned his baccalaureate, and married the young woman, Édith Follet. He started studying medicine at Rennes, transferred to the University of Paris, and became a doctor in May 1924.

Soon after, he joined the Geneva-based health department of the League of Nations. Leaving his wife and daughter in Rennes, he travelled around Europe, and to Africa, Canada, the United States, and Cuba. Édith divorced him in 1926 and he took up with Elizabeth Craig, an American dancer with whom he would live for six years. Late in 1927, he set up a medical practice in a working-class suburb in Paris. When that failed, he moved with Elizabeth to Montmartre and worked at various clinics while also writing his first novel, *Journey to the End of the Night*.

Published in 1932, this controversial work was celebrated for its anarchy, language, and anti-colonialism, and reviled for its vulgarity and obscenity. When it failed to win the France's foremost literary prize, the Prix Goncourt, the outrage and scandal drove sales to 50,000 in the next two months. Céline continued to work as a doctor. In 1933, interviewed as an author, he declined to take a stance on Nazism and the rise of fascism in France, explaining that he had always been an anarchist and had never voted for anyone: "The Nazis loathe me as much as the socialists and the commies too."

In May 1936, Céline's second novel, *Death on the Installment Plan*, appeared with numerous blank spaces, visibly redacted where the publisher feared being prosecuted for obscenity. It received mostly negative reviews—for its gutter language, its pessimism, its contemptuousness—but still sold 35,000 copies. That August, curious about Russia, Céline spent a month visiting Leningrad. Stalin's Great Terror was getting underway, a bloodbath designed by the dictator to eliminate suspected political enemies. This purge would claim millions of lives. Back home, Céline wrote and published "Mea Culpa," an autobiographical essay in which he criticized the violent repressiveness of Soviet society. He offered no comprehensive analysis, but after returning to France swung sharply and finally to the right.

In 1937, Céline revealed his fully adult ideology with the first of several anti-Semitic pamphlets, *Trifles for a Massacre*. In it, he advocated a military alliance with the Nazis to save France from war. Applauded by the French far right, Céline unleashed still more vitriolic anti-Semitism in a pamphlet called *School for Corpses*. By now he was writing full-time and living with Lucette Almansor, a French dancer he would later marry. When war erupted in September 1939, Céline was again declared unfit for military service—70 percent disabled. He was allowed to work as a ship's doctor on a French troop transport but was back in suburban Paris when the Nazis marched into the city. He and Lucette helped evacuate an elderly woman and two newborn infants to the west coast, but then returned to Paris.

In 1941, working in Montmartre as the head doctor of a public clinic, Céline published *The Beautiful Sheets*, a third book-length polemic. He ranted about Jews, Freemasons, the Catholic Church, the educational system, and even the French army. The Vichy government regarded this last denunciation as defamatory and so banned the book.

In October 1942, Céline's first two anti-Semitic rants appeared in new editions. Three months before, though he had been in Paris at the time, he had said not a word about the infamous Vél d'Hiv Roundup—the Great Roundup during which French gendarmes, acting on Nazi orders, had arrested more than 13,000 Jews, among them 4,100 children and 5,900 women. The police herded them into the Vélodrome d'Hiver, a winter stadium for bicycle races near the Eiffel Tower. They confined them in horrendous conditions—no sanitary facilities, little water, nothing to eat but scraps of bread—for an average of five days. After that, they put them on trains and shipped them east in cattle cars to concentration and extermination camps, among them Auschwitz, in Poland, where they would be murdered by poison gas.

By 1944, identified as a collaborationist writer, Céline was receiving anonymous death threats. When the Allies landed in France, he and Lucette fled to the Sigmaringen enclave in Germany, 650 kilometres east. They holed up with Vichy leaders and other French collaborators. In March 1945, Céline obtained visas for German-occupied Denmark and stayed on after the war ended. He lived there for the next six years—eighteen months of which he spent in prison after the new French government sought his extradition for collaboration.

Céline was tried in absentia, found guilty, and sentenced to a hefty fine and one year in jail. A French military tribunal granted him amnesty as a disabled war veteran, and in July 1951 Céline returned to France. He signed a deal with the publisher Librairie Gallimard to republish all his novels and bought a villa in Meudon, situated on the Seine just outside Paris. In 1957, a novel he wrote about his time in Sigmaringen, *From One Castle to Another*, sold 30,000 copies in its first year and revived the controversy over his wartime activities. Céline finished his final novel, *Rigodon*, on June 30, 1961, and died the next day, age sixty-seven, of a ruptured aneurysm.

Some literary critics, among them the Franco-American George Steiner, regard Céline as one of the two most important French novelists of the twentieth century—the other being Marcel Proust. Steiner credited these two with creating "the idiom and sensibility of twentieth-century narrative." Céline renovated literary language, incorporating the spoken French of the working class, neologisms, obscenities, and the slang of soldiers, sailors, and criminals.

How could Steiner ignore the writer's rabid anti-Semitism? Even the far-right French journalist Robert Brasillach thought it so extreme that it might be counterproductive. Some Nazis agreed, among them Abetz, the German ambassador, who argued that Céline "started from correct racial notions" but his "savage, filthy slang" and "brutal obscenities" spoiled his "good intentions" with "hysterical wailing." German novelist Ernst Jünger, stationed in Paris during the occupation, reported a 1941 conversation in which Céline said he was stupefied that the Nazis did not exterminate the French Jews. The following year, certainly, with the Great Roundup, they began a significant attempt.

Decades later, in 2018, following a public outcry and threats of legal action, Gallimard shelved plans to republish a thousand-page compendium of Céline's most virulently anti-Semitic works. Then in 2022, Gallimard did publish two long-lost novels, *War* and *London*, which Céline wrote in the early 1930s, before he was so driven by racist hatred that he could no longer think straight.

24 / A Human Wrecking Ball of Hatred

DURING THE 1930S and '40s, those three influential writers—Jouvenel, Drieu, and Céline—did terrible ideological damage. But I would argue that a fourth racist collaborator, American expatriate poet Ezra Pound, caused more harm than those three French writers combined. Pound was a human wrecking ball of anti-Semitic hatred.

He has his literary champions, of course. One of his most influential apologists was Canadian literary scholar Hugh Kenner, who in his 1971 book *The Pound Era* situated him as the central figure of Modernist literature. Having been introduced to Pound's work by Canadian media theorist Marshall McLuhan in 1948, Kenner ignored the poet's fascism, anti-Semitism, and treason and took a New Critical approach, arguing that only "the work" mattered, not the man. In this Kenner was joined by several others, among them Carroll F. Terrell, who added a two-volume companion to Pound's major works and, between 1975 and 1990, organized four major conferences around the poet's work.

Some scholars rejected this approach as hagiographic. Others recognized and lambasted Pound's fascism. And several critical biographers tried to find a middle ground. On the one hand, on the other. So, what about Ezra Pound? Is he to be absolved? Or is he to be weighed and found wanting? Certainly, he was an influential poet and editor. In the early 1920s, after he moved to Paris from England,

Pound helped guide the careers of several emerging writers, among them James Joyce, Ernest Hemingway, and another American expat poet, T.S. Eliot. Flash forward two decades, to the early 1940s, and we find Pound in Italy, transformed now into a raving anti-Semite doing international radio broadcasts on behalf of the Fascist Italian government, mainly to Axis-power populations. He attacked Churchill and Roosevelt and Roosevelt's family while celebrating Hitler and Mussolini.

During these broadcasts, he referred to Jews as "filth" and slandered them as "a parasitic race, draining the lifeblood of nations and civilizations." He denounced Jewish intellectuals for "having corrupted the cultural and artistic institutions." From April 1941, for thirty-three months of broadcasts, Pound received the equivalent today of more than $240,000 from the Mussolini government—this while denouncing Jewish bankers as "the root cause of economic inequality and the enslavement of the working class." He had become not just a lunatic racist-for-hire but a fascist sellout.

Born in 1885 in Hailey, Idaho Territory, Pound was the son of a land office registrar and the grandson of a Republican congressman. He was descended from Quakers and Puritans who had arrived from England in the seventeenth century. He grew up mostly in Wyncote, Pennsylvania, published a political limerick in 1896, and at twelve entered a military academy, where he wore an American Civil War–style uniform and learned how to shoot. He entered the University of Pennsylvania in 1901 and, with his parents, went on a three-month tour of Europe (his second) before transferring to Hamilton College in Clinton, New York.

After losing a fellowship due to a conflict with teachers, he taught at a Presbyterian college but lost that post because he flouted academic norms, refusing, for example, to give his students final grades. In 1908, Pound headed for Europe to immerse himself in the cultural scene. In London he got to know literary figures like Wyndham Lewis, George Bernard Shaw, and Hilaire Belloc. Back in the US, his anti-Semitic views surfaced when, at twenty-five, he wrote a series of essays called *Patria Mia*: "The Jew alone can retain his detestable qualities, despite climatic conditions."

His parents agreed to finance another voyage to Europe. He planned a sojourn, sailed in February 1911, and did not return to the US until April 1939. In London, he began writing a weekly column for the socialist *New Age*. During the next decade, he rubbed shoulders with such writers as Katherine Mansfield and H.G. Wells. He also met C.H. Douglas, an engineer developing an economic theory of Social Credit—one that would later underpin right-wing parties in Alberta and British Columbia. Douglas saw the Jews as needing to abandon a vision of themselves as the "dominating race."

Meanwhile, Pound developed a theory of Imagist poetry, which advocated the use of concrete language and cutting superfluous words to achieve clarity and precision while concentrating meaning. In 1913, he became literary editor of *The Egoist*, run by the British political activist Harriet Shaw Weaver, and worked as a secretary to Irish poet W.B. Yeats, who was twenty years older than Pound and losing his sight. Yeats introduced him to the work of James Joyce, who sent along the first chapter of his novel *Portrait of the Artist as a Young Man*. Pound declared it "damn fine stuff" and relayed it to Weaver, who published it. This led another publisher, Grant Richards, to reverse his previous rejection of Joyce's short story collection, *Dubliners*—an outcome that moved the young Irishman to credit Pound as "a miracle worker."

By the outbreak of the First World War, Pound had established himself in literary circles, though he alienated some with his abrasive arrogance. In 1914 he married the well-connected artist Dorothy Shakespear. After seven years in London, the Pounds decamped to Paris, where they moved in avant-garde circles.

In February 1922, Ernest Hemingway came calling, and the two men struck up a friendship. Pound also received an early draft of T.S. Eliot's groundbreaking poem "The Waste Land" and, applying his keen editorial eye, cut it in half. That summer, at age thirty-six, Pound began an affair with Olga Rudge, ten years younger, the daughter of a wealthy steel family from Ohio. She became pregnant and, when the Pounds relocated to Rapallo, Italy, in 1924, she joined them.

In 1932, influenced by fascist writings from *Action française*, Pound wrote the first of 180 articles for a Social Credit journal called

The New English Weekly. The following year, after making more than one request to share his Social Credit economic theories, he managed to gain an audience with Mussolini. He amused the dictator with anti-Semitic jokes and an eighteen-point draft of his economic plan.

Back in Rapallo, Pound knocked out a book celebrating the idea of the fascist state and produced articles praising Mussolini for the *New York World-Telegram*, the *Chicago Tribune*, and *The Criterion*, a British literary journal founded and edited by Eliot, who was also something of an anti-Semite. Pound wrote dozens of short pieces for a newsletter published by the Italian embassy in London.

In 1938, he hailed Mussolini's *Manifesto of Race*, which removed Italian citizenship from Jews, and thrilled to hear the Italian dictator declare Judaism "an irreconcilable enemy of fascism." The following year, during the spring and summer, Pound wrote a dozen articles for the *Japan Times*. He denounced Winston Churchill, asserted that in Europe, democracy was defined as "a country run by Jews," and discussed the "essential fairness of Hitler's war aims." In September, when war broke out, he kicked his racist rhetoric into overdrive with a letter-writing campaign. Then came the hateful radio broadcasts—hundreds of them between January 1941 and March 1945.

In July 1943, a US federal court indicted Pound in absentia for treason. Undaunted, Pound urged the secretary of Italy's Republican Fascist Party to compel bookstores to showcase *The Protocols of the Elders of Zion*, knowing full well it was an anti-Semitic hoax. Created in Russia in 1903 during a series of pogroms, it outlined a purported Jewish conspiracy to take over the world. "The arrest of Jews will create a wave of useless mercy," Pound wrote, "thus the need to disseminate the *Protocols*."

Nazi troops arrived in Rapallo in May 1944 to guard the Italian coast against Allied incursions, compelling the Pounds to vacate their apartment. For the next year, until the end of the war, the couple lived with Olga Rudge in her house above the town. Early in May 1945, Italian partisans arrested Pound, then transferred him at his request to the US Army Counterintelligence in Genoa.

On May 8, the day Germany surrendered, Pound produced a statement: "I am not anti-Semitic, and I distinguish between the Jewish usurer and the Jew who does an honest day's work for a living. Hitler and Mussolini were simple men from the country. I think that Hitler was a saint and wanted nothing for himself. I think that he was fooled into anti-Semitism and it ruined him." In a baffling echo of a statement made by Canadian prime minister King, Pound told a reporter that Hitler was "a Jeanne d'Arc . . . [L]ike many martyrs, he held extreme views."

Pound was sent to an American army centre north of Pisa, where he was penned up in an outdoor steel cage measuring six feet square. In stifling heat, denied communication, he slept on the concrete floor. After three weeks, he went on a hunger strike. Medical staff moved him to a tent of his own, where he began drafting poems for what became *The Pisan Cantos*. This poetry collection explores a wide range of topics, including his wartime actions, his controversial broadcasts, and his support for fascism.

Late in 1945, Pound was returned to the US and examined by three court-appointed psychiatrists. They found him mentally unfit to stand trial—"abnormally grandiose . . . expansive and exuberant in manner." A fourth doctor, hired by Pound's lawyer, declared him a psychopath and therefore unfit for trial. A hearing in February 1946 judged him to be of "unsound mind." From the floor he shouted, "I never did believe in Fascism, God damn it. I am opposed to Fascism." But soon enough, he resumed championing it.

Over the next dozen years, Ezra Pound remained in custody at St. Elizabeths Hospital in Washington, DC. From early 1948, he became so comfortable—he had a large room with a desk, a typewriter, and floor-to-ceiling bookshelves—that he wished only to remain. The following year, hoping to secure his release, a literary jury of mostly supporters decided to overlook his racist politics and recognize his *Pisan Cantos* with the inaugural Bollingen Prize for poetry. This caused an uproar within literary circles. George Orwell, for one, wrote that he considered Pound a mediocre writer who certainly did not deserve to be so honoured.

In July 1953, one psychiatrist, noting the poet's "profound, incredible, over-weaning narcissism," suggested that he had narcissistic personality disorder—the same diagnosis many experts would later apply to Donald Trump. Because this disorder was not viewed as a mental illness, and would have allowed him to stand trial, the hospital superintendent changed it to "psychotic disorder, undifferentiated."

While incarcerated, Pound became friends with John Kasper, a Ku Klux Klan member who set up a "white citizens' council" in Washington whose members had to be white, support racial segregation, and believe in the divinity of Jesus. During the mid-fifties, Pound wrote at least eighty articles for the Social Credit–linked *New Times* of Melbourne. In one he alleged a "Jewish-Communist plot" and likened it to syphilis. He also dismissed the concept of equality as "anti-biological nonsense." According to Pound, "the fuss about 'de-segregation' in the United States has been started by Jews." The country needed "race pride."

Against this backdrop, friends like Olga Rudge lobbied for Pound's release. In 1950, Hemingway told her the poet had "made the rather serious mistake of being a traitor to his country, and temporarily he must lie in the bed he made." But four years later, after being awarded the Nobel Prize in literature, Hemingway wondered if "this would be a good year to release poets." And in 1957, he signed a letter seeking Pound's release. Several publications got on board. And in May 1958, declaring the poet incurably insane and beyond treatment, the hospital discharged Pound.

He lived on for another fourteen years, during which time those who met him gave conflicting reports. T.S. Eliot said that Pound had recanted his "stupid, suburban prejudice of anti-Semitism," while poet and critic Allen Tate him as "cheerfully unrepentant" and regretting nothing he had ever said. Pound died in Venice on October 31, 1972—one day after his eighty-seventh birthday—of "a sudden blockage of the intestine."

Pound's friends strove to rehabilitate his reputation, claiming that his anti-Semitism arose out of mental illness. Others rejected this rationalization. Historian and poet Robert Conquest argued that Pound had a "minimal talent" and a "fantastic arrogance," and accused the critical establishment of having set up "a system of apologetics which the slyest Jesuit of the seventeenth century would have baulked at." Pound chose deliberately to collaborate with Nazis and earned a handsome living by making viciously anti-Semitic broadcasts. He championed fascism, celebrated racial purity, scapegoated Jewish people, and propagated conspiracy theories. What else do we need to know?

25
Arendt Fights Back

WHAT ABOUT THE targeted scapegoats of all this hatred? Millions of Jews were slaughtered. Of the many who fought back, few articulated their resistance more eloquently than Hannah Arendt. Looking back from the 1960s, Arendt would pinpoint February 27, 1933, as the date she turned from philosophy to politics and resistance. "The burning of the Reichstag," she told an interviewer, "and the illegal arrests that followed during the same night." Twenty-six years old at the time, shocked, she could no longer remain a simple bystander.

As a German Jew, Arendt became a target with the ascension of Hitler. But she refused to play victim. And when, soon after the Reichstag fire, the leader of the Zionist Federation of Germany asked her to do some risky research, she jumped at the chance. The Federation wanted to collect materials—"horror propaganda"—that would reveal systemic anti-Semitism in various business and professional circles. To assign one of their members to this task would have jeopardized the whole organization. But the academic Arendt, unaligned in Berlin and already doing related research at the Prussian State Library, was merely friends with Zionist leaders.

She went to work and, within weeks, put together a damning collection of evidence. But this was Berlin in the spring of 1933 and a librarian blew the whistle. With her mother, Arendt was on her way to attend a luncheon when the Gestapo arrested her—and, for good measure, her mother, Martha Arendt. The agents took the two women

Hannah Arendt in 1944, when she landed her first full-time salaried job in New York City. *dpa picture alliance / Alamy*

to a police station, separated them, then proceeded to search their apartment. They soon released Martha but held Hannah in custody. "I got out after eight days," she said, "because I made friends with the official who arrested me." He was "a charming fellow" who had just been promoted from the criminal to the political division. What was he supposed to do with this young woman? He had no idea. The Zionist Federation of Germany got her a lawyer, but she sent the man away. The arresting officer kept promising to get her released, and he "had such an open, decent face" that she relied instead on him. Sure enough, he set her free to await trial.

Next time, Hannah understood, she could hardly expect to encounter an equally sympathetic jailer. So, with her mother, she left Germany without travel documents, fleeing south over the Erzgebirge (the Ore Mountains) through a thick forest known as the Green Front. They crossed the border through a house that had a front door in Germany and a back door in Czechoslovakia.

They proceeded to Prague and then to Geneva, where, through a family friend, Hannah landed a job as a recording secretary and speech writer at the League of Nations Jewish Agency for Palestine. At this she excelled—but, as a brilliant young intellectual, recently politicized, she wanted more.

Born in Linden (now a district of Hanover) in 1906, Johanna Arendt had grown up in Königsberg in a comfortable, secular Jewish family of Russian extraction—community leaders, highly educated—though her father died when she was seven. By the age of fourteen, she had read the work of Søren Kierkegaard, Karl Jaspers, and

Immanuel Kant. At fifteen she was expelled from a school for leading a boycott against a teacher who had insulted her.

After finishing high school in Berlin, she studied at the universities of Marburg and Heidelberg, earning a doctorate in philosophy from the latter in 1929. At seventeen, she had begun a four-year affair with philosopher Martin Heidegger, who at the outset was thirty-five and married with two young sons. She would end her relationship with him after he became a Nazi. She herself wed a fellow student of philosophy, Günther Stern, in 1929.

Arendt spent two years in Berlin writing articles and reviews (on topics ranging from Jewish politics to the status of women). Confronting systemic anti-Semitism, Arendt wrote: "If one is attacked as a Jew one must defend oneself as a Jew. Not as a German, not as a world citizen, not as an upholder of the Rights of Man."

In 1933, after escaping to Geneva following her arrest, she moved to Paris, that great cosmopolitan magnet. While learning French, Hebrew, and Yiddish, she gave lectures and worked for Youth Aliyah, which rescued thousands of children from Nazi persecution and resettled them in Palestine. Here in Paris she became friends with her husband's cousin, the German Jewish philosopher and Marxist critic Walter Benjamin.

In 1938 Arendt finished her first book, *Rahel Varnhagen: The Life of a Jewish Woman*—a biography of a passionate nineteenth-century German intellectual. Arendt took this strong, independent woman, active in cultural discussions, as a role model. She had divorced her husband in 1937, after Germany deprived Jews of their German citizenship. In January 1940, she married philosopher Heinrich Blücher, attracted by his political activism.

On May 5, 1940, anticipating the Nazi invasion of France, the military governor of Paris went after "enemy aliens"—people who were citizens of countries at war with France, mainly German and Austrian Jews who had sought refuge. All those between the ages of seventeen and fifty-five were to report for internment (excepting only mothers with children). Days later, in what would look like a dress rehearsal for the Great Roundup of 1942, these mostly Jewish exiles were gathered—the men into the Stade Buffalo, the women into the Vélodrome d'Hiver. People were told to bring food for two days, their own eating utensils, and luggage weighing no more than 30 kilograms. The men, including Blücher, were sent to Camp du Vernet in the French Pyrenees, and the women, Arendt among them, to Camp Gurs, farther west.

Both areas were coming under control of the collaborationist Vichy government. Communications broke down and, "in the resulting chaos," Arendt wrote, she and two hundred of the seven thousand women at Gurs "succeeded in getting hold of liberation papers with which we were able to leave the camp." She managed to walk and hitchhike some 260 kilometres to Montauban, an unofficial headquarters for Jewish exiles where she had a close friend. Blücher turned up soon after, having escaped from a forced march. That fall, at Camp Gurs, another six thousand women joined those who had stayed behind. In 1942 and 1943, as conditions grew worse, the Nazis transported the remaining women to the death camp at Auschwitz.

At Montauban, through July and August of 1940, Arendt read voraciously and began envisioning a comprehensive book on anti-Semitism, "racial imperialism," and the suppression of minorities by the ruling nations of sovereign states. In September, bent on acquiring visas to America, she and Blücher made their way to Villa Air-Bel, a château in Marseille where a group of Americans were helping stateless Jews escape from France. There they met their old friend Walter Benjamin, who entrusted a valued manuscript to Arendt—*Theses on the Philosophy of History*—before he attempted to get out of France.

In January 1941, with all papers in order, Arendt and her husband travelled by train through Spain to Lisbon, Portugal. In May, they sailed on a Portuguese ship to New York City. There, starting with nothing, Hannah Arendt would turn herself into one of the most respected political thinkers of the twentieth century.

After settling in New York City and devoting a couple of months to learning English, Arendt worked as a research director for the Conference on Jewish Relations. She published articles on such topics as the plight of European Jews and the political situation in Europe. In 1944, she became a naturalized US citizen, solidifying her commitment to her new home. She took up various teaching positions, including one at the New School for Social Research, where she would teach for many years.

In her writing, Arendt explored diverse themes, such as authority, power, violence, judgment, and the nature of political action. She challenged conventional wisdom and provoked critical thinking about the nature of politics, society, and human behaviour. In 1951, she pulled it all together in *The Origins of Totalitarianism*, a groundbreaking analysis of the rise of totalitarian regimes that remains one of her most widely read books. Focusing mainly on Nazism and Stalinism, the book underscores how demagogues rise to power by exploiting societal vulnerabilities and political discontent. It shows how they use populist tactics—propaganda, manipulation, and divisive ideologies—to erode democratic values and establish authoritarian regimes. This seminal work solidified Arendt's reputation as a political thinker and brought her international recognition.

Meanwhile, in the 1950s, Arendt was shocked to see red-baiting senator Joseph McCarthy raging around the United States, smearing individuals with groundless allegations of communist affiliations and suppressing dissent by instilling fear. The country's long tradition of open debate, she explained later, "was being threatened by McCarthyism and the fear it generated." The silencing of disagreement created a climate of conformity, stifled critical thinking and undermined democracy itself—one of her highest values.

Hannah Arendt died in 1975 and so did not witness the rise to power of Donald Trump. Certainly, she would have deplored his barefaced lies and self-serving conspiracy theories. By his methods, she would have been appalled but not surprised. Arendt had observed that loneliness and isolation can make individuals more susceptible to totalitarian ideologies, and explained how, to stay in power, autocratic regimes exploit terror, surveillance, ignorance, and the herd mentality. "The ideal subject of totalitarian rule is not the convinced Nazi or the dedicated communist," she wrote, "but people for whom the distinction between fact and fiction, true and false, no longer exists."

26 / Benjamin Takes to the Pyrenees

LATE IN SEPTEMBER of 1940, the German Jewish philosopher Walter Benjamin set out from Villa Air-Bel in Marseille to escape France. A friend at the Institute of Social Research in Frankfurt had managed to get him a "non-quota visa" that would allow him to enter the United States. In Marseille, the American consulate gave him transit visas for Spain and Portugal. Benjamin lacked only an exit visa for France. This, he knew, the Vichy government would never grant. As a known anti-fascist, and a Jew, he was an obvious candidate for incarceration and everything that followed.

At Villa Air-Bel, Benjamin entrusted an important manuscript to Hannah Arendt, who had also turned up at the château. He told another would-be escapee, the Hungarian writer Arthur Koestler, that he was carrying enough morphine "to kill a horse." And on September 25, with a particularly cherished manuscript in a black briefcase, he boarded a train that took him to meet a guide in a small town near the border between France and Spain.

Benjamin, one of the most brilliant intellects of the early twentieth century, had never secured an academic position. He was too wild and unruly, nonconformist, uncontainable. Yet he was also a leading critic of Europe's cultural life. Literature, theatre, philosophy, theology, language, media, painting, architecture, photography, radio—he wrote about all of them definitively.

Outside the academy, which was more rigid then even than now, other leading intellectuals recognized his brilliance. Gershom Scholem, a prominent scholar of Kabbalah and other Jewish mysticism, recalled the "immediate impression of genius" and "the lucidity that often emerged from his obscure thinking." Benjamin's distant cousin Günther Stern, Arendt's first husband—later famous as Günther Anders for his work on the atomic bomb—said that next to Benjamin, "we are all unsubtle barbarians."

The apperceptive genius had become a Marxist in the mid-1920s, after spending two months in Moscow. He participated in interwar debates on mass media and mass culture, arguing that technical media could put an end to the pervasive bourgeois culture and create a new mass culture featuring new forms of imagination and expression. In a show of defiance, he appropriated the Nazi epithet "cultural Bolshevism" to describe his own position.

As he watched the Nazi party gain ground in the 1930s, he produced a series of critiques. In *Theories of German Fascism*, for example, he assailed the champions of paramilitary politics, charging that what these authors meant by "nation" was a ruling class supported by dependable fascist warriors—a ruling class "accountable to no one, and least of all to itself, enthroned on high."

Born in Berlin in 1892, Benjamin grew up in a prominent Jewish business family. He studied philosophy at the University of Berlin, where he first encountered Zionism, a political movement with the goal of establishing a Jewish homeland in the region of Palestine, then part of the Ottoman Empire. Benjamin developed a unique idea of "cultural Zionism," which highlighted spirituality and the furthering of European culture.

In 1914, Benjamin volunteered to serve in the German army but was rejected because of a heart condition. He resumed studying at the University of Munich, then transferred to the University of Bern, where he married and fathered a son. In 1919 he earned his PhD cum laude with a thesis on art criticism in German Romanticism.

Between the wars, Benjamin produced penetrating essays on everything from metaphysics and philosophy to theatre, radio, and politics—insightful, even dazzling, but also idiosyncratic. Instead of deploying conventional linear argument or narrative, he would create a montage and weave together a collage of diverse ideas, quotations, and observations. Hoping to qualify as a tenured university professor, he wrote a dissertation on *The Origin of German Tragic Drama*. It proved too original for the hidebound committee, whose members rejected it as eccentric.

His father declined to go on supporting his academic pursuits, so Benjamin devoted himself to criticism, translation, and writing for highbrow newspapers. In 1927 he started working on his magnum opus, a study of nineteenth-century Parisian life known as *The Arcades Project*. It would be published in 1982, a dazzling gallimaufry of notes and stand-alone articles running to more than one thousand printed pages. Ranging widely, Benjamin presents a devastating critique of the Nazi regime, arguing that it was oppressive, violent, and designed to maintain power and suppress the masses.

In 1932, as Hitler gained prominence, Benjamin, now divorced, lived several months on the Spanish island of Ibiza. After his return to Berlin, he perceived the 1933 Reichstag fire as marking the beginning of the end for Jews in Germany and left the country for good, eventually making his way to Paris. He joined a German émigré community that soon grew to more than 30,000.

Moving among artists and intellectuals, he grew close to his cousin Günther and his wife, Hannah Arendt, as in the evenings they frequented cafés and played chess. While living with emigrants as a lodger, Benjamin received financial aid from a support network run by the Institute for Social Research, which was affiliated with the University of Frankfurt.

In 1936, Benjamin published the essay "The Work of Art in the Age of Mechanical Reproduction," a groundbreaking study of how human perception changes in response to technological advance. He championed film as encouraging a more democratic, engaged audience, and encouraged surrealistic techniques that went beyond the real, anticipating computer-generated imagery. This essay, like many of his others, also lays out a critique of fascism. As early as 1921, in an essay called "Critique of Violence," Benjamin had remarked that "fascism aims at the substitution of the totalitarian state for the liberal state" and that "fascism is itself less 'ideological' than it is opportunist."

He also argued that "violence, naked and pure, is the only logical conclusion of fascism." Now, in 1936, he wrote that "fascism attempts to organize the newly created proletarian masses without affecting the property structure which the masses strive to eliminate." He added that "fascism sees its salvation in giving these masses not their right, but instead a chance to express themselves" and that "the logical result of fascism is the introduction of aesthetics into political life . . . Communism responds by politicizing art."

Late in August 1939 came a hammer-blow: the signing of the Nazi–Soviet non-aggression pact. On September 3, following the Nazi invasion of Poland, placards appeared in Paris ordering Germans to report to the city's Olympic stadium. After ten miserable days there, Benjamin was sent by train, along with three hundred others, to the Château de Vernuche near the town of Nevers, 250 kilometres south. On the last leg of this journey, he struggled during a forced march. The château was cold and empty and the men slept on the floor. Luckily, Benjamin had a support network that included bookseller Adrienne Monnier, life partner of Sylvia Beach of Shakespeare and Company, who with the help of PEN International secured Benjamin's release in November.

Back in Paris, Benjamin drafted an essay later published as "Theses on the Philosophy of History." Often cited as his last finished work, it strives to reconcile the idea of progress with the chaos of history. It also contains critiques of fascism and the totalitarian state. Benjamin writes that "behind every fascism is a failed revolution" and that "the tradition of the oppressed teaches us that the 'emergency situation' in which we live is the rule." The socialist workers' movement had too easily accepted notions of progress, so weakening the left's ability to confront fascism. Finding hope in the past requires a historian "who is firmly convinced that even the dead will not be safe from the enemy if he wins."

Benjamin knew that this political and social critique, so lucid, so on point, had enraged those Nazis who read it. On June 13, 1940, one day before the storm troopers entered Paris, he fled first to the town of Lourdes, 830 kilometres south of Paris in the foothills of the Pyrenees. He was determined to escape to the US via Spain and Portugal. From Lourdes he proceeded to the Villa Air-Bel in Marseille, where he took that train along the coast to Banyuls-sur-Mer, south of Perpignan.

There he called on Lisa Fittko, a young anti-Nazi from Berlin. Fittko and her husband, Hans, had known Benjamin in that city and, after 1933, in Paris. Now she agreed to lead him and two others—a mother and her sixteen-year-old son—into Spain along a mountain path, *la route Lister*. During the Spanish Civil War, the Republican general Enrique Lister had used this route to evacuate troops. The only alternative to well-guarded tracks and trails, it ran just a dozen kilometres from Banyuls to the Spanish town of Portbou—but it did involve steep grades and difficult climbing.

Physically, Walter Benjamin was in no condition for hiking. He was only forty-eight but his heart condition reduced his mobility to that of a much older man. When Fittko expressed concern that he was not fit for the arduous journey, he insisted that "the real risk would be not to go." And so, at the end of September, the party of four set out hiking. Benjamin established the pace. He would walk for ten minutes, then pause to catch his breath. Clearly, he was struggling. But he clutched his black leather briefcase and refused to relinquish it.

This continued for seven hours. Then the travellers came upon an almost vertical climb through a vineyard. More than once, Benjamin struggled upward and slid back down. Finally, Fittko and the teenage boy dragged him and his briefcase to the crest of the mountain. From that height, they could see the Mediterranean coasts of both Spain and France. There, directly below, lay the border crossing and, just beyond it, the town of Portbou.

Fittko did not have the necessary papers to go farther. Her mission accomplished, she said goodbye and turned back. The three hikers proceeded down the mountain to the Spanish border control. But now disaster struck. Spanish officials said that while countless others had passed this way without problem, they had just received orders to close the border crossing. The three new arrivals could stay in Portbou that night, but tomorrow they would be sent back to France.

Benjamin collapsed. His fellow travellers found a doctor, who bled him and administered injections. But that night, alone in a small hotel room, and knowing what would happen if he fell into the hands of the Gestapo, he administered the morphine he had brought. He scrawled a note. Unable to escape, he felt he had no choice. "It is in a tiny village in the Pyrenees, where no one knows me, that my life must come to its end."

Next morning, when locals found his body, they were shocked. The guards reopened the border. Later Hannah Arendt wrote, "One day earlier Benjamin would have got through without any trouble; one day later the people in Marseille would have known that for the time being it was impossible to pass through Spain. Only on that particular day was the catastrophe possible."

The manuscript that Benjamin carried in his briefcase has never been recovered.

27 / Némirovsky Guilty of Being Jewish

HANNAH ARENDT AND Walter Benjamin were activist Jewish intellectuals. They decried fascism and the rise of Hitler and actively opposed the occupation of France. They were communicators. They wielded influence. The Nazis would pursue them to the ends of the earth—or at least to the boundaries of Europe.

The situation of fiction writer Irène Némirovsky was more complex. It reveals more about the depth of racial hatred driving the Nazis because Némirovsky, born in Kyiv in 1903, the daughter of a wealthy Jewish banker, avoided activism and protest. She avoided confrontation—kept her mouth shut—and ended up dying at Auschwitz just the same.

In 1939, while seeking to obscure her Jewish roots, assimilate, and be recognized as French, Némirovsky converted to Catholicism. During the Nazi occupation of France, as a well-known novelist and the mother of two daughters, she sent letters seeking the protection of officials within the Vichy regime. She approached the rabid anti-Semite Xavier Vallat, the head of the Commissariat-General for Jewish Questions, requesting an exemption from anti-Jewish measures while expressing her loyalty to the regime. She also received financial support from a Vichy government literary foundation.

Meanwhile, Némirovsky continued to publish—albeit anonymously—in the far-right newspaper *Gringoire*, which juxtaposed fascist opinion pages with apolitical fiction. It was the only outlet that would have her.

Some critics have argued that, as a way of avoiding scrutiny, she perpetuated negative stereotypes that reinforced anti-Semitic sentiments. But the controversy around Némirovsky's response to persecution is less dramatic than the way in which, long after her death, she became a celebrated novelist.

For decades, Némirovsky's eldest daughter, Denise, had held on to a microscopically handwritten notebook her mother had left behind when arrested. She had always assumed it was a personal diary, not a literary manuscript. But then, in 1998, when she herself was sixty-eight years old, she took a closer look and realized that the notebook contained two short novels of a projected quintet, complete with notes for the final three. With her sister, Élisabeth, she transcribed them. She sent them to the French publisher Denoël, which in 2004 delivered them to the world in a single volume entitled *Suite française*.

The book, which portrayed life in France during the early days of the Nazi occupation, became an international sensation. It won awards and critical acclaim and sold more than 2.5 million copies in thirty-eight languages. In 2015, it was adapted into a successful film. Irène Némirovsky would have been astonished.

Growing up in Kyiv when that city was still part of the Russian Empire, Irina Leonova Nemirovskaya was fourteen when the Russian Revolution began. With her family, she fled to Finland, then settled in Paris. She graduated from the Sorbonne and, at eighteen, began madly writing—always in French. She married a Jewish banker in 1926, and with him would have two daughters.

In 1929, she published *David Golder*, a novel about a Jewish banker with family troubles. An overnight success, it hit the silver screen in France the following year, when Némirovsky struck again, with a novel called *Le Bal*, which became both a film and play. Through the 1930s, Némirovksy published ten more novels, so establishing herself as a French writer.

During this period, as the Nazis came to power in Germany, anti-Semitism intensified throughout Europe. In 1938, Némirovsky and her husband sought and were denied French citizenship. The following year, in a bid to gain some protection from persecution, Némirovsky became a Roman Catholic. She also baptized her daughters into the Catholic Church—one of them age ten, the other two. Then she sent them 330 kilometres south to live in the village of Issy-L'Évêque in the house of their nanny's mother.

In early 1940, Némirovsky still perceived herself as French in every way that mattered. But with the establishment of the collaborationist Vichy regime, that wasn't enough. No longer permitted to publish under her own name, Némirovsky received only rejections. The far-right *Gringoire* would publish her fiction without a byline— and, needing the money, she accepted that arrangement.

In May, with the Nazis closing in on Paris, Némirovksy joined her daughters in the south. Her husband would follow in 1941, having lost the right to work. Némirovsky had published at least fifty short stories and fifteen novels, yet now she had to publicly identify herself as a Jew and wear a yellow star when she left the house.

Soon after arriving in Issy-L'Évêque, Némirovksy outlined her most ambitious work yet—a five-part novel, inspired by *War and Peace*, that barely mentioned the Jews. Over the next two years she completed the first two parts—*Storm in June*, tracking the chaotic civilian exodus from Paris in 1940, and *Dolce*, treating the early period of Nazi occupation, and offering a sympathetic portrait of a billeted German soldier.

On July 17, 1942, days after finishing that second volume, thirty-nine-year-old Irène Némirovsky was arrested in front of her daughters as "a stateless person of Jewish descent." On one of the first convoys out of France after the Great Roundup, she was deported to Auschwitz. Her frantic husband wrote to the German ambassador in Paris, pleading for her release, insisting that even though his wife was of Jewish descent, "she does not speak of the Jews with any affection whatsoever in her works."

His pleas met only silence.

Némirovsky died in Auschwitz, supposedly from typhus, on August 17, 1942. Her husband was arrested soon afterward, taken from the girls, and sent to the same death camp. He was murdered in the gas chamber that November.

The posthumous publication in 2004 of *Suite française* gave rise to renewed controversy—notably, accusations that the portrayal of

Jewish characters in her earlier works show that Némirovsky was anti-Semitic. Olivier Philipponnat, the co-author with Patrick Lienhardt of *The Life of Irène Némirovksy*, dismisses these charges categorically. He argues that Némirovsky was driven to sort out the complexities of her Russian-Jewish bourgeois background and, above all, by a loathing for her vain, snobbish, and adulterous mother. Némirovsky's own older daughter, Denise, reported in 2007 that after the war, when she and her sister showed up at their grandmother's door, the woman refused to open it, shouting, "If you're orphans, go to the orphanage."

Charges of anti-Semitism had surfaced as early as 1929, when at twenty-six Némirovsky published *David Golder*. The title character is a greedy Jewish banker with a grasping wife and is even described as having a hooked nose. Némirovksy said she had based the characters loosely on her family: "I'm accused of anti-Semitism? Come now, that's absurd! For I'm Jewish myself and say so to anyone prepared to listen!" In 1935, Némirovsky pointed out how different the political climate had been when she wrote the novel. Had Hitler been in power, she said, "I would have greatly softened *David Golder*, and I would not have written it in the same way."

Némirovsky had considered herself a "respectable" writer and not an "unwanted foreigner," as she wrote to Marshal Pétain, the head of the Vichy government in 1940. In other words, she was a "French bourgeoise, pure and simple." But as Philipponnat and Lienhardt write in their final chapter, from the day the gendarmes arrested her, Irène Némirovsky "ceased to be a novelist, a mother, a wife, a Russian, a Frenchwoman: she was just a Jewess." In truth, that day came long before she was arrested. Némirovsky did everything conceivable to be accepted into French society. In the end, she was guilty of being Jewish. And for that, she was put to death.

28 / Hitler Makes a Mistake

IN JUNE 1941, with Ezra Pound just months into his career as a deranged radio broadcaster, Hannah Arendt having escaped to America, and Irène Némirovsky keeping a low profile in Vichy France, Adolf Hitler made a strategic blunder. Two years before, with Stalin, he had signed a German–Soviet non-aggression pact. The two dictators agreed to take no military action against each other for the next ten years. But on June 22, 1941, with the backing of Mussolini, Hitler attacked the Soviet Union with more than four million troops. Operation Barbarossa.

The Nazis took Kyiv, capital of Soviet Ukraine, and then pushed north toward Moscow, the nerve centre of Soviet communications networks, among them roads and railways. By taking Moscow, they would finish the Russians. As if to illustrate how fascism can spiral into something far worse, the murderous SS, the elite corps of troops led by Reinhard Heydrich, followed the German army into the Soviet Union, murdering Jews as they went. Heydrich created four *Einsatzgruppen*, special-purpose groups assigned to liquidate all Communist officials and all Jews serving the Soviet state.

Often the local non-Jewish population, keen to remain alive, assisted in the murders. In Ukraine, during two days in September 1941, the Nazis rounded up more than 33,770 Jews in Kyiv, marched them to a ravine known as Babi Yar, and shot them dead in cold blood. This mass murder, the worst to that point, signalled an escalation in the ongoing "Final Solution." The numbers murdered at Babi Yar would not be surpassed in a single extended episode until October 1941 when, after a gruelling siege, the Nazis captured Odessa in Soviet Ukraine. They subjected the city to pogroms, deportations, and mass shootings—a massacre that killed 50,000 Jews.

The previous month, the Nazis had begun what would become the seige of Leningrad, lasting 872 days. With that well underway, they launched the Battle of Moscow on October 2, sending some one million German troops toward the capital. The initial assault seemed successful, the Wehrmacht powering through Soviet defences and closing on the capital city by late November. Meanwhile, however, the autumn rains had turned the dirt roads to mud, slowing Nazi progress to a standstill—and giving the Russians time to regroup.

In late October, realizing that they were overextended and had reached what military commanders call the "culminating point of the attack," Hitler's generals advocated a strategic retreat, or at least a pause. Back in Berlin, the Führer would not hear of it. He was waging what historian David R. Stone calls "a gambler's war." In mid-November, the weather turned cold, the muddy roads froze solid, and the German tanks renewed their advance.

By now, however, through Richard Sorge, a Soviet spy in Japan, Stalin had learned that he need not fear a Japanese attack on the Soviet Union through Siberia. Instead, the Japanese were planning to assault US military sites in a bid to gain control of the Pacific theatre. In response, Stalin pulled eighteen divisions—roughly 270,000 troops—and tens of thousands of tanks and aircraft from the Far East to defend Moscow. As temperatures fell to forty below zero, the ill-prepared Nazis suffered frostbite, equipment breakdown, and logistical problems. They were taking heavy casualties.

Stalin had put the veteran Soviet general Georgy Zhukov in charge of the Red Army—one of the few Old Bolsheviks to have survived his paranoid purging of more than 40,000 officers. On December 5, 1941, after the exhausted German soldiers had surrounded Moscow, Zhukov mounted a massive counterattack. He used tanks and artillery to blast through the German lines north of the city. Next day, the Red Army overran the Nazis to the south. Soon the Germans were retreating in disarray, while Hitler was ordering that they stand fast.

Stalin tried to finish off the fleeing Nazis. He sent out a people's militia of untrained soldiers, who got almost completely wiped out. Still, by successfully defending Moscow and winning a crucial victory, the Red Army had handed the Nazis their first major defeat of the war. If the Germans had taken the capital city, the Soviets would probably have been forced to surrender. Then Hitler could have turned his full attention—and his formidable military resources—back to fighting the Allies in the West. Instead, the Nazis suffered 500,000 casualties and Hitler had to keep most of his troops in Russia.

By late 1941, Nazi leaders had realized that shooting Jews and tumbling them into open pits was inefficient, psychologically hard on those who carried out the executions, and far too publicly visible. Hitler and his lieutenants were looking for alternatives to using mobile killing squads. Mass sterilization? Deportation to the distant island of Madagascar? On January 20, 1942, they held a conference in the Berlin suburb of Wannsee to finalize "a general plan of the administrative, material, and financial measures necessary for carrying out the desired final solution of the Jewish question."

Reinhard Heydrich chaired the meeting. Heinrich Himmler had tasked him with implementing Hitler's plan for a systematic, continent-wide genocide. During the conference, fifteen high-ranking Nazi bureaucrats discussed the logistical aspects of deporting tens of thousands of Jews to extermination camps in occupied Poland. The conference highlighted the systematic and bureaucratic nature of the "final solution," detailing methods of transport, timetables, and treatment of different categories of Jews. Attendees agreed to annihilate approximately 11 million Jews, murdering not just those in Nazi-controlled territories, but residing anywhere in Europe.

The Wannsee Conference formalized the horrific scale of Hitler's genocidal plan. Attendees discussed and organized mass murder as a matter of state administration. They settled on turning some of the existing concentration camps into death camps, mostly in Poland, and on using poison gas to efficiently exterminate vast numbers of Jews. The officials then adjourned and, as if to illustrate Arendt's concept of "the banality of evil," went home to their wives and children.

LATE IN AUGUST 1942, having failed to take Moscow, the over-extended Nazis turned around, trekked a thousand kilometres south, and laid siege to Stalingrad. Hitler wanted to seize and destroy the city named for his adversary. The ensuing battle, one of the bloodiest in the history of warfare, would cost the lives of two million people. While bombing raids targeted civilians, soldiers engaged in hand-to-hand combat. Winter came early, driving temperatures to thirty-six below zero, exacerbating supply issues and causing significant casualties.

Back in Berlin, Nazi propaganda minister Joseph Goebbels produced newsreels featuring soldiers gambolling in the snow, apparently having a wonderful time. In truth, German troops were starving. In November 1942, Russian generals brought up reinforcements and launched Operation Uranus, cutting Nazi supply lines and surrounding the German 6th Army. Attempts to break the encirclement failed. Finally, on February 2, 1943, with Hitler raging that they should fight to the last man, the Nazi generals at Stalingrad turned their backs on the distant Führer and surrendered.

The Battle of Stalingrad marked a turning point on the Eastern Front. The destruction of an entire army dealt a severe blow to Germany's strategic position and boosted Soviet morale, marking the beginning of a series of counteroffensives that would eventually lead to Berlin. For Hitler, personally, this defeat was a disaster. He went into a tailspin and retreated to his heavily fortified "Wolf's Lair" in East Prussia, now part of Poland. Fifty-five years old, he suddenly looked much older, stooped and trembling, perhaps with Parkinson's. Normally front and centre at Nazi rallies, he made no public appearances. He walked his dog in the woods and talked only to his companion, Eva Braun, and his personal physician, who put him on a regimen of antidepressants and narcotics.

Worst of all, perhaps, from Hitler's perspective, Stalin was no longer on the defensive. He was ready to retaliate. And he was boiling for revenge. The remaining Nazi forces could not contain him. By the time D-Day rolled around, the great Allied invasion of June 6, 1944, two thirds of Hitler's soldiers would still be engaged on the Eastern Front.

PART FOUR

Here Come the Canadians

29 / America at War with Canada?

IT'S NO SURPRISE that Canada turns up in *The Handmaid's Tale*, given that Margaret Atwood herself is Canadian. That the country features in American Sinclair Lewis's dystopian novel *It Can't Happen Here*—that might sneak up on you. Yet nothing compares with Canada's appearance in *The Plot against America* by Philip Roth, because . . . because America at war with Canada? *What?*

Roth could see it coming almost two decades before Trump apologist Tucker Carlson wondered on Fox News why the US was "not sending an armed force north to liberate Canada from Trudeau." (We'll address that soon enough.) In 2004, during the presidency of George W. Bush, Roth published his alternate history in which the famous American aviator Charles Lindbergh, an unapologetic anti-Semite, runs for the presidency in 1940—and wins. The story focuses on how Lindbergh's victory impacts American Jews and, in particular, one Newark-based Jewish family. That family is Roth's own, which comprises his parents, his older brother, and himself, all fictionalized but bearing their real names, and with young Philip serving as the point-of-view character.

In the novel, the real-life Walter Winchell, an outspoken newspaper columnist and broadcaster, himself a Jew, becomes Lindbergh's chief antagonist and ends up paying a heavy price. As the newly elected, Nazi-sympathizing president inspires increasingly violent anti-Semitic attacks, eventually Winchell gets assassinated. Against this backdrop, Canada steps to the fore. Philip's cousin goes north to Montreal, joins the Canadian armed forces, and travels overseas to fight the Nazis.

In Detroit, meanwhile, attacks on synagogues and Jewish-owned shops escalate into a large-scale pogrom modelled on *Kristallnacht.* Several hundred of the city's 30,000 Jews flee across the border and take refuge in Windsor, Ontario. As the fictional Philip turns nine years old, his father repeatedly rejects his wife's pleas to join the exodus to Canada. He is an American. He won't be driven out of the land of his birth. By the time he agrees to flee, the Lindbergh government has closed the northern border.

Roth creates a riveting scene in which young Philip asks his mother why the school is closed. Why can't he go to school? The answer: because America may be going to war with Canada. What? When? Nobody knows. But it's best to stay home until people know more. But why? Why are we going to war with Canada? Please, Philip. The mother runs out of patience. She can't take much more tonight. She has told him everything she knows. We just have to wait and see.

Young Philip thinks it through. The reason is that Canada is at war with Nazi Germany . . . and Lindbergh's America might be entering that same war, but not on the side of Britain and the Commonwealth, as everyone expected when Roosevelt was president. This new America would enter on the side of Adolf Hitler. America would line up alongside the Nazis.

When he first published the novel, Roth clarified that he did not intend the work as an allegory or a roman à clef. Flash forward to 2018, when, during the Trump presidency, writer and filmmaker David Simon set out to adapt Roth's novel into a six-part television series. Simon—best known for creating HBO's *The Wire*—visited Roth and humbly explained that he was having a problem with the novel's ending. Roth read and reread the ending, then closed the book and handed it back, telling Simon that the ending was now his problem to solve.

Simon wanted the TV version of *The Plot against America* to resonate with contemporary viewers who, during the leadup to the

2020 presidential election, perceived President Donald Trump as a threat to democracy. That was the only reason to spend money on making the series, he explained at one point. How do you turn a functioning republic into a totalitarian state? It happens gradually, without anyone quite realizing.

Three years before, when in January 2017 Trump moved into the White House, Judith Thurman of *The New Yorker* emailed Roth a few questions. Self-identifying as a lifelong Roosevelt Democrat, the novelist said he saw much that was alarming during the presidencies of Richard Nixon and George W. Bush. But despite their apparent limitations of character and intellect, he said, they were nowhere near as ignorant as Trump, who knew nothing "of government, of history, of science, of philosophy, of art." He was just a con man who lacked subtlety or decency—a description that, to most Canadians, will seem mild enough.

In 2018, following a G7 summit held at La Malbaie, Quebec, Trump threw an unprovoked temper tantrum during which he castigated Prime Minister Trudeau as "very dishonest and weak." This was not quite sabre rattling—and not as consequential as, say, Trump's sudden imposition of tariffs on Canadian aluminum, steel, and other resources. But you don't have to be a Trudeau fan to consider the remark nasty and overbearing—certainly not what one might hope for from the supposed leader of the Free World.

Come to think of it, the dislike is mutual. Late in September 2020, during the run-up to the last American election, an exclusive Leger poll for 338Canada asked more than 1,500 Canadians, "If you could vote in the U.S. presidential election, would you vote for Joe Biden or Donald Trump?" The result? Seventy-two percent would have supported Biden, 14 percent would have voted Trump, and another 14 percent were undecided. Of decided voters, 84 percent supported Biden. No doubt 338Canada will again poll Canadians during the run-up to the 2024 American election. I wouldn't anticipate any major changes.

30 / Churchill Looks to Beaverbrook

OF THE TWO Canadians he knew best by the early 1940s, Winston Churchill tolerated one, William Lyon Mackenzie King, and looked to the other, Lord Beaverbrook, to handle a critical portfolio in his battle against Adolf Hitler. With King, Churchill travelled to Ottawa by train from Washington, where he had given a speech to Congress that impressed even President Franklin Roosevelt. On December 30, 1941, the British prime minister gave a similar speech to the Canadian parliament, though he knew enough to open by hailing Canada's magnificent contribution to the war effort "in troops, in ships, in aircraft, in food and in finance." He noted particularly the presence of Canadian troops in Britain and the gigantic Empire Air Training Scheme, which so far had instructed 125,000 aircrew in Canada.

Addressing the Speaker of the House, and through him the world, Churchill included Canadians when he declared that we did not make this war and did not seek it but instead went so far in avoiding it that, when it broke, it almost destroyed us. Having turned that corner, we would now confront the evildoers and drive them back. Churchill spoke of spending the past week with Roosevelt and agreeing with him to fight on in unity to "the total and final extirpation of the Hitler tyranny, the Japanese frenzy, and the Mussolini flop."

Pause for laughter, applause, and impish grin. And then more of the same. These gangs of bandits had sought to stand between the common people and their march into their inheritance and would themselves be cast into the pit of death and shame. Turning to the invasion and occupation of France, Churchill broke into rough but serviceable French, electrifying those francophones in the audience who spoke the language as their mother tongue. He insisted that France would rise again and retake her place in the company of free and victorious nations.

Few people could match Churchill in full oratorical flight, as awed newspaper reports would soon verify. Describing his voice as a gift from God, one reporter celebrated his poetic use of language, noted the influence of the King James Bible, and declared, "When we shout for Churchill, we shout for the human power to weather anything that comes."

Ironically, the most revelatory exchange came that evening. Prime Minister King had invited Churchill and his personal physician, Charles Wilson, to dine at Laurier House, that comfortable downtown home he had received as a gift from his predecessor, Sir Wilfrid Laurier. The doctor arrived early and, having met King in London, talked freely. Wilson found the Canadian "restive about the P.M." King said that there were many men winning the war, revealing a touch of jealousy, and confessed that he was "rather put off by a strain of violence" in Churchill. Wilson suggested that this was no more than a lack of verbal restraint, but King remained unconvinced.

Later, when chatting with the British prime minister, King remarked, "The great thing in politics is to avoid mistakes." Wilson wrote that he could almost see Churchill sniffing at this. As an aside, he noted that King had never been one to take risks, which no doubt accounted for "some lack of fervor" in Churchill's response. The two men were friendly, but Churchill was not much interested in King.

Wilson contrasted this with the way Churchill related to Roosevelt, when he became, for the first time in the doctor's experience, "content to listen." Churchill clearly felt it important to bring Roosevelt along, Wilson added, and so became a model of self-restraint—"a new Winston" who could sit quite silently. Once in a while, Churchill would say "something likely to fall pleasantly on the President's ear. But here, in Ottawa, he does not seem to bother."

BETTER THAN HE knew King, Churchill knew Max Aitken, Lord Beaverbrook, a British media mogul and sub rosa politician who was at once a fabulously wealthy expatriate and a self-made man from small-town New Brunswick. Churchill would hail his contribution to the war effort as indispensable—though their long friendship was not without rough patches.

In 1937, already a British lord with a media empire, Beaverbrook deplored Churchill's syndicated political columns warning that the Nazis were rearming for war. He believed that Britain should rearm but thought Churchill's strident articles were only exacerbating tensions with Germany. The following September, Beaverbrook hailed the Munich Agreement as guaranteeing that there would be no major war in Europe in the foreseeable future. He took Chamberlain at his word! In November, he wrote to an American editor suggesting that Churchill was a spent force in British politics, claiming that despite his brilliant talent, splendid abilities, and magnificent power of speech, Churchill no longer influenced the British public.

Beaverbrook revised that opinion after September 3, 1939, when the Nazis invaded Poland and Britain declared war on Germany. Beaverbrook, a man of many transformations, underwent yet one more. By the autumn of 1940, having re-established his friendship with Churchill and been appointed minister of aircraft production, he would be playing a critical role in the Battle of Britain, a turning point in the Second World War.

But this evolution cries out for unpacking. Born in 1879 in Maple, Ontario, a hamlet north of Toronto, William Maxwell Aitken was the son of a thundering Presbyterian minister, William Cuthbert Aitken, who had emigrated to Canada in 1843 after a schism in the Church of Scotland known as the "Great Disruption." Aitken's mother came from a wealthy family of Ulster Scots. When Max was one year old, his father moved the family from Ontario to Newcastle, on the Miramichi River in New Brunswick, where the St. James Presbyterian Church had become one of the richest in the province.

Max Aitken grew up in a multi-storey manse and distinguished himself at school as a "conspicuously naughty and idle boy." After a short stint at the University of New Brunswick in Fredericton, he dropped out to work with lawyer R.B. Bennett, an ex-schoolteacher friend of his father and a future prime minister of Canada. He ran Bennett's first political campaign in New Brunswick and then followed him to Alberta, where he briefly became a partner in a Calgary bowling alley.

At twenty-three, after selling both insurance and bonds door to door, Aitken moved to Halifax to work at Royal Securities for John F. Stairs, a leading Scottish-Canadian businessman. Under the veteran Stairs, the wily Aitken was wheeling and dealing in stocks when, in 1904, suddenly his mentor collapsed and died. Aitken seized control of Royal Securities, moved to Montreal, the country's financial centre, and never looked back.

In 1910, he made a small fortune by amalgamating several cement plants into the Canada Cement Company and then selling shares he had acquired while creating the deal. Critics claimed Aitken had "watered" the stock and skimmed off more than $10 million. Fearing incarceration, he decamped to England. He was facing a trial set for 1913, but in Canada the Crown's case collapsed when a crucial witness died.

Aitken stayed in England. Still in his early thirties, he was already wealthy enough to assist the British Conservative Party by helping to finance the *Daily Express*, a Tory newspaper. For this, the Tories not only allowed him to run for Parliament in a safe seat, but in 1911, honoured him with a knighthood.

After trying and failing to gain control of automaker Rolls-Royce, Sir Max Aitken sold his shares at an enormous profit and then began creating a newspaper empire, building on the *Daily Express* and the London *Evening Standard*. Through the First World War, he ran the Canadian War Records Office in London. As an honorary colonel in the Canadian army, he visited the Western Front. And in 1916, with the war raging, he published *Canada in Flanders*, a chronicle of Canadian achievements on the battlefields. He also established a fund that produced a notable collection of war art.

In 1917, Aitken was granted a peerage and became the 1st Baron Beaverbrook. The next year, as Britain's first minister of information, Lord Beaverbrook became responsible for Allied propaganda—a posting that involved him in considerable wrangling over the use of intelligence. In 1918, with an armistice looming, Beaverbrook resigned.

That year, too, he founded the *Sunday Express*, which featured innovative photographic layouts and became immensely profitable. By the end of the Second World War, Beaverbrook's *Daily Express* would have a circulation of 3.7 million across Britain—easily the largest in the world.

He himself would be known as the First Baron of Fleet Street—a figure famous enough to be lampooned by satirist Evelyn Waugh. Starting in 1930, a Beaverbrook caricature surfaces in three of Waugh's novels—*Vile Bodies, Scoop,* and *Put Out More Flags.* He appears as a pushy newspaper publisher who barks orders down the telephone lines to London editors from his estate in Surrey, south of the city.

As a young man, Waugh had worked briefly for the Beaverbrook-owned *Daily Express*. In the 1930s, after he got a rise out of the press baron, he declared, "I am suing Lord Beaverbrook for libel and hope for some lovely tax-free money in damages. He has very conveniently told some lies about me." He never did sue, but later, in response to a jocular question, Waugh said, "Of course I believe in the Devil. How else could I explain Lord Beaverbrook?"

Sometimes an elected politician, always the most powerful media mogul in England, Beaverbrook played a significant role in British politics for more than fifty years. He moved in the highest circles and became friends with Winston Churchill. The two men drifted apart in the later 1930s as Churchill became increasingly bellicose. They stopped speaking after they disagreed about the Munich Agreement of September 1938. One year later, when Hitler invaded Poland, Beaverbrook realized that he had been wrong.

That December, with Russia having invaded Finland, Beaverbrook reached out to rekindle relations with Churchill. He wrote to the politician, now First Lord of the Admiralty, suggesting that Britain should send "a competent man" to the United States to rouse Scandinavian expatriates against Stalin's aggression. Given that the US was still a neutral country, Beaverbrook knew this would be regarded as too radical, but he was signalling that he was keen to get involved in the war.

In May 1940, following the invasion of Norway, Holland, and Belgium, Chamberlain resigned as prime minister. On May 10, Churchill followed him into that office as leader of a coalition government. That same night, the convivial Beaverbrook hosted a celebration of the leadership change—not at Cherkley Court, his splendiferous 370-acre estate south of London, but at the Vineyard, his Tudor mansion in the upscale suburb of Fulham.

Churchill arrived with a mission. For the past six months, he had argued that Britain needed more air power. As prime minister, he would act immediately to divide the Air Ministry in two—one part to wage war, the other to build, acquire, and develop airplanes. Knowing that Beaverbrook was relentless, and that he had served in the First World War, Churchill invited him that evening to become minister of aircraft production. Beaverbrook waffled: Would this be the best use of his abilities?

Churchill swept aside his hesitations and, on May 14, announced the appointment. So Beaverbrook entered what he later described as the most glorious period of his life. The following month, in the House of Commons, Churchill reiterated that the Battle of France was over but the Battle of Britain was about to begin. Because the Royal Navy remained far stronger than the German one, he perceived that Hitler would set out to destroy the Royal Air Force.

Having appointed Beaverbrook to what he regarded as the most important of all portfolios, he later explained that the Canadian was at his best "when things are at their worst." Britain had developed two outstanding airplanes, and Beaverbrook immediately scored a propaganda coup by appealing to the British public to donate aluminum to build more: "We will turn your pots and pans into Spitfires and Hurricanes."

He also set up the Civilian Repair Organisation, which built new planes out of pieces from those that had been shot down. Whenever he encountered a closed door, he kicked it down. According to one member of the British parliament, Beaverbrook swept through government departments like Genghis Khan.

On taking office, Beaverbrook was astonished to learn that bombers built in the United States were being flown to Halifax, Nova Scotia, disassembled, and put on ships to cross the Atlantic, only to be reassembled when they reached England. He soon put an end to that. After getting clearance from Churchill, and while the British brass howled, he built a runway at Gander, Newfoundland, hired bush pilots from Canada, the United States, and Australia, and put them to work flying the bombers from Newfoundland to England.

Military historians argue about numbers. But most agree that in 1940, Beaverbrook's big year, Great Britain increased aircraft production by 250 percent, producing 4,283 fighters to Germany's 3,000. At this crucial moment, Beaverbrook increased fighter and bomber production so prodigiously that many historians have suggested that without him, the pivotal Battle of Britain might have gone the other way. Later Churchill would declare, "This was his hour."

According to British historians, this decisive battle—the first major campaign fought exclusively by air forces—ran from July 10 to October 31, 1940. German historians date it from mid-August 1940 to May 1941. Whatever the dates, the failure of the Luftwaffe to defeat the Royal Air Force—largely because of Beaverbrook's planes—prevented Hitler from launching his projected invasion by sea and made a crucial difference to the outcome of the Second World War. Canadian biographer David Adams Richards goes further, crediting Beaverbrook with saving Western civilization almost singlehandedly.

31 / A Canadian
Called Intrepid

ON THAT MOMENTOUS evening of May 10, 1940, at Lord Beaver-brook's London residence, Churchill also approached a second expatriate Canadian with an offer the man could not refuse. The newly appointed prime minister wanted someone working in the US to confront isolationist attitudes and convince the Americans to join the British war effort. Having chatted with Beaverbrook, he drew aside William Stephenson, a businessman then running British Pacific Trust, which made investments around the world.

Socially, Stephenson moved in the upper echelons of British society, rubbing shoulders with H.G. Wells, George Bernard Shaw, and Greta Garbo, as well as Beaverbrook and Churchill. Details remain vague, but it appears that around 1936, Stephenson began drawing on his wealthy international connections to provide Churchill, then an outspoken backbencher, with details about how the Nazi government was flouting the Versailles Treaty and building up its armed forces at an extraordinary rate. Over the next few years, Churchill realized what this "quiet Canadian" could do.

At the mansion in Fulham, he drew Stephenson aside and asked him to be his personal representative in the US, promising to support him without reservation. The Canadian said yes. And over the objections of the head of British Secret Intelligence Service (SIS), who had his own man in place, Churchill appointed Stephenson passport control officer in New York City—really a cover occupation for secret service operatives abroad.

By late June, Stephenson and his wife were ensconced at the Waldorf Astoria Hotel, and he was acting on his assignment to do all that could not be done overtly to aid the British war effort and eventually bring America into the war. Before long he was talking frequently with US president Franklin Roosevelt, discussing the "developing horror" driven by the Nazis.

Stephenson wrote to Churchill, informing him that Roosevelt wanted a close relationship between the American Federal Bureau of Investigation and the British SIS—though this was to be kept secret. Stephenson called this an essential first step, noting that the Nazis were already well entrenched in the US and working hard to shore up a wall of isolationism around Roosevelt.

Stephenson convinced Roosevelt to put lawyer and soldier William J. "Wild Bill" Donovan in charge of US intelligence services. He had become friends with Donovan in the 1930s, when both were engaged in gathering intelligence about the rise of fascism in Europe. Roosevelt acted on Stephenson's advice, and Donovan then founded the Office of Strategic Services, which later became the Central Intelligence Agency. With Stephenson running British Security Coordination (BSC) in the US, the two were able to coordinate the gathering of information on German activities in North America.

Who was this Stephenson? He represented himself as the son of a Scottish lumber mill owner. In fact, born in Winnipeg in 1897, he was adopted by the Stephensons after his parents—Icelandic and Orcadian immigrants—struggled to support him and two siblings. His birth name was William Samuel Clouston Stanger, and his is yet another Canadian rags-to-riches story.

The boy left school early and worked as a telegrapher. In January 1916, with the First World War raging, he joined the Winnipeg Light Infantry. In June he sailed to England, where a series of transfers took him to the Canadian Training Depot Headquarters in Shorncliffe. The following August, he gained a commission in the Royal Flying Corps. In 1918, he became a flying ace, scoring twelve victories in his Sopwith Camel.

That June, however, he got shot down behind enemy lines. Captured by the Germans, he was held as a prisoner of war until he escaped in October and made his way back to England. By the end of the war, at twenty-two years of age, Stephenson had become a captain and earned the Military Cross and the Distinguished Flying Cross for conspicuous gallantry, devotion to duty, and great courage and skill in attacking the enemy from low altitudes. His citation for the DFC noted that he had "proved himself a keen antagonist in the air," and that his reports were notable for their valuable and accurate information.

After the war, Stephenson returned to Winnipeg and, with a friend, launched a business that manufactured can openers based on a German one he had stolen from his POW camp. When this quixotic venture went bust, he returned to England, where in 1924 he married an American tobacco heiress. Wealthy and well-connected overnight, Stephenson teamed up with an American civil war hero and patented a system to transmit photos wirelessly. Over the next eighteen years, this patent generated £100,000 a year in royalties, the equivalent today of more than $2 million a year.

Meanwhile, Stephenson diversified into manufacturing radios, airplanes, and automobile bodies. In 1931, he launched Shepperton Studios, which soon became the world's largest moviemaking concern outside Hollywood. And in 1934, as owner of General Aircraft Limited, he built an airplane that won the King's Cup race, using a pilot he had hired.

In the mid-1930s, while moving in international circles and building airplanes, Stephenson gleaned that the Germans were making enormous progress in developing their air force far beyond the limits prescribed by the Treaty of Versailles. He brought this news to Churchill, with whom he rubbed shoulders in London, and so became a conduit of secret information to that politician.

His service was such that, once Churchill took office, his appointment to his senior position in New York followed ineluctably. As a spymaster, Stephenson was one of the few people in North America authorized to view transcripts of German ciphers decrypted at

Bletchley Park, home of Britain's codebreakers. He decided what information to pass along to the American and Canadian governments. He established the BSC, a clandestine organization that would play a significant role in the war effort. Stephenson arranged for all trans-Atlantic mail from the US to be routed through the British colony of Bermuda, off the North Carolina coast. BSC censors, working closely with the FBI, were able to discover and arrest Axis spies operating in the US.

Collecting no government salary, and often financing operations out of his own pocket, Stephenson also influenced American public opinion through his newspaper friends, among them columnists like Walter Winchell and Drew Pearson. After the US entered the war in December 1941, galvanized by Japan's surprise attack on Pearl Harbor, BSC led propaganda efforts throughout the Americas. From a new base in Bermuda, Stephenson hired hundreds of people to staff his operations, most of them Canadian women eager to join the war effort.

To gather and analyze information, Stephenson used innovative methods. Drawing on his experience in filmmaking, he adapted cinematic techniques to create espionage training films while developing a vast network of undercover agents. They included a University of Toronto professor whose electronic wizardry helped win the Battle of the Atlantic. Another of his spies infiltrated the German spy network in both the United States and Europe and played a significant role in the counter-intelligence efforts of MI6. One of Stephenson's most successful spies was the American Betty Pack, the so-called "Mata Hari of Minnesota," treated in Chapter 33.

Occasionally, Churchill grew frustrated with Stephenson's initiatives, as when his lieutenant ordered the bugging of the US embassy in London. A bridge too far? Churchill worried about diplomatic fallout that never came. Ultimately, he supported Stephenson's action, recognizing that it was necessary to maintain the security of the Allied forces.

In November 1942, Stephenson played a key role in the planning and execution of Operation Torch, the Allied invasion of North

Africa. It featured the first major airborne assault by the United States and enabled the Free French eventually to dominate the government in Algiers. A year and a half later, Stephenson orchestrated the even more crucial Operation Bodyguard, a campaign of deception designed to conceal the D-Day invasion of Normandy. Stephenson used his network of agents to provide misinformation to the Nazis.

Meanwhile, while the war was unfolding, Stephenson created and supervised North America's first training school for covert agents, Camp X, in Whitby, Ontario. From 1941 to 1945, as many as two thousand agents trained there. Among them was Stephenson's friend Ian Fleming, who later wrote the James Bond novels. Some historians contend that the raid on Fort Knox in *Goldfinger* was based on a Stephenson plan, never acted upon, to steal almost $3 billion in Vichy French gold reserves stashed on the Caribbean island of Martinique.

After the war, Britain, the United States, and Canada all recognized Stephenson's extraordinary wartime service. Recommending him to King George VI for a knighthood, Winston Churchill wrote, "This one is dear to my heart." And in a letter to the *Sunday Times* in October 1962, Ian Fleming himself wrote that James Bond "is a highly romanticized version of a true spy. The real thing is . . . William Stephenson."

32 / Among the Foreign Nationals

AFTER THE WAR ended, while interrogating Rudolf Höss, ex-commandant of Auschwitz-Birkenau, spymistress Vera Atkins shuddered at the man's response to one question in particular. She had remarked that 1.5 million people had been killed in that death camp. "Oh, no," he said. "It was 2,345,000." That testimony would be used at the Nuremberg trials. In 1947, Höss—not to be confused with Rudolf Hess—was executed by hanging at Auschwitz, where he had committed countless atrocities.

The brilliance, commitment, and courage of his interrogator became public knowledge only after the Allied victory in Europe. During the war, while officially second-in-command of the French section of the British secret military organization Special Operations Executive (SOE), Vera Atkins had recruited and deployed 470 secret agents. Of those, 118 had disappeared behind enemy lines, including 14 women. By the end of 1945, Atkins had learned the fate of 57 lost agents. Early the next year, she set out to trace what had happened to all the rest. Before she was done, Atkins had traced all but one of the missing agents. And she had established what had happened to all 14 missing women, 12 of whom had died in concentration camps. She detailed their bravery before and after capture and persuaded the British government to honour them as having been killed in action.

Born Vera May Rosenberg in 1908, Atkins grew up on a large estate in Romania. Her German Jewish father was a wealthy businessman,

192 · HERE COME THE CANADIANS

and with him in Bucharest she moved among the city's business and political elite. Her father went bankrupt in 1932 and died soon after. Vera went to work for an oil company. She travelled widely, making useful contacts, among them diplomats and British secret agents. She excelled in modern languages at the Sorbonne.

In 1937, as the persecution of Jews increased throughout Europe, she emigrated to Britain with her British Jewish mother, whose family name was Atkins. While based in London and moving in wealthy industrial circles, Vera met Canadian spymaster William Stephenson, soon to become head of British Security Coordination. She was keen to fight what she could see coming, and he gave her a cover job so he could send her on fact-finding missions to supply Winston Churchill with details of the rearming of Nazi Germany.

In May 1940, Atkins got temporarily stranded in the Netherlands when Germany invaded. With the help of a Belgian resistance network, she made it back to Britain later that year. In February 1941, she joined the French section of the SOE—the F Section, set up by Churchill to "set Europe ablaze" by sabotage and subversion. Thanks to her memory, mastery of the French language, and organizational skills, she soon became assistant to section head Colonel Maurice Buckmaster.

Atkins was meticulous in gathering and analyzing intelligence and had an uncanny ability to piece together fragmented information and identify patterns. She recruited and deployed hundreds of British agents in occupied France, among them thirty-seven women SOE agents who worked as couriers and wireless operators. One report rightly described them as "a clandestine army of unconventional women," among them newlyweds, homemakers, public school graduates, and an Indian princess.

The enlistment process for both men and women started with training at a sixteenth-century country house in Beaulieu, Hampshire, that had no contact with the outside world. Then came a commando course in the Scottish Highlands, where recruits learned about guns and explosives. Finally, they faced a survival course and parachute training. Along the way, they practised keeping their cover stories straight under interrogation. Atkins herself, who often worked eighteen-hour days, briefed the agents on how to survive in occupied France amidst curfews and regulations, and gave them French mementoes, ticket stubs, letters, and keepsakes. She was heavily involved in Operation Jedburgh, a joint venture that supported the French Resistance by parachuting teams of agents into occupied France to conduct guerrilla warfare, sabotage, and intelligence gathering. She also managed the logistics of agents' movements, organized safe houses, and maintained secure lines of communication.

Despite this meticulous attention to detail, scores of F Section agents were caught and killed after the SOE networks in the Netherlands and Belgium were compromised by a traitor. After the war, in January 1946, working as a squadron officer in the Women's Auxiliary Air Force, Atkins set out to learn what had happened to her lost agents. She was renowned for the effectiveness of her interrogation techniques, and she proved relentless in uncovering the truth. Most details did not become public knowledge until 2003, when Britain's National Archives released a huge tranche of secret documents. They revealed that Atkins had run a network of outstanding agents.

· Noor Inayat Khan, an Indian princess by birth, had written and published children's books. In November 1940, at twenty-six, Khan joined the Women's Auxiliary Air Force in the UK and was sent to be trained as a wireless operator. Assigned to a bomber training school in June 1941, she found the work boring and applied for a commission. She joined F Section of the SOE, and in early February 1943 took special training as a wireless operator. She was the first woman to be sent to France as such, and her SOE instructors determined that she was both fast and accurate. Khan's gentle manner and "childlike" qualities had worried some of those who trained her. One instructor described her as very feminine in character—kind-hearted, emotional, imaginative.

Vera Atkins did not question Khan's commitment and, although her final training in field security and encoding had to be cut short, judged her ready to go. The two met at an upscale restaurant in London's affluent Mayfair district. Atkins wanted to evaluate Khan's self-confidence, which she believed was the secret of success in this line of work. She told Khan she had received mixed reports and offered her a chance to back out gracefully. Khan insisted adamantly that she wanted to go and could do the work.

In mid-June 1943, Khan was flown into northern France. A few days after her arrival, Nazis began to round up the members of Prosper, SOE's largest and most important network in France—a network to which Khan was attached. She remained in radio contact with London. When Buckmaster told her she would be flown home to Britain, she told him she would prefer to remain, as she was the only radio operator left in Paris. Buckmaster agreed to this, though she was told only to receive signals, not to transmit. During the next few months, she helped thirty Allied airmen escape with vital intelligence. But on or around October 13, 1943, Khan was arrested and interrogated by Gestapo officials in Paris. Twice she tried and failed to escape. Later, an interrogator testified that she did not give the Nazis a single piece of information.

By 1946, Atkins had determined that Khan was executed in Dachau concentration camp on September 13, 1944. Five years later, she saw to it that Noor Inayat Khan was awarded a posthumous George Cross, the highest civilian decoration in the United Kingdom.

- Yolande Beekman, the Hampstead-educated wife of a Dutch freedom fighter, joined the SOE in February 1943 and in September transferred to Tours, France, as a radio operator. She worked in a dangerous region, and her great courage made possible the delivery of arms and explosives to resistance forces. Captured by the Gestapo in January 1944, she was interrogated and imprisoned at Dachau. On September 13, 1944, she was handed over to a camp official and spent the night in the cells. Between eight and ten the next morning, she was taken to the crematorium compound, shot through the head, and immediately cremated.

- Andrée Raymonde Borrel, code named "Denise," was one of the first two women agents to arrive in France from F Section by parachute. Born and raised near Paris, she worked as a nurse and then with an escape network in the French Resistance until December 1941, when the network was compromised and she fled to England. The following May, she joined the SOE and began training to become a field agent in F Section. The men she trained with found her easygoing, playful, and unhardened by war. On the night of September 25, 1942, "Denise" was one of the first two women to parachute into occupied France to set up resistance networks. After landing in a field near the village of Mer, about 160 kilometres southeast of Paris, Denise went to work as a courier with the Prosper network. An important figure in its leadership, she was arrested by the Gestapo in June 1943 and executed in July 1944 at the Natzweiler-Struthof concentration camp.

DECADES AFTER THE events described here, some critics alleged that Vera Atkins had been a Soviet agent, while others charged that she had actually been working for the Nazis. Biographer Sarah Helm repudiated both claims and argued that Atkins had been secretive and defensive because she was vulnerable, not only as a Jew and a non-British national, but as a woman.

Atkins remained a staunch defender of F Section's wartime record and ensured that the twelve women who had died in Nazi concentration camps were properly commemorated. She received the Croix de Guerre and, after becoming a knight of the Legion of Honour in France, became a Commander of the Most Excellent Order of the British Empire (CBE). Atkins died in hospital in 2000 at the age of ninety-two.

33 / The Mata Hari of Minnesota

EARLY IN 1939, while living in Paris, American spy Betty Pack seduced Count Michael Lubienski, chief aide to the Polish foreign minister. She let him make love to her as often as he wanted, she said later, because that kept the flow of useful political information coming. From Lubienski she learned that Polish experts were wrestling with Germany's Enigma enciphering machine. Her contribution to the resolution of that challenge, which gave the Allies a crucial edge, remains a matter of debate among historians.

But there is no doubt that Pack, code name "Cynthia," completed crucial missions for the British Security Coordination (BSC) and the American Office of Strategic Services (OSS), using her personal allure and magnetism to glean intelligence from high-level foreign diplomats. In time she became known as the "Mata Hari of Minnesota," so named for the Dutch exotic dancer and German spy who seduced men into giving up state secrets during the First World War.

Born in 1910 into a wealthy family in Minneapolis, Amy Elizabeth ("Betty") Thorpe was the daughter of a distinguished officer of the US Marine Corps and a Minnesota socialite. The family travelled extensively during her childhood, exposing her to different cultures and social settings. While still a teenage debutante, she developed a reputation for romantic entanglements with older foreign diplomats. At nineteen, while pregnant with his child, she married Arthur Pack— second secretary at the British embassy and a man twice her age.

She accompanied Pack when he was transferred to Madrid at the outbreak of the Spanish Civil War. In a move that would have outraged Martha Gellhorn, Betty supported the anti-democratic Nationalists. She smuggled rebels to safety, transported Red Cross supplies, and became involved in diplomatic affairs. She also had an affair with a Spanish priest.

In the fall of 1937, denounced as a Republican spy, she moved to Paris bent on joining, as she later put it, "his Britannic Majesty's Secret Intelligence Service." The following year, her husband told her that he had fallen in love with another women. Unconcerned, she started a relationship with a politically active Pole named Edward Kulikowski. He told her that Nazi Germany had plans to annex Czechoslovakia and that Poland was conspiring to claim a portion of the country. She shared this information with Jack Shelley, an agent of Britain's Secret Intelligence Service. He recruited her into the SIS and provided an allowance to enable her further investigations. Now came her relationship with Lubienski.

In April 1939, after she had gleaned all she could from him, Betty left Europe with her husband when he was posted to Santiago, Chile. She wrote articles for Spanish and English newspapers and came to the attention of William Stephenson, the Canadian head of the BSC. Impressed by her ingenuity and connections, Stephenson recruited her as a spy and gave her the code name "Cynthia." In November 1940, leaving her husband and daughter in Chile, Betty moved back to the US. Based in Washington and posing as a journalist, she worked to influence prominent American senators to support lend-lease legislation, which aimed to provide military assistance to Britain and its allies.

Betty was also charged with obtaining Italian naval ciphers, which would assist the Allies in their fight against Italy in the Mediterranean Sea. As a teenager in the 1920s, she had enthralled an Italian naval attaché named Alberto Lais, who called her his "golden girl." Now an admiral based at the Italian embassy in Washington, the sixty-year-old Lais refused to give her the ciphers but did disclose the name of the cipher clerk at the Italian embassy. Betty convinced the clerk to hand over the ciphers for a small sum of money.

In another version of this story, which later prompted lawsuits for defamation, Betty said that with Lais's permission, she received access to the sensitive materials from his assistant. Either way, the intelligence she provided allowed the British to decode Italian messages and played a significant role in the Allied victory at the Battle of Cape Matapan in March 1941.

By 1942, Betty was working jointly for both BSC and the OSS. They challenged Betty to acquire more naval code books by infiltrating the embassy of Vichy France—an assignment that, successfully completed, would turn her into a legend. Betty seduced Charles Emmanuel Brousse, an anti-Nazi press attaché at the Vichy embassy, and when the time was right, told him what London wanted. The ciphers comprised several volumes. They were locked in a safe in a code room guarded by a watchman with a dog.

After Betty and Brousse tried and failed to lay hands on the code books, William Stephenson hired someone to assist them—a thug known as the "Georgia Cracker." With his help, and after a couple of failed attempts, they drugged the watchman and his dog, got into the code room, opened the safe, removed the cipher books, delivered them to another agent, waited while he took photos, then returned them to the safe. That November, the Allies put the ciphers to good use when, in North Africa, they routed the Vichy French.

Cynthia wanted to keep spying but had become too well known. Was she ashamed, journalists asked, of the way she had elicited secrets? Not at all, she said. Her superiors had affirmed that her work had saved thousands of Allied lives.

When the war ended, her estranged husband, Arthur Pack, killed himself. Brousse and his wife got a divorce. Betty married Brousse and settled in France in a medieval castle. She would die there in 1963 of throat cancer, but not before publishing excerpts from a never-finished memoir. In one of them, she wrote that her first child, Anthony, had been raised in England by a country doctor and his wife and later died fighting in the Korean War. Her daughter, Denise, was happily married in America.

34 / The Creole Goddess

HER MOST AMBITIOUS cloak-and-dagger adventure went sideways in Casablanca, North Africa. Back in Marseille days before, with the occupation of France well underway, Josephine Baker had learned that the Nazis were looking for her. The superstar singer and dancer—the embodiment of Jazz Age liberation—had been performing a series of sold-out concerts at the Alcazar d'Été music hall. She still had two nights to go.

By this time, January 1941, Baker's singing and dancing had become an occupational disguise. The thirty-four-year-old entertainer was secretly working as an "Honorary Correspondent"—an unpaid agent—for the *Deuxième bureau*, the French military intelligence bureau. Now the Marseille chief told her that, with the Nazis closing in, the boat departing for Algiers on the day after tomorrow might be the last.

She and Jacques Abtey—the French professional agent with whom she travelled—needed to be on that boat. The chief produced a thick dossier of top-secret intelligence that had to go to Portugal, and from there to London. Stressing the importance of its contents—information on Nazi airfields, munitions, troop placements—he wanted them to deliver the portfolio to Lisbon themselves.

While Josephine dashed around packing—and organizing ways to house her travelling menagerie of pets—Abtey went to the music-hall managers and explained that the Nazis were pursuing Baker because she had been working secretly for Free France. She had to "put herself out of reach of the invader." They understood and asked for a medical certificate stating that she was too ill to perform. Sure enough, Baker was not entirely well. She had a nasty chest infection due to days of cold weather, months of stress, and a relentless performing schedule. The doctor instructed her in writing to leave for sunnier climes.

At her Marseille hotel, an assistant arrived from home—the Château des Milandes on the outskirts of Paris—with the pets she adamantly refused to leave for long: Bonzo the Great Dane; Glougou the monkey; Mica the golden-lion tamarin; Gugusse the marmoset; and two white mice, Bigoudi and Point d'Interrogation. Next morning, with Abtey—who was masquerading as her tour manager—Baker boarded the *Gouverneur-Général Gueydon*. Her first-class cabin, suddenly overrun with animals, "was indescribable hustle and bustle," Abtey wrote later, "as well as the funniest show I ever saw."

The Mediterranean crossing was unusually rough. Bonzo was seasick and howled when, with the ship's heaving, a trunk came loose

Josephine Baker wearing the uniform of the French Air Force in 1948. *Studio Harcourt Paris*

and fell on his head. In Algiers, the moment she stepped off the ship, Baker was arrested. Was her cover blown? Were her spying days ended? No. But the managers at the Marseille music hall had decided to sue Baker for breach of contract.

Eight days later, after the spy chief in Marseille pulled strings, and probably produced some cash, Baker and Abtey and their entourage boarded a train for Casablanca, from where they would proceed to Lisbon. That 1,200-kilometre journey, with the animals running amok, tested even Baker's patience. And when, upon arrival, officials refused Abtey's visa application, she stormed into the Portuguese consulate. She received her own visa free of charge. But as regards Abtey, though Baker pleaded that she needed him to organize her Lisbon shows, the consul refused to budge. No explanation.

Had his cover been blown? They couldn't see how. Nor could they see how to get Abtey into Portugal. They debated any number of harebrained schemes—maybe he could stow away on a steamship or a fishing boat?—before they faced the truth. Up until this point they had worked together, the volunteer and the professional. Now, for the first time ever, Baker would have to embark on a solo mission—the lone courier of a highly secret intelligence dossier. Carrying that file, Josephine Baker boarded the night train to Tangier, 340 kilometres away. From there, she would have to make her own way.

With that much, at least, she was all too familiar. Baker was born Freda Josephine McDonald in St. Louis, Missouri, in 1906, to washerwoman Carrie McDonald. Her vaudeville-drummer father soon abandoned them. Carrie—whose own mother was Native American—married a gentle but perpetually unemployed man and gave birth to a son and two more daughters. Josephine grew up cleaning houses and babysitting for wealthy white families.

At thirteen, she got a job waitressing at the Old Chauffeur's Club. She met and was briefly married to one Willie Wells. She would marry (and later divorce) three more men—American Willie Baker in 1921, Frenchman Jean Lion in 1937, and French orchestra leader Jo Bouillon in 1947. But at fourteen, having discovered that she had a gift for performance, she toured the US doing comical skits with the Jones Family Band and the Dixie Steppers.

When the latter group developed a show called *Shuffle Along*, she auditioned to be a chorus girl but was rejected as "too skinny and too dark." While working as a dresser, she learned the chorus line's routines. When a dancer left, she was the obvious replacement. Onstage, she brought a comedic touch, rolling her eyes and pretending to be clumsy. The audience loved it.

After *Shuffle Along*, she enjoyed some success at the Plantation Club in New York. But her career didn't take off until 1925, when she travelled to France to be part of *La revue nègre*. Baker became an overnight sensation when, wearing nothing but a feather skirt, she threw off all inhibitions in *La danse sauvage*. Ernest Hemingway described her as "the most sensational woman anybody ever saw. Or ever will." Picasso painted portraits of her repeatedly, and Jean Cocteau, the poet and filmmaker, raved about her.

For the first time in her life, Baker was raking in money. She bought clothes, jewellery, and, because she loved animals, pets: a cheetah (Chiquita), a chimpanzee (Ethel), a pig (Albert), a snake (Kiki), a goat, a parrot, parakeets, fish, three cats, and seven dogs. When *La revue nègre* closed, Baker starred at the Folies Bergère theatre. Her exotic eroticism—she did a wild dance in a skirt made of sixteen bananas on a string—fed her celebrity. Admirers hailed her as the "Black Venus," the "Black Pearl," and the "Creole Goddess." She was showered with gifts, including diamonds and cars, and received a whopping 1,500 marriage proposals.

By 1927, when she turned twenty-one, Josephine Baker was the highest-paid entertainer in Europe. She rivalled actresses Gloria Swanson and Mary Pickford as the most photographed woman in the world. In the early 1930s, she became the first Black woman to star in a movie, and then did so in a second. In *Zouzou* and *Princesse Tam-Tam*, she danced and sang songs. She moved her extended family from St. Louis to the Château des Milandes, an estate she bought outside Bordeaux in southern France.

Josephine returned to the US in 1936 to star in the Ziegfeld Follies. But American audiences failed to welcome this sophisticated Black woman with overwhelming star power—the *New York Times* even called her a "Negro wench." Heartbroken, Josephine returned to France. By 1939, given to walking the Paris streets with her pet cheetah on a diamond-studded leash, she was one of the wealthiest women in France.

In Paris, Jacques Abtey doubted that Baker would become an Honorable Correspondent—an unpaid secret agent. But a colleague convinced him to pay her a visit at Le Beau Chêne, her turreted villa in Le Vésinet, one of the wealthiest suburbs of Paris. When he arrived, she was working in her garden, wearing a battered felt hat and an old pair of gardening trousers—completely upending his expectations.

He remained dubious. Baker was not French, born and bred. How could she have the passion needed to drive a volunteer agent? But, as he laid out why he had come and what the agency expected of an Honourable Correspondent, she listened attentively. Turned out she had performed in Germany not long before and had learned to hate the Nazis. Not only that. She said, "France has made me all that I am. I shall be eternally grateful to her." She paused. "I gave my heart to Paris, as Paris gave me hers. Captain, I am ready to give my country my life. Dispose of me as you will."

Baker quickly proved herself. She moved in the highest social circles in Europe and around the world, gathering information from conversations at parties and events. First assignment: Italy—become friendly with an attaché at the Italian embassy and pump him for information. Now that the Second World War was underway, world leaders were trying to figure out what Mussolini meant to do. Baker found out by provoking and challenging the attaché's every utterance. She found out that when the time came to opt one way or the other, Il Duce had zero intention of backing the Allies. He would strike an alliance with Germany.

Second assignment: Japan. By now, Baker had close friends among the movers and shakers of the international community—including the Japanese. Working her high-level contacts at the Japanese embassy, she ferreted out the truth: the Japanese would not forge a coalition with the Allies, as they had done during the First World War. In 1936, Japan and Germany had signed an "an anti-communist" pact. Going forward, Tokyo would march in lockstep with Berlin. Not good news, but mission accomplished.

Next assignment: What of Portugal? The Free French worried because this avowedly neutral country, long a faithful British ally, was now run by António Salazar, a dictator of fascist bent. Josephine Baker turned up, ostensibly bound for Brazil to perform, bringing forty boxes of musical scores, all of which had been overwritten with top-secret intelligence in invisible ink. These she and Abtey put on a plane to London, hoping soon to follow. But no. Having established this connection, Lisbon to London, they were wanted again in Paris.

Next came that assignment in North Africa—the voyage to Algiers and the train to Casablanca, whence for the first time Baker would have to carry on alone, making her way to Tangier and then to Lisbon. The trouble for Abtey, she found out, had started at that far end, with someone arousing suspicion by clamouring to let him enter. She completed the assignment anyway—delivered that great trove of top-secret reports from France to agents who relayed them to London.

Even then, Josephine Baker was far from done. Again with Abtey, she embarked on a marathon performance tour of North Africa and the Middle East, dancing and singing her way from Tunis to Alexandria, Cairo, Jerusalem, Damascus, Beirut, back to Cairo and Alexandria. Along the way, she gathered intelligence and reported what she learned: North Africa was a powder keg set to explode. This intelligence proved crucial to Allied victories in that part of the world.

As the war ended, Charles de Gaulle praised Baker for her heroic devotion and said she "has given her all for France." Winston Churchill called her "the most glamorous heroine of the French Resistance." When Allied commanders put out a call for an entertainer to visit and perform at the now liberated Buchenwald, Baker stepped up. She went to that horrific death camp, she sang, she saw faces light up. And then she wept.

During the 1950s and '60s, Baker visited the US several times. She refused to perform in segregated clubs and wrote newspaper articles about the racism she encountered. In New York, when the Stork Club refused her service, she stormed out, prompting columnist Walter Winchell—then backing Senator Joseph McCarthy—to smear her as having "communist sympathies." She lost her work visa and had to leave the country, even though a civil rights organization established May 20, 1951, as Josephine Baker Day.

In 1963, back in the US for the civil rights March on Washington, Baker walked alongside Dr. Martin Luther King Jr. and gave a powerful speech overshadowed only by King's legendary "I have a dream" exhortation. A decade later, she agreed to perform at New York's Carnegie Hall. She worried about her reception but received a standing ovation when she walked out on stage—a welcome that reduced her to tears.

On April 8, 1975, at sixty-eight, Baker gave a high-energy premiere at the Bobino theatre in Paris and drew rave reviews. Mere days later, she would slip into a coma. She died from a cerebral hemorrhage on April 12. More than 20,000 people crowded the streets of Paris to observe the funeral procession. The French government honoured her with a twenty-one-gun salute, making Josephine Baker the first American woman buried in France with military honours. She had already received the Medal of the Resistance with Rosette and the Croix de Guerre, and been appointed a Chevalier of the *Légion d'honneur*. In November 2021, almost five decades after her death, Baker would be interred in the crypt of the Pantheon in Paris, an honour reserved for the nation's foremost national heroes—fewer than one hundred individuals, among them only five women.

35 / Mowat Fights
in Sicily

FEW EXPERIENCES MARKED Farley Mowat like his wartime involvement as a young man in Canada's Italian campaign. Mowat would travel the world and become the most successful Canadian author of his generation. His forty-five books, translated into fifty-two languages, would sell more than 17 million copies. His avalanche of bestsellers would include *Never Cry Wolf*, *Owls in the Family*, *Woman in the Mists*, and *Sea of Slaughter*. Mowat would mention his Second World War experience in several works and focus on the Italian campaign in two of them—a regimental history, *The Regiment*, and a shattering memoir, *And No Birds Sang*.

That campaign lasted twenty months, from July 1943 to February 1945, and was the longest undertaken by the Canadian army in the Second World War. Was it essential to the defeat of the Nazis? Probably not. But it certainly represents Canada's commitment to fighting fascism and Nazism. It tied down significant German military resources, including divisions that might have been used in France following the D-Day invasion, or else on the Eastern Front against the Soviet Union. It also stretched Nazi resources to the limit and aided the Allies in strategic bombing by providing airfields closer to Germany.

In July and August of 1943, as part of Operation Husky, Canadians seized control of Sicily. Then they proceeded to the mainland. The 1st Canadian Infantry Division and the 1st Canadian Armoured Brigade were seeing combat together for the first time as I Canadian Corps, an integral part of the British Eighth Army.

Landing at Reggio Calabria on September 3, 1943, the Canadians overcame their first major challenge. They pushed on despite the harsh terrain and German resistance and managed to establish a solid front. The Canadians then moved north to seize the Moro River and Ortona, a strategically important town on the Adriatic Sea.

The Battle of Ortona in December 1943, often referred to as "Little Stalingrad" due to its intense urban combat, was a defining moment for the Canadians. The fighting was fierce, with both sides suffering heavy casualties. The Canadians employed a tactic known as "mouse-holing," where they blasted holes in walls to move from building to building without being exposed to enemy fire. After eight days of ruthless combat, the Canadians finally captured Ortona on December 28, marking a significant victory. Farley Mowat was there. Five months before that, in July 1943, he had scrambled ashore at Pachino in southern Sicily. As a twenty-two-year-old junior officer in charge of a rifle platoon, he then slogged north with the Hastings and Prince Edward Regiment (the Hasty P's).

Farley Mowat was born in Belleville, Ontario, in 1921. A great-great-uncle, Sir Oliver Mowat, had been premier of the province, and his senior-librarian father—active again in this Second World War— had fought in the 1917 Battle of Vimy Ridge. In the 1930s, the family moved to Saskatoon, where in his teens Mowat wrote a column about birds for the local newspaper. He studied zoology at the University of Toronto and, in the summer of 1939, travelled west to collect data on birds.

That fall, when war broke out, Mowat applied to join the Royal Canadian Air Force and was rejected, he wrote later, as a "peach-faced kid." The following May, the day after he turned nineteen, he tried again—and was again rejected. Finally, in July 1940, he was accepted into the infantry in his father's old regiment—the Hasty P's. He repeatedly sought a transfer to active service but was denied because, as he wrote, he looked "so damn young."

In the spring of 1941, Mowat was finally sent for officer training to Fort Frontenac near Kingston, and then to Camp Borden,

100 kilometres north of Toronto. The following July, after taking a train to Saint John, New Brunswick, Mowat boarded a troop transport that took him to Greenock, Scotland. End of the month found him in southern England joining the 1st Canadian Infantry Division Reinforcement Unit. He served as an intelligence officer and then became a platoon commander.

Finally, on July 1, 1943, after practising assault landings, he sailed south from Greenock on a crowded troopship, the *Derbyshire*, destination unknown. Ten days later, as commander of a rifle platoon in Operation Husky, Mowat arrived off the southwestern tip of Sicily. There he would join battle with the enemy, as the brigadier announced, "in this first dagger-thrust into Fortress Europe." In his war memoir *And No Birds Sang*, Mowat writes that some four hundred Allied vessels had gathered in heaving nighttime waters seven miles off the coast.

Then came the landing in a small boat that, because of sirocco winds, pitched and yawed as enemy guns opened fire. The landing craft caught on a sandbar, and Mowat jumped over the gunwales to lead his men ashore, quickly discovering that the water was eight feet deep. He marched forward until his head emerged, then stumbled through the shallows until he saw "little spurts of sand racing down the beach" toward him. He dropped onto his belly but a huge wave picked him up and swept him, helpless, "toward the stitching machine-gun bullets."

It dropped him just short of that deadly stitching. Mowat rolled onto his back, looked seaward, and saw a hundred men wallowing ashore "like a herd of seals hurrying to land upon a mating beach." He also saw that a sergeant-major within arm's reach had been killed by a bullet through his throat. Now came a long march inland, during which Mowat heard a "scream of horror" from a man who lost his grip while riding on the front of a tank "and slid into the roaring vortex of dust between its churning treads."

Few writers can paint a picture like Farley Mowat. He vividly describes beating across Sicily, taking casualties, losing men he knew well, picking up and carrying on. Early in December 1943, Mowat was present when two Canadian battalions lost 164 men—though he observes that they lost more than men. Badly beaten in the field for the first time, the regiment itself felt broken. Soldiers knew they had failed themselves and each other—"knowledge that knifed into them." Only gradually did some of them realize that much of the fault lay elsewhere—with the "stupid high-level planning," one major wrote, by senior officers ignorant of the wretched terrain and of fighting among dikes.

In mid-December, the Hasty P's held a bridgehead through fourteen counterattacks. They were mentioned in a BBC news report and received a message of congratulations from the army commander. But the losses were devastating: three men killed, seven wounded, fifty-nine taken prisoner. This broke the regiment, Mowat wrote. The survivors were empty of emotion, beyond praise or condemnation. The medical officers called it "battle exhaustion."

For Mowat himself, Christmas Day proved still more devastating. Outside the town of Ortona, with the men holed up under fire from three machine guns, a giant friend named Alex grabbed a Tommy gun, gave a great bellow, and went charging out the door at the shooters. He managed three or four paces before he was cut down in a hail of bullets and crashed face first into the mud, his body jerking spasmodically.

Minutes later, someone thrust aside a blanket covering the cellar door and stretcher-bearers came into the room. On one of the stretchers lay Mowat's closest friend and fellow platoon commander, Al Park. He was alive but not for long—already unconscious, a bullet in his head. As Mowat looked down at the crimson bandage, the empty face, he began to weep uncontrollably. Looking back later, he wondered: Were his tears for Alex and Al and all the others who had gone and would go? Or was he weeping for himself . . . and those who would remain?

Battle stress. Combat fatigue. It's a short-term condition, but early in January the regiment commander sent Mowat to battalion headquarters to serve as an intelligence officer. He was back in action soon enough and stayed in Italy with the 1st Canadian Infantry Division through 1944. Promoted to captain, he moved with the division to northwest Europe. In early 1945, Mowat went through enemy lines and organized food drops that saved thousands of Dutch lives. In April 1946, the war over, he declined a promotion to major rather than remain in the military. He received six different medals for his service.

Yet the war years had taken a toll. For a time, Mowat felt himself to be in limbo. Having done some writing before and even during the war, he saw that pursuit as the only way to go forward into the future. But now he had to beat his way through writer's block. He would sit down to write and produce a paragraph or two, but no story would come. In a fury he would rip the paper to shreds. He got through this period of cynicism and disgust and then, still just twenty-four, enrolled to study biology at the University of Toronto.

For the Royal Ontario Museum, he roamed around Saskatchewan collecting birds. Then he agreed to assist an American naturalist in studying the barren-ground caribou around Nueltin Lake and beyond in what is now Nunavut. This six-month expedition would change his life. Outraged by the conditions under which he saw Inuit living, he wrote his first book, the angry and accusatory *People of the Deer* (1952). A blazing success, that work launched Mowat on a multi-faceted career.

To survey his body of work is to witness the emergence of a major writer. The rough carpentry of *People of the Deer* evolves into the equally searing but masterful *Sea of Slaughter*. Down through the decades, while remaining true to his singular vision, Mowat displayed an astonishing versatility. He did trail-blazing work in a variety of subgenres that other Canadian writers have taken up and developed: environmental polemic, political polemic, autobiography/memoir, exploration narrative, adventure travel, cultural advocacy, cross-gender biographical narrative . . . the man never stopped writing. His permutations and combinations represent a master class in the possibilities of creative non-fiction. But the books he fashioned out of the Second World War stand among the best he ever wrote.

36 / Born to Be
a War Hero

IN JANUARY 1944, as part of Operation Shingle, Canadians led an amphibious landing near the port at Anzio, located on the west coast of Italy about 50 kilometres south of Rome. The objective was to out-flank the formidable German defences known as the Winter Line (or the Gustav Line), and then push on to Rome. The hope was that the landing would also draw German forces away from the Gustav Line, where the Allies were bogged down in a standoff.

The operation did not proceed as planned. The Nazis contained the Allied forces in the Anzio beachhead for four months. The pro-tracted and bloody stalemate didn't end until May 1944, when in conjunction with an offensive against the Hitler Line farther south, the Anzio forces broke out from the beachhead and started the drive toward Rome.

One Canadian instrumental in achieving the breakout was a ser-geant named Tommy Prince. Early in February 1944, near Anzio, Prince volunteered to run a telephone wire 1,400 metres from the Allied trenches to an abandoned farmhouse overlooking a German artillery position. He made his way there, then hid in the house and turned it into an observation post, using the phone to report on shift-ing German positions.

When during an artillery exchange the line got cut, Prince dug some work clothes out of a closet and found a hoe near the back door. Disguised as a peasant farmer, he shuffled outside and pretended to

Sergeant Tommy Prince
of the Brokenhead
Ojibway Nation and 1st
Canadian Parachute
Battalion in 1945. *Alamy*

work the land around the farmhouse. While German soldiers looked on, not knowing what to think, Prince located the break in the severed wire. Kneeling and pretending to tie his shoelaces, he reconnected the two ends.

When he was done, he stood and shook his fist at the Allies, then at the Nazis, as if calling down the wrath of God on both sides. Then he returned to reporting enemy movements. This action—so creative, so characteristic—led to the destruction of four German batteries that had been raining hellfire on Allied troops. If Prince had been caught, he would have been executed as a spy. Instead, he received the Military Medal, the citation noting that "Sergeant Prince's courage and utter disregard for personal safety were an inspiration to his fellows and a marked credit to his unit."

And that is just one example of why, during the Second World War, Tommy Prince—born in a canvas tent near Lake Winnipeg—became the most decorated First Nations soldier in the Canadian army. The irony here is that he fought for king and country abroad while at home he had grown up as a marginalized citizen living on unceded territory.

Prince came into the world in 1915, one of eleven children born to Henry and Arabella Prince. He was descended from Peguis, a renowned Salteaux leader, and grew up as part of the Brokenhead Ojibway Nation. Thanks to his father, a hunter and trapper, he became an expert tracker and marksman. As a youth, he could shoot five bullets through a playing card at 100 metres. He went to Elkhorn Residential School, then joined the Army Cadets, hoping eventually to become a lawyer. But the sudden, crushing onset of the Great Depression forced him to quit high school at sixteen to work, mostly as a tree faller.

In September 1939, when war broke out, Prince sought to enlist with the Canadian army. Like Farley Mowat, he was repeatedly turned down until June 1940, when the fall of France caused the army to be less prohibitive in accepting new recruits. Originally assigned to the Royal Canadian Engineers, Prince sailed to France and trained as a sapper or field engineer. Promoted to lance corporal in February 1941, Prince grew bored with desk duties and volunteered to join a parachute unit—really a secret First Special Service Force of men preparing to raid targets in Nazi-occupied Norway. Instead, the men would end up in Italy.

In autumn 1942, now a sergeant, Prince trained with a joint US–Canada commando unit—later known as the "Devil's Brigade"—in Georgia and Montana. This elite unit, initially 1,800 strong, received intense training in stealth tactics, hand-to-hand combat, explosives, rock climbing, and mountain fighting. With his tracking and hunting background, Prince shone. He became a "reconnaissance sergeant" or scout, responsible for venturing ahead and ferreting out enemy positions.

Whenever he needed to move quietly during the Anzio campaign, Prince would remove his army-issue boots in favour of moccasins. At night, he would sneak past Nazi security guards and leave messages, steal boots, or use his knife to kill enemy soldiers. He would also venture out into no man's land, find a vantage point, and pick off any German who wandered out.

In the days leading up to Prince's farmhouse caper in Italy, the Devil's Brigade had won the Battle of Monte la Difensa by scaling a steep cliff at night and surprising the Nazis at the summit. To the Canadian contingent fell the task of taking Monte Majo, where the steep slopes were layered with machine-gun emplacements. Previous attempts to take the mountain had failed disastrously.

The brigade commander assigned his best man, Corporal Prince, to lead a night patrol in creating an invasion pathway up the mountain by taking out enemy gun emplacements on the lower and middle slopes of Monte Majo. Prince led his men partway up the steep hill, then told them to wait in case he needed covering fire.

Alone, he scrambled upward, working his way silently from one gun pit to another, dispatching every soldier he found without sparking so much as a single shot. He then collected his men and, before dawn, returned to camp and reported his mission accomplished. The only remaining Nazis were those on the summit, and they were soon taken by complete surprise.

On June 4, 1944, two days before D-Day, the Devil's Brigade led the way in liberating Rome from Nazi occupation. Then, as part of Operation Dragoon, it moved to Sylvabelle on the French Riviera. By September 1, Prince was sent forward with a private to scout enemy positions north of Nice at L'Escarène. They came across an enemy reserve battalion, and Prince hid in the trees and bushes to avoid detection while conducting detailed observations. Heading back to rejoin the brigade, Prince heard shooting and found a battle raging between a Nazi patrol and a group of French partisans.

While remaining hidden in the long grass, he and the private killed a dozen of the enemy. When the Germans withdrew in confusion, Prince met the French Resistance leader, who asked where the rest of his company were. Prince pointed to the private and said, "Here." The partisan said that, like the departed Nazis, he had thought fifty men were firing from the bushes. He recommended Prince for the Croix de Guerre, but the courier was killed en route and the message never reached General Charles de Gaulle.

Prince rejoined the Devil's Brigade. He led it back to the Nazi reserve battalion—one thousand men who were soon dead or taken prisoner. By this time, while hiking and scrambling more than 70 kilometres over mountainous terrain, Prince had gone without food, water, or sleep for seventy-two hours. For this wildly successful action, he was awarded the American Silver Star. This made him one of only three Canadians to receive both that and the Canadian Military Medal. Prince would be mentioned several more times in dispatches and would receive six service medals for his outstanding work in the Italian and North West Europe theatres of war.

In June 1945, with Hitler dead and the war winding down, Sergeant Prince was honourably discharged and returned to his home on the Brokenhead Reserve. He moved to Winnipeg the following year and, with some business funding from the Department of Veteran's Affairs, started up a successful cleaning service.

In 1946, he was elected vice president of the Manitoba Indian Association and became chairman of the national delegation representing First Nations at a parliamentary committee in Ottawa. He advocated abolition of the *Indian Act* and insisted that Crown treaties should form the basis of a new system for First Nations peoples— positions that were decades ahead of their time.

But life was not always easy. Frustrated at his inability to effect change, Prince returned to Winnipeg and discovered that his cleaning business had gone under. His friends had crashed his truck and sold the parts as scrap metal, then sold his other equipment and spent the money. Tommy Prince reverted to working jobs that presented little challenge.

In 1950, when the Korean War broke out, he rejoined the Canadian Army as a sergeant and, able once more to use his special talents, again distinguished himself by leading stealth missions and earning three more medals This was a man born to be a war hero. When he died in financial difficulties at age sixty-two, having refused to move in with one of his five children, more than five hundred people attended a provincial state funeral in his honour. In October 2022, Canada Post issued a postage stamp depicting Tommy Prince in his Korean War uniform, behind him a wilderness of pine trees and an array of northern lights.

37 / Finding Big Brother
in the Ruins

AFTER SPENDING SIX months in Morocco recovering from tuberculosis, George Orwell was back home in England in September 1939 when the Nazis started the Second World War. As anticipated, the British Army rejected him as unfit for service on medical grounds. He managed to join the volunteer Home Guard, became a sergeant, and in British magazines published what he hoped were inspiring articles on weaponry and street-fighting tactics.

In the early 1940s, Orwell worked at the BBC as a "talks assistant" or assignment editor—an experience that gave him an inside view of toiling in a bureaucracy. He also developed his political vision in several notable essays—a vision that put him at odds with most leading European intellectuals, who were so horrified by fascism that they embraced communism, Joseph Stalin notwithstanding.

In his essay "Inside the Whale," Orwell used the Biblical story of Jonah to distance himself from the anarchistic passivity of Henry Miller. In "The Lion and the Unicorn: Socialism and the English Genius," he argued that to defeat Nazi Germany, Britain needed to undergo a revolution that would introduce a democratic socialism radically different from the oppressive communism of the Soviet Union. And in "Fascism and Democracy," he wrote that "Communism was from the first a lost cause in western Europe, and the

Communist parties of the various countries early degenerated into mere publicity agents for the Russian regime . . . [T]he Communists were obliged to pretend that the purges, 'liquidations,' were healthy symptoms which any right-minded person would like to see transferred to England."

In 1943, when a young Farley Mowat was training in England, avid to see action, Orwell resigned from the BBC, feeling that as he was assigned to writing broadcasts for an audience in India, he was contributing little to the European war effort. He became literary editor of the *Tribune*, a left-wing weekly, and wrote a regular column, "As I Please," which gave him room to cover a wide array of subjects. In March of that year, he finished a book that would transform his career—though not overnight.

Since escaping Spain, Orwell had been ruminating about writing a political fable. Later he would explain, "Of course I intended it primarily as a satire on the Russian revolution. But I did mean it to have a wider application in so much that I meant that that kind of revolution (violent conspiratorial revolution, led by unconsciously power-hungry people) can only lead to a change of master." *Animal Farm* emerged as an allegorical barnyard rebellion in which characters had obvious historical counterparts—a pig named Napoleon was Stalin; his porcine rival, Snowball, was Trotsky; a next-door farmer was Hitler.

Four British publishers rejected the book. By 1943, Russia had become a crucial British ally in the war against fascism, and editors worried about stirring up controversy. Victor Gollancz, who had published Orwell previously, ran *Animal Farm* past an acquaintance at the British Ministry of Information and received a thumbs-down. In *The Tribune*, Orwell observed, "Circus dogs jump when the trainer cracks his whip, but the really well-trained dog is the one that turns his somersault when there is no whip."

In June 1944, after German saturation bombing destroyed the ceilings of his London flat, George Orwell rescued the crumpled typescript of *Animal Farm* from the rubble. He smoothed it out, sent it off through his agent, and this time received an offer from the publisher Secker & Warburg. The British edition, which appeared in August

1945, attracted rave reviews and sold 25,000 in its first five years—
ten times what anybody had expected. The American edition came
out in 1946 and sold 590,000 copies in four years.

Meanwhile, in February 1945, despite his poor health, Orwell
jumped at a chance to serve as a war correspondent in France for
the *Observer*. He found Paris "horribly depressing compared with
what it used to be" but set up shop at the Hotel Scribe, a favourite
among foreign journalists, and began writing articles. One afternoon,
on learning that Ernest Hemingway had checked into the hotel, he
knocked on his fellow writer's door. Hemingway was packing his bags
and Orwell awkwardly introduced himself as Eric Blair, a writer for
the *Observer*.

"Well, what the fucking hell do you want?"

The visitor laughed at the two-fisted predictability of this. "You
might know me as George Orwell."

"Orwell? Why the fucking hell didn't you say so?" Hemingway
pulled a bottle of whisky out of one of his bags and insisted that
Orwell have a drink. "Have a double. Straight or with water, there's
no soda."

The meeting was brief, what with Hemingway halfway out the
door. But in 1950, in one of many letters he exchanged with English
literary critic Cyril Connolly, the American wrote of his admiration for
the British author. Orwell also introduced himself to André Malraux,
by now advising French president Charles de Gaulle, and arranged
to meet philosopher and novelist Albert Camus at the iconic Parisian brasserie Les Deux Magots. Camus was laid low by tuberculosis
and couldn't make it. As Dorian Lynskey observes in *The Ministry of
Truth: The Biography of George Orwell's 1984*, that meeting would have
brought together "two natural rebels who put principles before political expediency and turned political writing into art." Orwell would
send Camus a copy of *Animal Farm* in French translation.

Orwell was still in Paris when, at the end of March 1945, tragedy
struck. His wife Eileen, just thirty-nine years old, went into a London
hospital for routine surgery. She had an allergic reaction to an anaes-
thetic and died of a heart attack. A devastated Orwell hurried home.

He and Eileen had recently adopted a baby boy, loved by both, and Orwell struggled for months with moving forward, even to making a couple of ill-considered marriage proposals, both rejected.

Finally, unable to think straight in the flat he had shared with his wife, Orwell left the baby with Eileen's sister and returned to the Continent to write articles. Finding refuge in overwork, he produced 130 articles and reviews in the year that followed Eileen's death. The destruction he saw in Germany—the cities in ruins, the refugees in flight—took his mind off his own grief. Orwell spent that Christmas at a cottage in Wales owned by his friend Arthur Koestler.

Orwell had long dreamed with Eileen of retreating to a Scottish island. In August 1946, without her, he moved into an isolated house called Barnhill on Jura, accompanied by his baby son and a succession of housekeepers. At some point in the 1940s, according to biographer Michael Sheldon, Orwell read Yevgeny Zamyatin's dystopian novel *We*. In it he found a future nation living in OneState, a totalitarian society ruled by the Benefactor. Citizens wear uniforms, identify not by name but by number, and behave according to equations and formulas. The plot circles around a doomed love affair.

At Barnhill, Orwell began writing what would become *Nineteen Eighty-Four*, the book that would cement his reputation as one of the great writers of the twentieth century. As early as 1940, when he reviewed *The Totalitarian Enemy*, a non-fiction book by Austrian writer Franz Borkenau, and as Lynskey points out in *The Ministry of Truth*, he had begun to see "Nazism and Stalinism as two faces of the same monster." In reviewing Borkenau's book, Orwell wrote that the "sin of nearly all left-wingers from 1933 onwards is that they have wanted to be anti-Fascist without being anti-totalitarian."

With *Nineteen Eighty-Four*, Orwell was finally able to show that the ultimate enemy, totalitarianism, subsumed both fascism and communism. In depicting his fictionalized regime, Orwell drew on both Nazi Germany and Stalinist Russia. He symbolized the enemy in the figure of Big Brother: hate-filled, ruthless, all-powerful. Thematically, the novel addresses his concerns about extensive surveillance, the manipulation of truth, and total control over individual behaviour.

The narrative unfolds in the future, apparently 1984. The world is engulfed in perpetual warfare. Airstrip One, formerly known as Great Britain, is a province in the all-encompassing totalitarian superstate known as Oceania. It is dominated by Big Brother, a dictatorial figurehead kept in power by the Thought Police. Through the Ministry of Truth, the Party enforces omnipresent government surveillance, historical revisionism, and relentless propaganda to suppress independent thought.

Winston Smith, the novel's protagonist, toils diligently as a mid-level worker at the Ministry of Truth. He loathes his life, yearns to rebel, and keeps a secret diary that he fills with sometimes subversive observations. He and a co-worker, Julia, embark on a clandestine affair and discover an underground resistance called the Brotherhood. Their contact betrays them. After months of brainwashing in the Ministry of Love, Smith succumbs to loving Big Brother.

The novel, a dystopian classic, would turn "Orwellian" into an adjective and would introduce into the public lexicon such indelible terms as "Big Brother," "doublethink," "thought police," "thoughtcrime," and "newspeak." Orwell finished the first draft of the book in his sick bed at Barnhill in November 1946. When the novel appeared in 1949, astute readers hailed the book, among them John Dos Passos, E.M. Forster, and Lawrence Durrell. Koestler called it "a glorious book," Aldous Huxley pronounced it "profoundly important," and Margaret Storm Jameson wrote that this was "the novel which should stand for our age."

The book would sell 50,000 hardcover copies in the UK in its first two years. In the US, where the novel remained a *New York Times* bestseller for twenty weeks, it would sell 170,000 in hardcover, 190,000 through the Book of the Month club, 596,000 as a Reader's Digest Condensed Book, and more than 1.2 million as a North American Library paperback. *Nineteen Eighty-Four* would become a fixture on high school reading lists throughout the Western world. Then, with the election of Donald Trump in 2016, it would skyrocket to the top of bestseller lists.

Orwell considered the work not a prophecy but a warning. He did not think something like the totalitarian society he depicted "necessarily will arrive . . . but that something resembling it could arrive." As for lasting influence, one example will suffice. Margaret Atwood described *The Handmaid's Tale*—which she started writing in West Berlin in 1984—as "speculative fiction of the George Orwell variety."

In October 1949, aware that ill health would soon end his life, and looking for someone to protect his legacy, the forty-six-year-old author married Sonia Brownell, a thirty-year-old who is thought to be the inspiration for the fictional Julia, Winston's love interest in *Nineteen Eighty-Four*. In January 1950, she managed to charter a plane to take him to a sanatorium in Switzerland. They were due to leave in four days when on January 21, while in hospital in London, satisfied that he had issued a final warning with his dystopian novel, George Orwell passed away.

PART FIVE

The French Resistance

38 / Jack London: Vive la Revolution!

IN ONE OF the most prescient dystopian works ever written, the narrator describes how the party in government, having lost an election, declined to leave office. "The incumbents refused to get out. It was very simple. They merely charged illegality in the elections and wrapped up the whole situation in the interminable red tape of the law. The Democrats were powerless. The courts were in the hands of their enemies."

Okay, in quoting that passage, I cheated. I changed the fictional "Grangers" to the real-world "Democrats." But let's admit that Jack London's *The Iron Heel*, published in 1908, shows uncanny foresight in anticipating the end game of the 2020 election, when MAGA Republicans fought tooth and nail to retain control of the White House.

Readers who know Jack London only as the author of the classic animal stories *The Call of the Wild* and *White Fang* will be surprised by the political engagement of *The Iron Heel*. Published almost three decades before Sinclair Lewis's *It Can't Happen Here*, this was the first American novel to warn against the rise of fascism and the emergence of a right-wing dictatorship in the United States. In *The Iron Heel*, London refers repeatedly to "the people of the abyss." He had already

Jack London—American author, journalist, and social activist.

Arnold Genthe / Alamy

used that expression as the title of a non-fiction book—one that influenced Orwell to write *Down and Out in Paris and London*. But in this book, London offers a footnote saying that he took his title from a phrase "struck out of the genius of H.G. Wells."

While harking back to Wells, London's dystopian novel also looks forward. It anticipates Orwell, who himself described *Iron Heel* as "a very remarkable prophecy of the rise of Fascism." Orwell also asserted that London was a better prophet "than many better-informed and more logical thinkers." He could foresee the cruel struggles that lay ahead "because of the streak of brutality which he had in himself." London knew the ruling class was tough and would hit back because he himself was tough. The best of London's stories, Orwell wrote, "deal with prison, the prize-ring, the sea, and the frozen wastes of Canada—that is, with situations where toughness is everything."

In *The Iron Heel*, London uses a futuristic framing device now familiar from later dystopian novels, such as *Nineteen Eighty-Four* and *The Handmaid's Tale*. In this case, a scholar by the name of Anthony Meredith, writing from the vantage point of around 2600 CE, supplies a short foreword introducing an ancient manuscript (early twentieth century)—a long-lost memoir by Avis Everhard. Throughout, Meredith adds the occasional footnote to clarify allusions and correct errors.

The story covers the period from 1912 to 1932 and treats the evolution of the powerful "Oligarchs" in the US into the ruling dictatorship of the *Iron Heel*. The Oligarchy comprises a few massive and growing "trusts" run by individuals who have become obscenely rich and powerful by squeezing small and middle-sized businesses into capitulation. The contemporary reader cannot help but think of the top 1 percent of Americans, billionaires said to control 40 percent of the nation's wealth—though some say that figure is much higher.

Jack London drew heavily on the theories of Karl Marx, who had argued that capitalism is unsustainable and would destroy itself. In 1937, the Marxist revolutionary Leon Trotsky would write of *The Iron Heel* that "London already foresaw and described the fascist regime as the inevitable result of the defeat of the proletarian revolution." By then, of course, fascists were in the ascendant—not in the US, but in Spain, Italy, Germany, and even France. Those in France during the Second World War who opposed the fascists, and instead championed the people of the abyss, would comprise the French Resistance.

On one level, London's narrative becomes a journey of discovery for Avis as she investigates her lover's highly articulate contention that the existing social order is built on the exploitation of labour. She sees her father, a prominent physician, who because of his outspoken opposition, his resistance, has lost his medical practice and faces financial hardship. She sees a family friend, a reformed priest, driven into a mental asylum for challenging the Oligarchy. She opens her eyes to the "people of the abyss"—and to what they are up against.

While Avis writes in the belief that she and her fellow revolutionaries will succeed in overthrowing the Iron Heel, the latecomer Anthony Meredith reveals that their revolution will end in failure. But London lays out a scenario in which such setbacks are to be expected: the class revolution fails repeatedly until the 2200s. It remains possible that London's three-century scenario, as outlined by Anthony Meredith, will prove more eerily prescient than anyone could have imagined.

That is because *The Iron Heel* anticipates Trumpism and its unwillingness to concede defeat. As Orwell observed, Jack London foresaw that "when the working-class movements took on formidable dimensions and looked like dominating the world, the capitalist class would hit back. They wouldn't simply lie down and let themselves be expropriated, as so many socialists had imagined." London's main achievement, he wrote, was to foresee "that the menaced capitalist class would counterattack and not quietly die because the writers of Marxist textbooks told it to die." Neither London nor Orwell would be surprised to see Donald Trump and far-right Republicans manning the barricades for the billionaire class.

39 / The Resilience of Agnès Humbert

THE FRENCH RESISTANCE was a diverse and diffuse network of groups and individuals, most of whom operated in secrecy and many of whose actions went unrecorded. Estimates vary, but the armed *maquisard* fighters—those who formed rural guerrilla bands—may have numbered up to 100,000. As many as 400,000 more people, out of a national population of 41 million, participated less directly. The Resistance incorporated men and women from all walks of life— intellectuals, workers, teenagers, the elderly. They came from across the political spectrum: communists, socialists, conservatives, mon- archists. This diversity sometimes led to conflicts within, but the common goal of defeating the Nazis held the movement together.

Those involved engaged in sabotage, disrupted German opera- tions, provided crucial support to the Allies, distributed pamphlets and newspapers, and served as beacons of hope and defiance to the French people. In so doing they faced enormous risks. Between 15,000 and 35,000 Resistance members lost their lives—either in combat or after some combination of capture, torture, and deporta- tion to concentration camps.

To tell the full story of the French Resistance and the thousands of diverse figures that filled its ranks in a few short chapters is impossible. But by approaching this history through the lives of key individuals, perhaps we can capture the spirit of the movement.

Agnès Humbert, for example, was primarily a writer and intellectual—an art historian. She was not a soldier. Four days after the Nazis occupied Paris, Humbert heard a BBC radio broadcast that changed her life. At forty-five, she had fled 400 kilometres south to check on her mother in a small town near Limoges. The museum where she worked as an art historian had shut down. Divorced for the past six years, Humbert was the mother of two young men in their twenties—one serving in the French navy in Newfoundland, the other living independently in Paris, beginning a career in journalism.

The Nazi occupation had left her feeling hopeless, suicidal. On June 18, 1940, as she wrote in her journal, she turned on the wireless set, which was tuned to London, and "by a pure fluke [found herself] listening to a transmission in French." A French general, whose name she didn't catch, was urging all Frenchmen to rally around him, to regroup and carry on the struggle. In *Resistance: Memoirs of Occupied France*, Humbert writes that she felt hope stirring. There was one man, at least, who understood what she felt: the battle was far from over.

She hurtled outside, crossed the garden "like a lunatic," and charged up to an old military man. She told him what she had heard and he nodded and identified the general she had heard as Charles de Gaulle: "Oh, we know all about him, don't you worry. It's all a lot of nonsense . . . [H]e's a crackpot, that de Gaulle, you mark my words."

Thanks to that "crackpot," Humbert wrote that night, she had decided to live on. De Gaulle had given her hope. Within days, Agnès Humbert was back in Paris. On hearing that the sympatico Jean Cassou, director of the museum where she worked, had reopened the museum, Humbert rushed off to see him. In his office they compared impressions and Humbert blurted that she would go mad if she didn't do something in response to the invasion.

Cassou confided that he felt the same way. The two decided they should form a group of perhaps ten like-minded comrades. They would meet regularly, and at the very least write, print, and distribute pamphlets. The two drew up a list of candidates and identified a place to meet, and Humbert returned home "with a lighter heart."

So began the *Groupe du musée de l'Homme*, one of the earliest of countless Resistance groups that arose in France during the Nazi occupation. Humbert, the prime mover, had been born in Dieppe in 1894, the daughter of a French senator and an English writer. She grew up in Paris, studied painting and design, and in 1916 married one of her fellow students. She bore two sons—one of whom would grow up to become an adviser to Charles de Gaulle—and divorced in 1934. After advanced studies at the Sorbonne, she worked as an art historian at a national museum and library. In 1936, she published an acclaimed book on the neoclassical French painter Jacques-Louis David. After the fall of Paris in June 1940, she began keeping a diary and barely managed to suppress her outrage at seeing Nazis remove books by French authors and replace them with those by Germans.

Early in August she began approaching like-minded souls. Within a few months, the original members had developed a considerable network. They created a clandestine newsletter, *Resistance*, and published five issues between mid-December 1940 and mid-March 1941, all of them denouncing the collaborationist Vichy regime. They also fed information to the British government.

That April, one member betrayed the group leaders, Humbert among them. They were arrested by the Gestapo and jailed in Fresnes Prison, south of Paris, known for its horrific conditions. There they were tried by the Nazi Wehrmacht (the unified armed forces) and in February 1942, sentenced to death.

Along with the other women from her group, Humbert had her sentence commuted to five years of slave labour. She was sent first to the Prison de la Santé, where she learned that her seven male colleagues had been interrogated, tortured, and killed by firing squad at the Mont-Valerién execution site. In their last moments, they sang "*Vive la France*."

Humbert was then sent to Anrath Prison in Germany and made to work in horrendous conditions at a rayon factory in Krefeld. Many of her fellow French women prisoners died, went blind, or developed skin diseases. Agnès Humbert survived and refused to succumb to despair. She took notes as a means of coping and resisting. This served as a cathartic outlet, enabling her to process her emotions, maintain a sense of identity, and hold on to her principles. She also drew strength from her sense of purpose and her unwavering commitment to the cause of resistance, maintaining hope even in the face of adversity. At Anrath, despite the strict regulations that separated men and women, prisoners devised a clever method to communicate using a ball of string. Tying small notes to the string, they would toss it from cell to cell, allowing them to exchange messages, share information, and offer words of encouragement, fostering a sense of connection and solidarity.

In defiance of the oppressive conditions, the prisoners managed to create a secret library within the prison walls. They smuggled books and shared them, finding solace, escape, and intellectual nourishment amidst the bleakness of their confinement. During a period of hunger and limited food rations, one prisoner managed to lay hands on a potato. Instead of consuming it alone, she divided it into equal portions and distributed them to her comrades—an act of selflessness that raised everyone's spirits. Prisoners also found ways to inject humour into their lives, sharing jokes and anecdotes and bringing levity into the darkness.

In June 1945, after four years at Anrath, Agnès Humbert was among those finally liberated by the US Army. Later that year, she set up soup kitchens for refugees and insisted that everyone was welcome, even German civilians.

After the war, Agnès Humbert went to work with an old colleague at the new National Museum of Modern Art. In 1946, she published her book *Notre guerre*, which combined diary entries and reminiscences based on her prison notes. Three years later, Humbert received the Croix de Guerre with silver gilt for heroism. She spent her final years living with her son Jean Sabbagh, an adviser to the president of France—the same man who, in 1940, had made a broadcast that turned her into a *résistante*. She died in Valmondois, north of Paris, in 1963, at age sixty-nine. In 2008, her wartime book appeared in English translation: *Resistance: Memoirs of Occupied France*.

40 / The Martyrdom of Jean Moulin

TWO DECADES AFTER the end of the Second World War, French president Charles de Gaulle presided over a ceremony celebrating the martyr Jean Moulin as the greatest hero of the French Resistance. On December 19, 1964, outside the Pantheon in Paris, resting place of the heroes of the French Republic, de Gaulle called upon culture minister André Malraux to deliver a eulogy.

Malraux picked up the story in October of 1941, when Moulin flew to London to ask de Gaulle not only for money and arms, but also for moral support and closer links. Already, Moulin had gone on record as declaring that if the Allies came to fight on the continent, it would be crazy not to deploy determined troops who, already familiar with the landscape, were ready to risk their lives in battle.

Moulin was a bureaucrat and an organizer. He was not the one, Malraux said, who created the various Resistance networks, but he was the one who united them into an army. In what is considered one of the greatest speeches in French history, Malraux swept his listeners away, back to July 8, 1943. That was the day when, having refused to betray his comrades despite being brutally tortured, Moulin died. That day, Malraux cried, his poor battered face was the face of France.

Born in 1899 in Béziers, in southern France, the son of a history professor, Jean Pierre Moulin studied law at Montpellier, where his sister lived. In 1918, toward the end of the First World War, he joined the French army—an engineering regiment—and was preparing to go to the front lines when the war ended. In November 1919, he resumed his law studies while serving as a government attaché.

In 1930 Moulin became subprefect of Châteaulin in Brittany—a local administrator responsible for implementing government policy. A talented artist, Moulin published political cartoons and illustrated books. In 1932, the socialist politician Pierre Cot, then serving as foreign minister, made Moulin his second-in-command.

Four years later, while helping Cot assist the Republicans during the Spanish Civil War, Moulin supervised the delivery of planes to the Republican forces. And in 1937, he became France's youngest prefect or regional administrator in the south of the country. He moved to a larger department based in Chartres, but after war broke out, requested a demotion that would take him nearer the action.

No need. In June 1940, Nazi troops entered the city. Now came Moulin's first great test: on June 17, Nazi troops ordered him to sign a false document stating that Senegalese troops had killed several French women. This was really a test to see if he would collaborate with the Vichy regime. Moulin refused, and the troops beat him to a pulp. Left alone in a cell, fearing that under further torture he might yield, Moulin cut his own throat. He did so near the chin and eventually recovered. But in November, the Vichy government ordered him to fire any remaining left-wing officials. He refused and was himself sacked.

In 1941, while visiting his parents on the French Riviera, Moulin joined Free France, which de Gaulle had set up as the French government in exile. He visited Marseille, met other leaders of the Resistance, and then, in September 1941, travelled to London. He met Charles de Gaulle in October, described the splintered state of the Resistance, and secured the assignment he wanted: to unify and coordinate the various Resistance groups.

Early in the new year, Moulin parachuted back into France, landing in a low mountain range south of Avignon. He met with Resistance leaders and spent a year uniting three major groups—*Combat, Libération, Franc-Tireur*—into the *Mouvements unis de la Résistance* (United Resistance Movements). In February 1943, Moulin again flew to London and consulted de Gaulle. He returned to France the following month with orders to unify the military wings of the various groups by forming the *Conseil national de la Résistance*.

Incredibly, given the strong personalities involved, he succeeded. The council comprised representatives from eight resistance movements, two labour unions, and six political parties. Moulin convinced even communist Resistance groups to accept de Gaulle as their leader. He laid out a two-part program featuring an "immediate action plan" and "measures to be applied after the territory is liberated." This described how to purge Nazi influence while restoring universal suffrage, freedom of the press, and the right to unionize.

Less than one month later, the Gestapo arrested Moulin and seven fellow Resistance leaders during a meeting at a home in suburban Lyon. A ninth man, René Hardy, managed to escape—and, despite denials, was almost certainly the traitor. Hardy had been seduced by a young woman at the urging of her real lover, a Gestapo officer, and betrayed his comrades because he believed that otherwise she would be arrested.

Along with the others, Moulin was taken to Montluc Prison, where he was tortured by German officer Klaus Barbie, the "Butcher of Lyon." While demanding answers to questions, the torturers used hot needles to remove his fingernails. They placed his hands in the door frame of the cell and repeatedly slammed the door, shattering his joints and knuckles. Then they beat him unconscious, rendering his face unrecognizable. Barbie ordered that, while comatose, Moulin be displayed to his fellow prisoners as an object lesson.

Today, the prevailing theory is that, while being transported to Berlin for further questioning, Moulin managed to kill himself on July 8, 1943, at or near the French town of Metz. An alternative hypothesis is that he died before being put on the train, killed by overzealous torturers who wished to avoid the wrath of Hitler for failing to make him talk. Either way, as Laure Moulin wrote in a biography of her brother, the savagely beaten Moulin had reached the limits of human suffering without betraying a single secret.

41 / Elusive Queen of French Spies

IN JUNE 1944, shortly after D-Day, the Gestapo caught up with her. Marie-Madeleine Fourcade had eluded them for four years. She had moved her base of operations frequently, while also changing her hair colour, her style of dress, her identity. The men who arrested her knew she was an Allied spy, but her phony papers identified her as a homemaker named Germaine Pezet. Tomorrow, the Germans said, a senior Gestapo official would arrive from Marseille to question her. Fourcade realized he would probably figure out who she was. She had to escape her jail cell if she could. As she assessed her options, she remembered a story her father had told her in Shanghai.

Her father was an executive with the French Maritime Service. Born in Marseille in August 1909, Marie-Madeleine Bridou had spent her childhood in Shanghai, that teeming metropolis, a city crowded with beggars and street vendors, white Russians, Chinese warlords, American gangsters, and international arms dealers. When she was eight, her father died of a tropical disease. The family moved back to France, but living abroad had already set the young girl on a singular path. At eighteen she met and married an army officer, and soon had two children. But she balked at settling into the traditional role of wife and mother and ended the marriage in 1933.

She left her husband in Morocco, brought the children back to Paris, and took to flying airplanes and driving in automobile races. Unusually for a woman of her time and social class, she got

Marie Madeleine Fourcade in 1959—one of the female war heroes overlooked by
General Charles de Gaulle. *Getty Images*

a job—going to work as a producer at a Paris radio station. In 1936,
while attending an afternoon tea at her sister's upscale apartment,
she caught the eye of a military man while sharing her views on the
threatening rise of Adolf Hitler. As it happened, this man, Major
Georges Loustaunau-Lacau (code name "Navarre")—formerly a
French army intelligence officer—was equally concerned.

He told the twenty-seven-year-old woman he was launching a
journal aimed at opening French eyes and asked if she would travel to
Belgium to retrieve sensitive documents detailing German intentions
in Europe. Outraged by the idea that Hitler would roll into France
and destroy the country she loved, she agreed. She began working
with Navarre on his espionage magazine, *L'ordre national*. She stayed
with him in 1940, when the Nazis occupied France. They went underground and set about creating an atypical Resistance group—one not
given to acts of sabotage or assisting people to escape, but devoted to
gathering intelligence: a spy network called *Alliance*.

Marie-Madeleine—henceforth Fourcade—left her children with caregivers and became deputy leader. In July 1941, when Loustanau-Lacau was arrested by Nazis, he appointed her number one. Would the mostly male agents accept a woman in this role? "She was young and very beautiful," one of them said later, "but there was an unmistakable aura of authority around her."

Fourcade set about growing the network, recruiting spies—radio operators, pilots, couriers—from Normandy and Brittany to Burgundy and the French Riviera.

At its height, *Alliance* had more than three thousand agents, making it the largest of all French Resistance organizations. The Nazis dubbed it "Noah's Ark" because for code names, Fourcade drew on the world of animals. She called herself "Hedgehog." *Alliance* comprised ordinary French citizens—shopkeepers and students, workers and businessmen, policemen, government workers, and homemakers. Almost 20 percent of them were women, the highest percentage of any network.

Alliance worked closely with British intelligence, and to ensure that money and supplies continued to flow, Fourcade travelled to Spain to meet a British MI6 agent. She agreed to be smuggled across the border in a jute mail sack hidden in the trunk of a car. She curled up into this small bag, all five foot six of her, and rode that way for nine excruciating hours. When she reached her destination, she stood up and fainted, and had to be revived with cognac and a cigarette. Soon afterward, when she met the MI6 man, he looked at the elegant woman introduced as the head of *Alliance*, and said, "This is a joke, isn't it?"

She won him over and the money kept coming. *Alliance* radioed crucial information to London as dozens of Nazi clerks searched furiously for suspicious radio transmissions. The work was dangerous because most of Fourcade's spies were untrained amateurs. Hundreds were captured or killed. Fourcade had an instinct for impending danger. More than once, she anticipated a Nazi raid and moved her headquarters. The next day the Gestapo would turn up at the old address.

Meanwhile, *Alliance* agents flooded the British and Americans with vital information, covering everything from troop movements to airfield locations and submarine sailing schedules. Two of Fourcade's most successful agents brought singular talents into the fray.

· Jeannie Rousseau was a brilliant woman in her early twenties. In Paris, she became an interpreter for a group of French businessmen who frequently met with German military officials to discuss commercial issues. She played the wide-eyed skeptic to induce a Nazi officer to share secrets about the latest flying bombs (v-1) and rockets (v-2), and even to show her a map of the main testing site. She had a photographic memory and after each meeting transmitted what she had learned to Britain, where it ended up on the desk of Winston Churchill. On August 17, 1943, thanks to her intelligence, more than five hundred RAF bombers obliterated the testing site, setting the projects back months.

· Robert Douin was a sculptor living in Normandy. In preparation for the D-Day landing, *Alliance* asked him to provide detailed information about German coastal defences. For weeks, he and his son and a few subagents cycled along the coast, sketching what they saw. Ultimately, Douin produced a hand-drawn map, fifty-five feet long, showing every German artillery placement and fortification along the coast. Three months before D-Day, he sent it to London. Soon afterward, he and fifteen of his agents were arrested. On D-Day morning, they were rousted, taken to the prison courtyard, and executed by firing squad.

BY THE SUMMER of 1944, Fourcade knew that dozens of her agents had been tortured and killed, among them some of her top lieutenants and close friends. Finally, in Aix-en-Provence, her own luck ran out. She was arrested and thrown into a jail cell to await the arrival, the next morning, of that senior Gestapo figure—no doubt an expert torturer. As she sat in her overheated cell with a single barred window, she remembered that story her father had told her, about how Chinese thieves would smear oil over their naked bodies and squeeze through the bars and windows of targeted houses.

Fourcade had no oil, but she was sweating profusely in the stifling heat. She waited until three o'clock in the morning, when the guards went off duty, then stripped off her clothes and rubbed herself down with her own sweat. Holding a light summer dress between her teeth, she managed to squeeze through the bars of the window. She slipped to the ground, crossed the street on her hands and knees, and put on her dress. Then she stood up, brushed herself off, and headed back to Paris, never to be captured again.

Despite her spectacular contributions, Fourcade was ignored when the time came to award honours. First, she was a woman, and when at war's end General Charles de Gaulle appointed "heroes" to the *Compagnons de la Libération*, he named 1,038 individuals, only 6 of them female. Second, Fourcade had worked closely with Navarre, a military figure with whom de Gaulle felt competitive.

Championing the agents in her network, and the 429 who had died, Marie-Madeleine Fourcade soldiered on. She remarried and became the mother of three more children. She published a memoir, *Noah's Ark*, in 1968, and died in Paris in 1989, just shy of her eightieth birthday.

42 / A Young Mother Survives Torture

THE STORIES OF operatives who lost their lives can be heart-wrenching. The narratives of those who managed to survive can make for equally difficult reading. Consider only Odette Sansom—also known as Odette Churchill and Odette Hallowes. Born in 1912 in Amiens, France, she was the married mother of three in 1942 and living in Somerset, England, when she responded to a British Admiralty request for photos of the French coastline.

By mistake, she sent her package to the War Office, where it elicited an invitation to a meeting with the Special Operations Executive (SOE). With her English husband already serving in the British army, she left her three daughters in a convent school and trained to go to France and work with the French Resistance. One instructor judged her "impulsive and hasty . . . excitable and temperamental, although she has a certain determination."

The SOE pushed her forward because she was desperate to do something for the country of her birth. Late in the autumn, a troop ship carried Sansom to the British base at Gibraltar. From there, in a 20-ton wooden sailboat, she sailed along the coast of Spain for ten days and landed on a beach near Marseille. There she met her contact, Captain Peter Churchill, who headed an SOE network called Spindle.

While working in Marseille, according to her secret file, Sansom arranged for several parachute drops of arms and supplies and, as they arrived, would always direct ground operations. Frequently

Odette Sansom was a Special Operations Executive agent, and was also known as Odette Churchill and Odette Hallowes. This photo was taken after her retirement, in about 1946. *Pictorial Press / Alamy*

stopped and searched by the Gestapo, she remained cool and unperturbed, contemptuous of danger.

In January 1943, Sansom moved north with the team to the Annecy area in the French Alps. Meanwhile, the Nazi spy-catcher Hugo Bleicher had ferreted out Spindle's location and, at two in the morning on April 16, arrested Sansom and Captain Churchill. The Gestapo took them to Paris, where, at a torture house (84 Foch Avenue) and in Fresnes Prison, Nazis interrogated Churchill only twice, but Sansom fourteen times. They scorched her back with a red-hot poker and pulled out her toenails.

She stuck to the cover story she and Churchill had fabricated—that they were married and that Churchill was related to the British prime minister. If this were true, the Gestapo would see value in keeping them alive to use as bargaining chips. Sansom revealed nothing. In

June, condemned to death, she was sent to Ravensbrück concentration camp. Confined in the punishment block, she could hear other prisoners being beaten.

In August 1944, when the Allies invaded southern France, the Nazis threw her into a dark cell, turned up the heat, and denied her food. At the end of one week, found unconscious on the floor of her cell, she was placed in solitary confinement near the crematorium. From her window, she saw starving prisoners eat a dead inmate.

Sansom would be recognized for her extraordinary bravery and resilience, her effective use of disinformation, her ability to resist and endure, and, later, for her postwar testimony. Believable disinformation? As the Allies approached Ravensbrück, the camp commandant, Fritz Suhren, forced Sansom into a car and drove out to surrender. Having bought her cover story, he hoped to avoid death by exploiting her supposed friendship with the British prime minister.

In 1946, at the Hamburg Ravensbrück trials, Sansom gave detailed testimony against those who had tortured her. Suhren, charged with war crimes, was among those executed. In 1947, having divorced her first husband, Sansom married Peter Churchill. A 1949 biography, followed by a film about her life, made her a celebrity heroine in both France and England.

She became the first woman to receive, while alive, the George Cross. She was also appointed a chevalier of the *Légion d'honneur*, the highest French order of merit, both military and civil. She would divorce Churchill and, in 1956, marry an ex-SOE officer. She died in Surrey, England, in 1995, age eighty-two.

43

The Original Partisan

ON THE NIGHT of February 12, 1941, under cover of darkness, Emmanuel d'Astier led a few fellow rebels in planting explosives at the train station in Perpignan, near the Mediterranean coast. In executing their carefully planned attack, the freedom fighters targeted vital points within the station and moved swiftly and efficiently, avoiding detection. The explosions destroyed railway tracks and derailed trains, forcing the Nazis to divert manpower to make repairs, hindering their ability to transport troops and supplies in the deep south of France.

Buoyed by this successful operation, which boosted the morale of the entire Resistance, d'Astier and his comrades targeted the more central train station in Cannes, situated between Marseille and Nice. In May, they carried out another meticulously planned operation. Executing with precision, they planted explosives on the tracks and caused substantial damage, crippling German transportation in the area.

These two attacks sent a clear message to the Nazi occupiers that the French could strike at the heart of their infrastructure. They highlighted the audacity and resourcefulness of the Resistance and served as powerful propaganda tools, instilling a broad sense of hope and defiance. They also showcased d'Astier's leadership skills and determination to disrupt the occupation and pave the way for eventual liberation.

Born in Paris in 1900, Emmanuel d'Astier de La Vigerie came from an aristocratic family. He attended the Naval Academy and joined the French navy but at twenty-three, lacking intellectual stimulus, grew bored and resigned. As a poet and journalist, he became friends with Pierre Drieu La Rochelle and wrote for *Action française*, France's leading right-wing journal. Then, after soul-searching during the Spanish Civil War, he moved politically leftward and supported the Republicans in their defence of democracy.

When the Second World War broke out, d'Astier rejoined the French navy and became head of naval intelligence. The following year, after the fall of France and the proclamation of the new Vichy government, he was fired for refusing to toe the pro-Nazi political line. He contacted André Malraux and other prominent dissidents, seeking to organize a Resistance group. Finally, in Clermont-Ferrand, some 400 kilometres south of Paris, he put together *La Dernière colonne*, which later evolved into *Libération-sud* (as distinct from *Libération-nord*). Leading members included Raymond and Lucie Aubrac.

In addition to sabotaging train stations at Perpignan and Cannes, the group orchestrated the distributions of thousands of flyers. These called for resistance, shared updates about the progress of the war, provided information on Nazi atrocities, and gave instructions for civil disobedience. The police caught one of the distributors, which led to the arrest of d'Astier's niece and uncle. The group lay low for a while, then began working on an underground newspaper, *Libération*. In July 1941, with the help of local typographers and trade unionists, they produced 10,000 copies.

The following year, with Jean Moulin, d'Astier discussed unifying the Resistance and eventually joined the *Conseil national de la Résistance*. He also travelled to London, where he met Charles de Gaulle and supplemented information provided by Moulin. In May, de Gaulle sent d'Astier to the United States to seek recognition and support for Free France from President Franklin Roosevelt. In this D'Astier stood no chance, but he met and gained qualified support from government officials and military leaders, among them General Dwight D. Eisenhower, who would become supreme commander of the Allied invasion of Normandy.

In July 1943, with Moulin having been taken by the Gestapo, d'Astier met de Gaulle in Algiers, his North African base. In November, he became commissioner of the interior for the Free French forces. He then worked with Winston Churchill to secure arms for the Resistance. Also in 1943, during a visit to London, the poet in d'Astier resurfaced briefly when he wrote the lyrics to a tune by Anna Marly, a Russian-born singer. Years later, Canadian Leonard Cohen would make it famous in English, slightly altered, as "The Partisan."

After the war, d'Astier became minister of interior in de Gaulle's provisional government. He continued to publish *Libération* and wrote memoirs about his experience in the Resistance, among them *Seven Times Seven Days* and *The Gods and Men*. He won a seat in the National Assembly as an ally of the French Communist Party, but in 1956, after the Soviet Union crushed the Hungarian Revolution, he cut ties with the Communists. Emmanuel d'Astier died in Paris in 1969.

44

Outwitting the Gestapo

THE GESTAPO'S ARREST of Jean Moulin and seven of his comrades in June 1943 would lead to one of the most spectacular rescues of the Second World War—not that of Moulin himself but rather of his friend Raymond Aubrac. Incredibly, this would be the third time Lucie Aubrac rescued her husband from prison, an action that came about because both Aubracs were core members of *Libération-sud*, led by Emmanuel d'Astier. While D'Astier was more involved in the political direction and organization of the Resistance, Lucie Aubrac was directly involved in operations. Her leadership role was also unusual, as most leaders were men. Nor did she come from a privileged background, despite a bizarre bog of misinformation—aristocratic parents, top-flight schools—designed to make her what she wasn't: a bourgeoise heroine.

In 1912, Lucie Aubrac—she adopted the surname during the Resistance—was born in a working-class Paris suburb as Lucie Bernard. She attended primary school near Rouen, where her parents worked as a gardener and a milkmaid. When Lucie received a scholarship to continue her studies, her parents moved to suburban Paris, where she could attend a normal school, which prepared students to become teachers.

In 1931, she passed the entrance exam but decided not to attend, rebelling against "the idea of being inside, prevented from circulating." This decision infuriated her parents, and nineteen-year-old

Lucie moved out on her own, taking a room in the Latin Quarter. She worked at various low-paying jobs and frequented an international youth circle founded by Quakers, which enabled her to visit Berlin and London.

Lucie joined Communist Youth in 1932 and, courageous and convivial, soon became a local leader. She set her sights on furthering her education at the Sorbonne, which meant she first had to pass the baccalaureate. By 1933, she had completed parts one and two and had begun studying to acquire teaching certificates in history and geography. For this she needed Latin and, having so far taken none, she failed three times before succeeding. She abandoned her left-wing activism to prepare for an exam that would allow her to teach history. This she passed on her first try in September 1938.

She landed a teaching job at Strasbourg, east of Paris, and there met and fell in love with Raymond Samuel, a young Jewish civil engineer doing his military service, who had also moved in Communist circles. The two went to bed together for the first time on May 14, 1939, a date that later in life they would commemorate with an annual dinner at the Eiffel Tower. They talked of travelling to the US. At twenty-five, Raymond had spent a year studying at the Massachusetts Institute of Technology and wanted to return to America. Two years older, Lucie had recently received a David-Weill scholarship to investigate the colonization of the Rocky Mountains from the south. They looked to be going in the same direction.

The Second World War disrupted their plans. Instead of going abroad, they married in Dijon in December 1939. Raymond had warned Lucie that it might be risky to marry a Jew, but she said, "That just made me even more keen." She taught for a few months in Brittany, where she had the future film star Simone Signoret as one of her pupils.

In August 1940, while serving in the French army, Raymond Samuel was taken prisoner by the Nazis at Sarrebourg, about 70 kilometres northwest of Strasbourg. Lucie didn't hesitate. From her husband's brother, who worked in a hospital, she acquired a drug that would provoke a fever. At Sarrebourg, she begged and received permission to see her husband. She slipped him the drug and, two days later, a feverish Raymond was transferred to a civilian hospital. Lucie visited again and gave her husband a cap and a pair of workman's overalls. Next day, when he hauled himself over the hospital fence, she was waiting.

The couple moved to Lyon, where Raymond found work in a patent office. In October 1940, Lucie ran into a colleague from Strasbourg—Jean Cavaillès, a philosophy professor. Shortly thereafter, he introduced her to Emmanuel d'Astier de La Vigerie, who as leader of *La Dernière colonne* was already plotting acts of sabotage against the Nazis. Soon she and Raymond were among the leaders of this group.

From May 1941, after the birth of their first child, the couple helped create a newspaper that gave rise to *Libération-sud*. Through 1942 and 1943, while teaching at a high school, Lucie remained furiously active in the Resistance. An assistant to d'Astier described her as an intellectual "endowed with excessive dynamism . . . amazingly brave and [doing] a tremendous amount of work." With a baby on her hip, she often worked at night, distributing leaflets and flyers non-stop.

In March 1943, the Gestapo arrested an inexperienced liaison officer who was carrying a list of names. That led to the detention of nine members of *Libération-sud*, among them Raymond Aubrac, appointed by d'Astier to lead the paramilitary branch of the movement. After this arrest, one colleague complained, Lucie Aubrac demanded that *Libération-sud* cease all other activities and focus exclusively on freeing the arrested men.

In May, after failing to convince her comrades of this, she went directly to the prosecutor of the case. She reasoned that he was a collaborator and, therefore, a coward. If she spoke loudly, she could browbeat him into doing what she wished. Lucie claimed she was an envoy sent by Charles de Gaulle and warned that if within twenty-four hours the prosecutor did not release François Vallet—Aubrac's assumed name—he would be assassinated. "Vallet" was released on bail.

With five associates previously freed under that arrangement, three remained in jail. The Aubracs provided those three with pharmaceuticals to make them sick enough to require transfer to the local hospital, which was not well guarded. From there, they orchestrated an escape.

Feeling that they had earned a brief vacation, the Aubracs travelled south with their two-year-old son and spent a few days in a boarding house on the French Riviera. Afterward, back in Lyon, Raymond Aubrac went to a strategy meeting set by Jean Moulin. On June 21, the Gestapo showed up. And while one man got away, René Hardy, the thugs arrested Moulin, Aubrac, and six others. These eight were taken to nearby Montluc Prison, which was headquarters to that infamous sadist Klaus Barbie.

Initially despairing, Lucie Aubrac pulled herself together. She sent her son to the countryside with a caregiver and set about hatching yet another rescue—one that would make her a legend. In September, passing herself off as a doctor, she visited four wounded Resistance members at the Saint-Étienne hospital, and told them of her rescue plan. Then she went to see Klaus Barbie himself, head of the Gestapo in Lyon. She presented herself as an aristocrat and begged to see her alleged fiancé, by whom she was pregnant (this last was true). She insisted that her fiancé was innocent and had been arrested by mistake. A woman of her position, she claimed, could not give birth without being married, and implored Barbie to let them wed in prison.

In her book *Outwitting the Gestapo*, she wrote that Barbie opened his desk drawer with "a queer smile" and took out a portfolio. It contained various papers and cards pertaining to her, as well as a small snapshot of her in a bathing suit on a beach with a baby by her side. The papers she carried identified her as unmarried. So either she was already married and her papers were fake, or she already had a child and did not care as much as she pretended about the public appearance of virtue. Barbie demanded to know how long she had known this terrorist, soon to be executed. She mumbled something about a few weeks and he threw her out of his office.

Lucie Aubrac remained undaunted. She called on a different Nazi officer, one who did not know she had seen Barbie, and bribed him to let her marry her "fiancé" in his office to legitimize her unborn child. This time, her plan worked. On October 31, 1943, after the wedding ceremony, the van transporting several prisoners back to jail "broke

250 · THE FRENCH RESISTANCE

down" in the street. Out of nowhere, Lucie Aubrac and her comrades fell on the unsuspecting Nazis, killing the driver of the truck and five guards, and setting free fourteen Resistance fighters, among them her husband, Raymond.

After this escape, the Aubracs went into hiding. They reached London in February 1944, and learned that Emmanuel d'Astier had turned Lucie into a legend. When she gave birth to a daughter, the child's godfather was Charles de Gaulle.

Over the next several decades, Lucie Aubrac remained active in left-wing causes and advancing women's rights in France. In 1984, she published *Outwitting the Gestapo*, a somewhat fictionalized version of her wartime diaries. She then saw her life portrayed in movies. And in 1998, she won a highly publicized libel suit against a historian who had questioned her heroism and that of her husband.

Lucie Aubrac died in Paris in 2007, at age ninety-four. She was eulogized by every leading French politician from the president down and was given a funeral with military honours. Her husband died five years later and was laid to rest beside her.

45 / Malraux Shines in Resistance

ON JULY 22, 1944, the sky was sunny and clear and the chauffeur was tooling along through the French countryside. Accompanied by a bodyguard and a British officer, André Malraux was dozing in the afternoon heat when *ratatat*, two machine guns caught the car in a crossfire. The back window exploded and the car spun off into a ditch.

The chauffeur had taken a bullet through the head. The bodyguard, too, was dead, slumped over his gun. The British officer, Captain George Hillier, was cut down as he crawled out of the car. He would be left for dead but found alive hours later and eventually nursed back to health. Malraux tumbled out of the car but took one bullet in the right leg and another in the left. He lost consciousness.

WHEN THE WAR had broken out almost five years before, André Malraux was already a celebrated writer. But he joined the 41st regiment (*41e dépôt de cavalerie*) as a lowly private. As a writer, he wanted an authentic experience, unmitigated by fame. He slept in a twelve-bed military barracks and did what he was told.

In April 1940, after several skirmishes with Nazi troops, Malraux and his companions were taken prisoner at Courtenay, south of Paris. The Nazis marched them to the nearby town of Sens and deposited them in a camp, Front Stalag 150, on the Yonne River. None of the Nazis recognized Malraux as a famous writer.

He found conditions tolerable and, when he was not working with others on farms, he spent his days writing a novel. Days became weeks and weeks, months. The prisoners were allowed to walk into Sens without guards. Malraux received visits from his common-law wife, Josette Clotis, and his half-brother Roland, who told him that, according to radio broadcasts, the Nazis were searching for him.

On November 1, after half a year as a prisoner, and accompanied by Roland, Malraux slipped away to the south of France. He retreated to a villa in Roquebrune-Cap-Martin owned by English friends of the French writer André Gide. Josette and their one-month-old son joined Malraux, and his American publisher sent money—an advance against his novel-in-progress. He flatly refused to publish anything in *La nouvelle revue française*, but newly appointed editor Pierre Drieu La Rochelle—a Vichy collaborator—drove south and visited anyway. Drieu and Josette had been intimate friends. Malraux saw Drieu as a crypto-fascist, nearly a crypto-Nazi, but such were the complexities of the time that the two men tolerated each other on a literary level.

Through Roland, Malraux received two manuscripts from an unknown writer based in Algeria named Albert Camus. Malraux told the younger writer, now thirty-one, that he was mightily impressed by *The Stranger* and *The Myth of Sisyphus*. The two became mentor and protegé, with Malraux declaring the first book "obviously something important" and urging his own publisher, Gaston Gallimard, to release it immediately. Other visitors to the villa included philosophers Jean-Paul Sartre and Simone de Beauvoir and Resistance leader Emmanuel d'Astier de La Vigerie, who set out to create one great umbrella organization.

In November 1942, the Germany army "reunified" France, ending the split between the Nazi-occupied zone in the north and the so-called Free Zone, controlled by Vichy collaborators. Feeling threatened, and with his anti-Nazi stance well known, Malraux moved from the French Riviera to Argentat in the mountainous Corrèze department, 220 kilometres north of Toulouse. He saw the ill-equipped Resistance as at last becoming "serious." Both Roland and his other half-brother, Claude, were taking part in operations, attacking factories and relay stations and derailing trains.

Still, whenever anyone invited Malraux to join the Resistance, he responded, "It isn't time yet." By spring 1943, however, he had gathered around him a small group of *maquisards*, or guerrilla fighters. He took the code name "Berger," after a colonel in the novel set in Alsace-Lorraine he was writing: *The Walnut Trees of Altenburg*. He had written to General de Gaulle, offering his services to the Free French in London, but the woman delivering the message was arrested and swallowed it in the van while travelling to prison.

In the Corrèze, Malraux was able to bring together the leaders sent by de Gaulle and the working-class fighters, previously at odds. He "made an indelible impression on us," one of the fighters wrote later, because he combined decisiveness and strength of character with "courtesy, an extraordinary facility of speech and a truly magnificent clarity." He deployed his men "according to their value without the least regard to their rank or social position. This is how real leaders work."

On July 22, 1944, after meeting with Resistance fighters and British officers responsible for parachute drops, André Malraux was taken prisoner in an ambush near the village of Gramat, north of Toulouse. Malraux had tasted victories. Six months before, his volunteer fighters had blown up the German arsenal at Tulle, putting it permanently out of commission. They used explosives provided by the London-based Special Operations Executive, with whom Malraux had made contact. Then, immediately after D-Day, June 6, his *maquisards* bombarded trains and blew up railway tracks to prevent a German panzer division from travelling north to join the fighting.

Meanwhile, he had lost both his half-brothers. The Nazis had captured Roland operating a secret radio and dispatched him to a concentration camp in Germany. He would die on a rescue ship torpedoed five days before the war ended. Claude, furiously active near Rouen, was captured and disappeared into the Nazi prison system.

That clear July day, when he regained consciousness, André Malraux found himself on a stretcher, his wounds roughly bandaged. Because he was in uniform and clearly a senior officer, the Nazis were taking him to intelligence officers in Gramat. When he saw tanks lined up in the street, he realized that Nazis had taken not just the town but the entire district.

A German officer interrogated him in a barn, then left. Malraux was bleeding from surface wounds but had no broken bones. He expected to die under torture. A different officer arrived and told him to get up and get out of the barn. He struggled to his feet and limped out into the yard where soldiers had lined up to form a firing squad. The officer told him to face the wall and extend his arms upward.

He did this but then changed his mind. None of this made sense. He dropped his arms and turned to face his executioners. The Nazis would never kill a French officer without first extracting what he knew. The German cried, "Present arms!" Then: "Aim." Malraux stood waiting. Finally, the officer said, "At ease!" And the soldiers, laughing, wandered off. Malraux limped back into the barn.

The Germans moved Malraux into a shed where he underwent the first of many interrogations. He confused the non-commissioned officers by telling the truth—that he was a novelist known even in Germany, here commanding a group of French *maquisards*. The Nazis took him south in an armoured car, passing through Albi, Castres, and Revel before installing him finally in Saint-Michel Prison at Toulouse, as dark and sinister a complex as existed in France.

The prison was well known as a place of savage beatings and executions. Every day around 6 p.m., Malraux waited with a dozen others in a room with barred windows. They waited for the footsteps along the corridor, for Gestapo officers to arrive, call out a name, and take one of them away to be tortured and shot or else transported to Germany.

After three weeks, Malraux heard his name called. The officers cuffed his hands behind his back and marched him off to a guardhouse. From behind a desk, a file in front of him, a German officer began asking questions. Was he thirty-three? Had he spent eighteen months in the Soviet Union? Now forty-two years old, Malraux realized that the man was mistaking him for Roland. The officer threw up his hands and sent Malraux back to the holding pen, where he told his companions, "They had the wrong dossier."

Next day, a stroke of luck: the Germans at Toulouse came under attack from Resistance fighters. The Nazis ushered five hundred prisoners into a huge room in the basement and then made haste to roll out of town. Outside in the courtyard, women began singing "La Marseillaise." Could this mean what they wanted it to mean? The men began banging and yelling. They picked up a heavy table, battered down the door, and stumbled outside into freedom.

A cry went up: "*Berger, au commandement! Berger!*" Was it because he alone was still wearing a uniform? No matter. He climbed up onto a packing crate and shouted orders, posted sentries, got the prisoners ready in case the Germans returned. Some tanks rumbled along the road. Prisoners prepared to hurl some of the hand grenades they had found, but the tanks rolled right on past. The Nazis were in retreat.

An unsympathetic biographer, Olivier Todd, observes that the novelist would sometimes get swept up into his own fictions. He doubts that Malraux was made to stand in front of a firing squad or that he jumped onto a packing crate to shout orders. And he writes that Malraux's "1944 Resistance was, at best, ill defined, and at worst, a failure." So it is significant that Todd pronounces the Alsace-Lorraine Brigade, which Malraux created after his stay at Saint-Michel Prison, "an epic success."

Back in the mountainous Corrèze department, Malraux learned that his radio connection to London was still functioning and that the young *maquisards* from Alsace-Lorraine wanted desperately to form their own brigade and retake their homeland. A young doctor from Strasbourg, Bernard Metz, was their main spokesperson. Malraux had just written a novel set in Alsace-Lorraine and understood completely.

Resistance leaders in London and Paris proved indifferent to the Alsatian yearning, so Malraux forged a fictional radio message from Paris, expressing approval. With Metz and lieutenant-colonel Pierre-Élie Jacquot, he went south to Toulouse and got clearance to organize a brigade from General Maurice Chevance-Bertin, commander of Free French forces in the southern zone.

Metz, who knew Malraux's novel *Man's Hope* almost by heart, urged the novelist to take command. General Chevance-Bertin signed off on this and Malraux called the new entity the Independent Brigade Alsace-Lorraine. It was no more independent than any other brigade, but it was tough and earned a reputation as the "Gangster Brigade of Colonel Malraux."

In the Toulouse area, fiction writer and museum curator André Chamson was leading 400 Resistance fighters, many of them from Alsace-Lorraine. In mid-August, he drew on a long-standing friendship with General Jean de Lattre de Tassigny to borrow forty trucks to carry his men north to join the fight for their homeland. Malraux found out and said, "We are going the same way, why don't we go together?"

The larger Malraux brigade joined the 400 already in the trucks. As they fought their way north, they added still more volunteers. When Chamson returned the trucks to General de Tassigny at Autun, he brought 2,400 *maquisards* in three battalions under the command of himself, the professional soldier Jacquot, and, overall, Colonel André Malraux.

In mid-September 1944, the Alsace-Lorraine Brigade reached the front lines. Malraux had hoped his guerilla fighters would have a period of training with the unfamiliar bazookas and machine guns, but they went straight into battle. For two weeks, the brigade fought to drive Nazis from the hills known as Bois le Prince. Malraux terrified his men by appearing at the front to gaze at the enemy, refusing to take cover. By the beginning of October, with the help of some Moroccan troops, the *maquisards* took the forested hills.

The brigade's next great challenge came late in November at Dannemarie when they took a town of about a thousand ringed with Nazi tanks. Early in December, the brigade went to Strasbourg. On the sixteenth, as demanded by the raging Hitler, German forces launched a sustained attack to retake the city, which had fallen to the French. American General Dwight Eisenhower was ready to abandon Strasbourg, but de Gaulle flatly refused. The Brigade Alsace-Lorraine undertook to hold certain especially difficult areas, fighting through ice, snow, and freezing cold. Eventually, with the Allies advancing into Germany, the Nazi forces had to withdraw.

Toward the end of January 1945, with the war's end in sight, Malraux made his way to Paris to fight a different kind of battle at a congress of the French Committee of National Liberation (*Comité français de Libération nationale*). Having realized that communist factions were fighting more for Russia than for France, he went determined to prevent a takeover. He urged the committee to abandon this idea of introducing "soviets" or revolutionary councils and organizing along Russian lines. Far better, he argued, to emulate the socialism of Britain. He enraged the communists by hailing the British parachute operations: "We must not forget that the Allies did help us; that we were armed by them; that without them we would have had nothing."

Having thrown the communists back on their heels, Malraux returned to the front by car. He was present in April when the French swept into the German city of Stuttgart. There, amidst the rubble, he added a fourth citation to his Croix de Guerre. More medals would follow. But already Malraux was turning his attention to "the new resistance" and the struggle against communist totalitarianism.

46 / Halton Revels in Liberation

ON AUGUST 24, 1944, while in Italy Canadian forces were fighting their way to Ravenna, Canadian journalist Matthew Halton was making for Paris behind Allied troops bent on liberating that city. At Rambouillet, he joined about eighty journalists in a small hotel. They were only about 60 kilometres southwest of the city, but German snipers and patrols made the road ahead impassible for the moment.

Ernest Hemingway had arrived and was making a commotion. He had strapped a .45 pistol to his side and was enlisting would-be Resistance fighters, revealing that he had stashed grenades and machine guns in his room. Several foreign correspondents protested that he was putting their non-combatant status at risk. Halton had recently had a testy exchange with Hemingway and stayed out of this altercation. But an American correspondent traded blows with the famous author before the two were dragged apart to go their separate ways. So began what Halton would later describe as the most unforgettable few days of the war—a time when he was "hand-in-hand with history" and present at the epochal liberation of the city he loved best.

The past few months had brought Halton any number of memorable moments. Based in London after spending months covering the war in North Africa and Italy, he had been singled out in Britain as one of the best war correspondents. No surprise, then, that he was one of the "assault journalists" chosen to land with the troops on the

CBC war correspondent Matthew Halton faced technical difficulties in Normandy in 1944, but is seen here broadcasting from Sicily during the previous year.

CBC / Library and Archives Canada

first day of the D-Day landings. On June 5, he and a few other Canadian reporters joined hundreds of soldiers from the 3rd Canadian Infantry Division to cross the channel overnight on a repurposed Irish ferry.

Next morning, the ship dropped anchor off the coast of Normandy, and Halton and Reuters correspondent Charles Lynch boarded a landing craft with troops from the Royal Winnipeg Rifles. A few hours earlier, the first assault had cleared a way through the mines, but still they came under sporadic fire. "I have been through many battles," Halton would say in his first CBC radio broadcast, "but I was never as excited as when my time came to go ashore for this was France and the beginning of the end." He jumped into water— six feet deep, and so had to swim a bit with his pack and waterproof typewriter before he could wade to shore. He saw dead Canadians floating in the water, and then more of them in lying in the soft sand.

Having crossed the beach, and with evening coming on, Halton and Lynch wandered down a lane and met an old farmer and his wife, who, unconcerned about the sporadic bursts of gunfire, invited them to stay in the farmhouse. Uniquely among all who landed, they spent the night in featherbeds. Next day, to his profound disappointment, Halton determined that no broadcast facilities existed. He watched in frustration as a Canadian press reporter filed a world scoop and a Canadian army cameraman sent off film that turned up in newsreels all over Britain and North America. Meanwhile, he had written a two-thousand-word account of the landing and sent it to London for another CBC reporter to read on air, only to have it get lost in Britain's censorship bureaucracy. "The hair-brained bastards!" he wrote his wife. "You risk your life covering the greatest story in history . . . and then it is lost in the Ministry of Information."

A week later, on June 13, Halton and four other correspondents were holed up in a manor house on the coast near Courseulles when the place came under attack and suffered three direct hits. The journalists escaped to the trenches and then moved 20 kilometres inland to a hotel in Bayeux. They arrived just in time to see the arrival of General Charles de Gaulle, who led thousands along the main street. "It was like a scene from a film," Halton reported, "the tall, handsome general and the people following, and France soon to be free."

Now came a series of skirmishes that culminated in a major assault at Carpiquet, just outside Caen. The night before, Halton and a colleague had moved to the front and set up their recording equipment in a stone barn. On July 4, with dawn approaching, Halton flicked a switch and began talking: "It's two minutes to five. Two minutes to five in Normandy and the sun hasn't risen yet, over our guys or over the Germans 800 yards away. It will rise on a fearful scene because at 5 o'clock precisely the Canadians are going to attack, and they'll attack with the support of the most enormous concentration of fire ever put down on a small objective."

Halton gave a countdown . . . and then came the barrage. Later, he described dense smoke and cordite fumes and "the incessant, earth-shaking and atrocious pounding of the hundreds of guns." After providing more such description, he said, "This is the morning we waited for. A morning in France. A morning in which the fair fields of Normandy are torn and rent and split apart . . ." According to his biographer-son, Matthew Halton wrote to his wife of being appalled one moment and responding the next to "a roaring glory and I want to be advancing across those wheat fields full of poppies with the assault troops."

A week later, to prepare for the liberation of the ancient city of Caen, the Allied forces sent 450 heavy aircraft over the town, blowing much of it to smithereens. After entering, Halton reported that amidst the ubiquitous ruins he found a famous thousand-year-old church miraculously undamaged. Later, in a *Star Weekly* article, he would complain that "we liberated—and obliterated—Caen."

The fighting around Caen went on for six more weeks. Early in August, having arranged to meet up with some fellow war correspondents, Halton drove south to Mont Saint-Michel, that famous medieval monastery on a tiny coastal island. Over a splendiferous lunch at La Mère Poulard, he found himself sitting with several of the best-known American correspondents, among them Hemingway.

That was where it happened. As the men quaffed champagne and vintage wines, the two traded impressions of working for the *Toronto Star*. Halton told the author how much he admired his novels. Their only weakness, he said, was in the descriptions of sexual desire. According to Charles Lynch, Halton realized too late how this was being received. The passages weren't bad, he backtracked, but they just didn't match the excellence of the rest. Too little, too late.

Hemingway banged his fist on the heavy oak table and roared, "Any fucker who fucking well says I can't write about fucking is a fucking liar!" He pushed away from the table. "And you, Halton, are full of shit!" With that he stormed out, and Halton didn't see him again until Rambouillet in late August, when at that crowded hotel he saw him pushing and shoving with other American correspondents and boasting about having stashed munitions in his room.

Early the next morning, word arrived that a French Resistance brigade had started filtering into Paris. With a few other Canadians, Halton jumped into a jeep and set off for the city. Nearing the capital, they joined a convoy of tanks and armoured vehicles. "Suddenly we could see the Eiffel Tower," Halton wrote in the *Star Weekly*, "and there before us was the most beautiful city in the world. And it had gone mad."

Jubilant Parisians swarmed the arriving Canadians. Sometimes the jeep couldn't move. "We drove for miles," Halton reported, "saluting with both hands and shouting *Vive la France* till we lost our voices. Every time we stopped for a second, hundreds of girls pressed round the jeep to kiss us, and to inundate us with flowers." Halton changed vehicles and described driving past Notre-Dame through wildly cheering crowds: "My friends were shouting *Il est Canadien* . . . And I knew what it was to feel like a king."

The Canadians made their way to the Scribe Hotel, which became the press centre for all the Allied correspondents. Halton watched as de Gaulle, who had spent most of the war in exile, led the parade down the Champs-Élysées. Accompanied by a cheering throng, de Gaulle marched to the Hôtel de Ville and there, shortly after 4 p.m., gave a rousing speech. "Why do you wish us to hide the emotion which seizes us all, men and women, who are here, at home, in Paris that stood up to liberate itself and that succeeded in doing this with its own hands? No! We will not hide this deep and sacred emotion. These are minutes which go beyond each of our poor lives.

"Paris! Paris outraged! Paris broken! Paris martyred! But Paris liberated! Liberated by itself, liberated by its people with the help of the French armies, with the support and the help of all France, of the France that fights, of the only France, of the real France, of the eternal France! . . . Since the enemy which held Paris has capitulated into our hands, France returns to Paris, to her home. She returns bloody, but quite resolute. She returns there enlightened by the immense lesson, but more certain than ever of her duties and of her rights."

At one point, caught up in the celebrations, Halton found himself lifted to the top of a military vehicle and giving a speech in his rough-and-ready French. He described how deeply he felt about being in the city of Paris, that shining symbol of democracy and freedom, at this bright moment in its history. Before returning to the front, he told his CBC listeners that to him, the Liberation of Paris was more important even than the freeing of Berlin would be, because it represented the triumph of the cause for which so many in Normandy had given their lives.

PART SIX

"What, Me Worry?"

47 / Burying One
Set of Tyrants

THE LIBERATION OF Paris in August 1944 marked the beginning of the end of one cycle of dictatorship. The citizens of France began to wake from the nightmare of occupation. But the war against the Nazis? In August 1944, that was still going strong. Hitler mounted one last desperate offensive in December, trying to split the Allied forces in the Ardennes Forest of Belgium and Luxembourg. The line bulged but did not break, the origin of the name Battle of the Bulge. As Allied troops then advanced into Germany from the west, they were shocked into silence, stunned into speechlessness, by what they discovered in the now liberated concentration camps of Bergen-Belsen and Dachau—countless dead bodies piled like cordwood, the few haunted survivors so weak and emaciated they could barely stand.

Hitler himself had lost touch with reality. By March 1945, having moved to his bunker in Berlin, he ordered the destruction of Germany so that it would not fall into enemy hands. On April 30, 1945, with the Red Army approaching from the east, Hitler killed himself with a shot to the head. On May 7, at Reims, France, Nazi generals surrendered to American general Dwight Eisenhower. Joseph Stalin refused to accept this as legitimate and, having occupied Berlin, forced the Germans to sign a second surrender the following day.

The Japanese refused to surrender until after the August atomic bombings of Hiroshima and Nagasaki, so the Second World War did not officially end until September 2, 1945. The war had killed so many people—50, 60, 80 million?—that we know only that the staggering total was three or four times as many as died in the First World War. The Nazis had systematically murdered more than 6 million Jews, driving a Polish-born lawyer who fled the Holocaust to coin a new word to describe what Churchill described as a crime without a name: genocide.

The war having ended, Charles de Gaulle organized a new French government, which arrested and tried 10,000 Parisians for collaborating with the Germans. Convicted: 8,000. Executed: 116. In the spring of 1945, thanks to their courageous resistance throughout the occupation, French women voted for the first time in the postwar municipal elections in Paris.

But what to do now with Germany? Hitler had led a gangster regime in the wholesale, industrialized slaughter of almost two-thirds of Europe's Jewish population. The victorious Allies set out to undo years of indoctrination, initiating a program of "denazification" of Germany. This encompassed war-crime trials, re-education programs, purging Nazis from positions of authority, enacting laws and regulations to remove Nazi influence from politics and the economy, and dividing Germany into occupation zones. This complex process encountered opposition, but it did lay the groundwork for transforming Germany into a leading democracy.

And it did produce one resounding success. In November 1945, in the German city of Nuremberg—formerly the site of massive Nazi rallies—the Allies mounted a series of tribunals to try twenty-four leaders of the Third Reich. Twelve were sentenced to death by hanging, but one (Martin Bormann) had died while trying to escape Berlin in May. All of Hitler's most senior henchmen—Goebbels, Himmler, Göring—took their own lives. The other eight were hanged.

Meanwhile, the uneasy alliance between the US and the USSR, which had evolved during the fight against Nazi Germany, did not long outlast the war. Differing ideologies (capitalism versus communism), competing geopolitical interests (especially in eastern Europe), and proxy conflicts in Korea and Vietnam all contributed to the emergence of the Cold War. The nuclear arms race gave rise to difficult decisions.

The Americans cut deals with some 1,600 guilty Nazis—mostly scientists, engineers, and technicians—whom they judged too useful to execute. For example, they falsified documents for Wernher von Braun and Nikolaus "Klaus" Barbie. Von Braun was a genius rocket scientist who ended up working for NASA and designing the *Saturn V* vehicle that sent the *Apollo* spacecraft to the moon. And the Butcher of Lyon had established a vast network of spies in the Soviet Union. This he handed over to the Americans, who in exchange secretly whisked him away to Bolivia. French Nazi hunters found Barbie in the 1970s and got him extradited to France in 1983. He was tried, convicted, and jailed, and in 1991 died of cancer in a jail cell in Lyon.

As for other mid-twentieth-century tyrants, Mussolini had already been dispatched by Italian partisans on April 28, 1945—two days before Hitler killed himself. The bodies of Mussolini and his mistress were deposited in a public square in Milan, where they were hung upside down from a metal girder above a service station. Francisco Franco lived on, but slowly changed Spain from a totalitarian dictatorship into an authoritarian state that allowed limited pluralism. Franco fell ill in the 1960s, resigned as prime minister in 1973, and died two years later, leaving Spain to enter a rocky transition to democracy.

The ruthless dictator Joseph Stalin ruled the Soviet Union with an iron fist until he died in 1953, just as the Cold War was commencing. Three years later, First Secretary Nikita Khrushchev gave a "secret speech" on the final day of the 20th Congress of the Communist Party. Calling his talk "On the Cult of Personality and Its Consequences," Khrushchev sought to launch a process of de-Stalinization of the Soviet Union. He unearthed Lenin's remarks criticizing Stalin, pointed to the purges of the 1930s, alluded to the mysterious murder of Sergey Kirov, and called on the party to eradicate the cult of personality that had grown up around Stalin and return to "the revolutionary fight for the transformation of society."

Khrushchev's speech shocked most Congress delegates as it flew in the face of Communist orthodoxy by insisting that Stalin did not possess "supernatural characteristics akin to those of a god." Some delegates laughed and applauded. Others claimed that Khrushchev's revelations induced heart attacks and precipitated suicides. In Georgia, Stalin's homeland, protests raged for days.

Not long after this controversial speech, the American Communist Party lost more than 30,000 members. The speech served as a stimulus to the severing of relations between China and Russia and as a catalyst for the 1956 uprisings in Poland and Hungary. Had George Orwell not died so young, surely he would have stepped forward to bear witness once more, and to warn that while Stalin was dead, he had established a tradition that might yet give rise to another rampaging totalitarian—a megalomaniac who, for example, might decide to invade Ukraine. Big Brother has many faces.

48 / McCarthy:
The Devil King

DONALD TRUMP HAS "the cruelty and power hunger of a dictator but not the discipline, intellect, or ideology." So writes Dorian Lynskey in *The Ministry of Truth: The Biography of George Orwell's* 1984. Don't compare him with Hitler and Stalin. For Trump, "a more apt comparison would be Buzz Windrip, the oafish populist from Sinclair Lewis's *It Can't Happen Here*, or, in the real world, Joseph McCarthy, a demagogue who displayed comparable levels of narcissism, dishonesty, resentment and crude ambition, and a similarly uncanny ability to make journalists dance to his tune even as they loathed him."

The Donald Trump presidency brought unabashed white supremacy, the confining of immigrant children in cages, and the storming of the Capitol by insurgents bent on overturning the results of a democratic election. That was the culmination of at least the first Trump presidency, though perhaps not of Trumpism. Before we explore that idea, we should look to where Trump came from—not personally, but politically. We should examine the trajectory that brought him to power.

Trump had predecessors like Louisiana governor Huey Long and the raving preacher Father Charles Coughlin. But politically, the first American public figure to take centre stage by adopting the tactics of the fictional Buzz Windrip was the opportunistic Joseph McCarthy. He began his political life as a Democrat but then saw that, in

Wisconsin, he had a better chance of advancing his career as a Republican. So he switched parties. In 1950, as a Republican junior senator, he began broadcasting false claims that Communists had infiltrated the United States government and the military. He created facts and figures out of whole cloth, used smear tactics against supposed homosexuals, and made hysterical and unsubstantiated allegations against innocent political opponents. In all this he saw nothing wrong.

McCarthy had grown up on a chicken farm in Wisconsin. By playing poker, he made enough money to put himself through law school. He knew how to sell a bluff. He knew that, no matter what you handed him, he could sell it to somebody. In 1939 he ran for the elected office of judge—and won. Three years later, considered too old to see action in the Second World War, he joined the Marines as an intelligence briefing officer for a bomber squadron. After flying twelve non-hazardous combat missions as a volunteer gunner-observer, he injured his leg when he fell off a ladder.

Now watch him leverage this pedestrian military record into a political career. When the war was over, he began telling people that he had been wounded in action. Before long, he was asserting that he carried ten pounds of shrapnel in his leg. Also, he said he had been in a plane that got shot down and burned. Well, no, never happened. In 1944, when he was first running for election to the Senate, he said he had flown fourteen missions. Two years later, he had flown seventeen. By 1951, the heroic Joe McCarthy had flown thirty-two missions.

In 1946, at age thirty-eight, glad-handing Joe got elected to represent Wisconsin in the Senate. Over the next few years, as the Cold War grew colder, Americans began to fear the "Red Menace"—and not entirely without reason. In August 1949, the Soviet Union tested its first atomic bomb. Then, in China, Communist forces won a civil war and created the People's Republic of China. The following year, backed by the Soviet Union, North Korea invaded the Western-supported South Korea, leading the US to enter the Korean War. Americans worried about Communist subversion at home.

This was not madness. A KGB memo from March 1950, which turned up later, regretted the loss of "more than forty most valuable agents" in the US. They had been exposed and were "impossible to replace." Nothing to do with Joe McCarthy. Senior Republicans had judged him too unsophisticated to succeed. He looked like a loser.

But in February 1950, almost by chance, McCarthy tapped into American fears with a speech he gave in Wheeling, West Virginia, to the Ohio County Women's Republican Club. Waving a piece of paper in the air, McCarthy claimed that he had a list of 205 known Communists who were "working and shaping policy" in the State Department. This was completely and utterly false—totally fabricated. Never mind. The press picked up the story and gave McCarthy the kind of attention he craved. In March, a Senate subcommittee investigated and found no evidence of subversive activity—the spies had been cleared out.

But McCarthy had seen a way forward and away he went with his Red-baiting campaign. President Dwight Eisenhower told his aides, "I will not get into the gutter with this guy." But in 1953, McCarthy gained the leadership of the Committee on Government Operations, which allowed him to launch grandstanding investigations into the alleged infiltration of the American government. At one hearing after another, he interrogated, bullied, and smeared witnesses, violating their civil rights, insinuating that they were disloyal and traitorous and causing more than two thousand government employees to lose their jobs. The Republican-led House Un-American Activities Committee (HUAC) sought to remove Communist subversion by targeting left-leaning liberals and Hollywood celebrities, who were always good for headlines.

When McCarthy began alleging Communist misdeeds in Bethel, Vermont, newspapers from the surrounding area would have none of it. Even the most conservative among them dismissed McCarthy, two of them running an interview with Dorothy Thompson, then a syndicated columnist with the Hearst newspapers. Under the headline NOTED AUTHOR DOUBTS BETHEL IS RED COLONY, Thompson said she was "extremely skeptical" of McCarthy's charges in one local case: "I see nothing strange in the transactions . . . I see nothing odd about two old friends buying a farm together and selling it when one of them needs the money."

Later, looking back at the 1950s, war correspondent Martha Gellhorn would write, "Joseph McCarthy, the junior Republican senator from Wisconsin, ruled America like a devil king for four years. His purges were an American mirror image of Stalin's purges, an unnoticed similarity."

By this time, McCarthy had found a devil smarter than he was to whisper in his ear—smarter and more devious. Almost twenty years younger, Roy Cohn had burst onto the national stage at age twenty-four, when he served as prosecutor in the controversial trial of Ethel and Julius Rosenberg, both accused of spying for the Soviet Union. He not only had them convicted but got them both sent to the electric chair—even though a lack of direct evidence and the use of questionable witness testimony suggest that Ethel, at least, was probably wrongly convicted.

Cohn's ferocious aggression appealed to FBI director J. Edgar Hoover, who commended the young man to Joseph McCarthy, who was then ratcheting up his anti-Communist campaign. McCarthy named Cohn his chief counsel, choosing him over Robert F. Kennedy. Cohn turned the questioning of suspected Communists into belligerent "off-the-record" sessions featuring false and unsubstantiated allegations. Adopted by McCarthy, this approach drew heavy criticism from intellectuals, academics, and civil libertarians who surfaced in newspapers and magazines and on television.

McCarthy's methods attracted attention, but they cost many decent people their jobs and livelihoods. Few dared to speak out against this flood of what came to be called McCarthyism. Finally, in March 1954, the celebrated journalist Edward R. Murrow risked his career to fight back on his national TV program, *See It Now*. He denounced McCarthy's "hysterical disregard for decency and human dignity and the rights guaranteed by the Constitution." He described the demagogue's proposition: "Anyone who criticizes or opposes McCarthy's methods must be a Communist. And if that be true, there are an awful lot of Communists in this country."

One month later, Murrow followed up, arguing that "congressional committees are useful" because investigation must precede legislation. "But the line between investigating and persecuting is a very fine one and the junior Senator from Wisconsin has stepped over it repeatedly. His primary achievement has been in confusing the public mind, as between the internal and the external threats of Communism. We must not confuse dissent with disloyalty. We must remember always that accusation is not proof and that conviction depends upon evidence and due process of law . . . We will not be driven by fear into an age of unreason."

Murrow sowed the first seeds of doubt in many minds. Also in April 1954, responding to a situation created by Roy Cohn, who had sought special treatment for his serviceman-lover, McCarthy set out to "expose" Communist infiltration in the American army. Always hungry for attention, he accepted that the "Army–McCarthy" hearings should be broadcast on national television. The event did not unfold as he and Cohn had intended.

At last people saw the agitator in action, intimidating witnesses and waffling in his own responses to questions. The key moment came when he slandered a young army lawyer, claiming he had ties to a Communist organization. This provoked the army's chief counsel, Joseph Welch, who responded with a denunciation that echoed Murrow and marked the beginning of the end for McCarthy: "Until this moment, Senator, I think I never really gauged your cruelty or your recklessness." McCarthy tried to interrupt but Welch had the floor: "Let us not assassinate this lad further. Senator, you have done enough. Have you no sense of decency, sir? At long last, have you left no sense of decency?"

This moment arrived too late to halt proceedings against the celebrated scientist J. Robert Oppenheimer, who in June 1954 lost the security clearance that allowed him to work for the US government. Historian Barton J. Bernstein summarized the case as "the triumph of McCarthyism without McCarthy himself." This travesty of justice, explored in the biography *American Prometheus* by Kai Bird and Martin J. Sherwin, and dramatized in the award-winning film *Oppenheimer*, put American scientists on notice that false accusations of disloyalty could derail even the most spectacular career.

In *Demagoguery and Democracy*, author Patricia Roberts-Miller argues that individual demagogues can be stopped, ultimately, only by in-group condemnation. So it was with Joe McCarthy. After the Army–McCarthy hearings ended, the Senate voted to condemn

McCarthy for his inexcusable, reprehensible, vulgar, and insulting conduct, which was "unbecoming a senator." Overnight, everything changed. No more was Joe McCarthy invited to meet with his colleagues at receptions and gatherings. As a political power, McCarthy was finished. He had always been a drinker; now he took heavily to alcohol and in 1957, at age forty-eight, he would drink himself to death. Politely put, he died of acute hepatitis exacerbated by alcoholism.

In the early 1950s, however, before McCarthy went into his tailspin, his protegé and secret whisperer Roy Cohn contrived to stir anti-Communist fervour by claiming that Communists overseas had convinced closeted homosexuals to pass on government secrets by threatening to expose their sexuality. Eventually, Cohn himself would stand revealed as gay. But now, as McCarthy's right hand, he orchestrated this so-called Lavender Scare against federal employees.

In *The Ministry of Truth*, while writing about Joe McCarthy, Dorian Lynskey notes that "McCarthy's protégé Roy Cohn became Trump's mentor in the 1970s, as if passing on a virus." In 1973, Cohn was at Le Club in upscale Manhattan when a young real estate developer asked him how to respond to Justice Department allegations that he was violating the *Fair Housing Act* at thirty-nine of his properties. Cohn responded, "Tell them to go to hell." That developer was Donald J. Trump. Already a racist, he was quoting different terms and making false "no vacancy" statements to Black people. Acting for Trump and deploying his usual strategy—attack, attack, attack—Cohn filed a countersuit against the government for $100 million . . . and helped Trump escape unscathed.

In the late 1970s and early 1980s, Cohn became a prominent New York City fixer. He introduced Trump to the "self-described 'dirty trickster'" Roger Stone, who after masterminding Trump's political campaign would need a presidential pardon to get out of jail. Meanwhile, Cohn's behaviour drew accusations of theft, obstruction, extortion, tax evasion, bribery, blackmail, fraud, perjury, and witness tampering. He would send threatening letters to anyone who dared to sue his clients, who included mafia bosses, the Roman Catholic Diocese of New York, and Nancy Reagan.

Senator Joseph McCarthy (left) confers with his attorney, Roy Cohn, during the Army–McCarthy hearings, in 1954. *Everett Collection / Alamy*

In 1984, Cohn was diagnosed with AIDS, though he managed to keep this hidden. Two years later, not long before his death, Cohn was disbarred as a lawyer for "dishonesty, fraud, deceit, and misrepresentation." Among the complaints that led to this action was that he visited a dying multi-millionaire, Lewis Rosenstiel, who was lying in hospital semi-comatose. Cohn helped the man sign a document naming himself co-executor of his will, claiming that the document dealt with his divorce.

As the end drew near, Republican president Ronald Reagan reached out to officials at the National Institutes of Health to see that Cohn received experimental treatments not generally available. Even so, Cohn died of complications from AIDS in 1986, still insisting that he was dying of cancer. In 2008, a *New Yorker* article quoted Trump adviser and convicted felon Roger Stone, saying, "Roy was not gay. He was a man who liked having sex with men. Gays were weak, effeminate . . . He was interested in power and access." Um, so glad you cleared that up.

Working with McCarthy, Cohn was responsible for the firing of gay men from government jobs and for bullying opponents into silence using rumours of their sexuality. Stone said that Cohn's "absolute goal was to die completely broke and owing millions to the IRS. He succeeded in that." One thing the Internal Revenue Service did not seize was a pair of diamond cufflinks Cohn received from Donald Trump.

Decades later, when Donald Trump found himself in legal trouble, he thought of Joe McCarthy and of his old mentor, and wailed, "Where is my Roy Cohn?" So there we have it. Trump did not spring out of nowhere. Joe McCarthy, Roy Cohn, Donald Trump. The trajectory, or this part of it, starts in a moral swamp and arches through time to the present day—to the demented authoritarianism that, under Trump, has taken control of the Republican Party.

49 / Finale: Big Brother Born Again

LATE IN APRIL 2023, Fox News fired Tucker Carlson—prime-time broadcaster and cheerleading Trumpist—after deciding not to air a TV documentary he had prepared advocating that the United States invade Canada to free the country from the tyranny of the Justin Trudeau government. The popular MAGA mouthpiece—"Make America great again"—lost his $20-million-a-year job after sending a racist text message during litigation over false voting system allegations. He had long been an enthusiastic supporter of the so-called Freedom Convoy that occupied Ottawa in February 2022.

By January 2023, Carlson was asking why the US government hadn't yet acted in response to Canada's vaccine mandates—most of which were relaxed by the time he spoke. "Why are we not sending an armed force north to liberate Canada from Trudeau?" Carlson insisted that he meant this, though later he chuckled and said, "I'm just talking myself into a frenzy here."

In recent years, Carlson had frequently referred to Canada in derogatory terms. "Canada is a sweet country," he said at one point. "It is like your retarded cousin you see at Thanksgiving and sort of pat him on the head. You know, he's nice, but you don't take him seriously. That is Canada." In the documentary, which the public has yet to see, he asks whether the US shouldn't "liberate" people living under authoritarian rule. "What if tyranny arrived right next door?" he asked in a promo for the Canada episode. "What would that look like? And what would our government do in response?"

Tucker Carlson took issue with the *Emergency Measures Act*, which the Canadian government used to shut down the truckers who parked big rigs out front of the Parliament Buildings, blaring horns and laying siege to an entire city. According to a national survey released in February 2023 by the Maru Group, 66 percent of Canadians applauded the invocation of the Act. Two-thirds of the populace had grown tired of loudmouth malcontents—heavily funded by American billionaires—taking over Ottawa. Some Canadians may have been swayed by a ruling in January 2024 that the invocation of the Act was illegal. Others see that as judicial nitpicking.

The point here is that, even if Carlson's documentary got shelved, the idea that the American military could invade Canada entered the mainstream news cycle. Reflecting on this, I found myself remembering that wealthy American woman I met in 2016, the one who wondered why I was taking such a keen interest in the presidential election. Surely, subsequent events, culminating in the Trump-inspired assault on the Washington Capitol, have more than justified my concern.

Looking back at the rise of fascism in 1930s Europe and then the Nazi occupation of France, I found myself thinking that when far-right Republicans take power in a flailing America, we'll be staring into the face of a born-again Manifest Destiny—an old familiar doctrine that the Nazis found useful as a justification for any run-of-the-mill invasion.

George Orwell anticipated the rationale in *Nineteen Eighty-Four*, when he introduced Newspeak as a way of using language to turn meaning upside down. In *Surviving Autocracy*, *New Yorker* writer Masha Gessen shows that until autumn 2016, the term "fake news" applied to false stories that appeared in *Breitbart* and similar outlets. Donald Trump flipped the epithet to refer to legitimate media that were critical of him. Trump's relentless assault on those newspapers and TV networks—and on political language itself—undermined the legitimacy of the press, which became "the enemy of the people."

Following Joseph McCarthy and Roy Cohn, Trump insisted that, awkward facts notwithstanding, his self-serving view of reality was the only correct one. And so, as if to vindicate *It Can't Happen Here*, four years of Donald Trump ensued—four years of both dismissing and vilifying mainstream media as "Fake News," of making up "alternative facts" and attacking science, expertise, and the very idea of verifiable truth.

This culminated in Donald Trump's Biggest-Ever Big Lie—that he, not Democrat Joe Biden, won the 2020 presidential election. You know where this led. On January 6, 2021, a joint session of Congress had begun counting Electoral College votes to formalize Biden's victory. Trump demanded that Vice President Mike Pence and Congress reject the election results and so keep him in power.

That morning, at a "Save America" rally held not far from the Capitol Building in Washington, the outgoing president urged thousands of right-wing activists to "fight like hell" in support of his false, unsupported contention that the election had been "stolen" from him. In response, a well-organized crowd of hundreds, many with military training, breached police perimeters and streamed into the heart of the United States Congress. They occupied, vandalized, and looted parts of the building. They erected a gallows on the grounds, and some, blaming the vice president for not acting illegally to reinstate Trump, wandered the building chanting "Hang Mike Pence." Others looted the office of Democratic House leader Nancy Pelosi.

Reports indicate that, safe in the White House, watching on television, Trump thrilled to see what he had instigated. Initially, he resisted dispatching the National Guard. He released a video calling the rioters "very special" and, while reiterating his false claim that the election had been stolen, urged them to "go home in peace." Meanwhile, five people lost their lives. The injured included 138 police officers—among them four who later took their own lives.

Initially, Republican House leader Mitch McConnell, a long-time Trump ally, called the storming of the Capitol a "failed insurrection" inspired by the president's lies and said the Senate "will not bow to lawlessness or intimidation." Soon enough, he himself would be bowing and scraping.

The House of Representatives voted to impeach Trump for "incitement of insurrection," making him the only US president to have been impeached twice. But because a guilty verdict required a

July 6, 2017: Donald Trump in Poland at the Monument of the Warsaw Uprising of 1944, when for 63 days the Polish Home Army battled the Nazis. *US State Department / Alamy*

two-thirds majority vote in Congress and Republicans were reluctant to vote against one of their own, the ensuing trial ended in acquittal. That was just the beginning. Ever since then, Trumpists have been working furiously to alter the legal system to subvert democracy.

Trump has declared that he intends to act like a dictator for a day. Some say he was joking, but I wouldn't bet on it. Certainly, he believes himself to be above the law. Most observers believe that early in another term he would target the Justice Department and seek to turn it into an instrument of vengeance against his political adversaries. He would also go after the intelligence community, which he considers the "deep state," and already has people drawing up lists of "disloyal officials." He would move quickly against immigrants, introducing a new *Insurrection Act* that would allow mass roundups and deportations of the undocumented.

Trump would probably withdraw the US from NATO and leave Ukraine to its own devices and the goodwill of Vladimir Putin. Would that be it on the international stage? At least one notable American historian thinks so. I draw your attention to Christopher R. Browning, who has written extensively about Nazi Germany. In a *New York Times* article published in July 2023, Browning writes that he has long resisted calling Trump a fascist, though he worries now "that if he wins another trip to the White House, he could earn the label." Browning explains that where Hitler and Mussolini "were ardent militarists and imperialists" bent on territorial expansion, Trump has shown no such inclination.

In his first term, Browning writes, Trump adopted a fascist style, complete with inflammatory, rhetoric-charged rallies. He encouraged a sense of grievance and victimization, endorsed violence, targeted vulnerable minorities, and revelled in a cult of personality. But his presidency "lacked any warlike, expansionist interest," and that made it different from twentieth-century fascism. A second term for Trump would be more efficient, Browning writes, and promises "something much closer to dictatorship at home." He anticipates an "isolationist fascism."

Speaking as a Canadian, I am less sanguine about the "isolationist" part. In January 2024, the Trumpist firebrand Tucker Carlson addressed a Calgary audience of four thousand at the invitation of Alberta premier Danielle Smith—and inspired numerous standing ovations. That reception suggests that a significant minority of Canadians would be ready to collaborate with any American occupation. I think of the French collaborators who surfaced during the Nazi occupation of France.

Carlson ridiculed Prime Minister Justin Trudeau and called Deputy Prime Minister Chrystia Freeland "a mentally deficient fascist." Without providing evidence, according to newspaper reports, he dismissed the storming of the US Capitol on January 6, 2021, as a "setup" orchestrated by "the left." And he urged people to "dislike and resist" the current Canadian government "to the maximum extent of your ability." He also offered up stupidly homophobic and transgender jokes.

Liberal cabinet members fired back, suggesting that Carlson's broadsides showed that Trumpism had arrived in Canada. "Don't ask the question if it's coming to Canada," said Transport Minister Pablo Rodriguez. "It's already here."

Most Canadians vividly remember the siege of Ottawa in February 2022, when big-rig trucks occupied the downtown core of the city. Here we had a different kind of invasion—not a military incursion from without but an ideological one from within, undertaken mostly by Canadians relying heavily on Trumpist funding. Would you believe $4.6 million came from the US—40 percent of the total?

A San Francisco billionaire, Thomas M. Siebel, made the largest single contribution. In Canadian dollars, he donated almost $115,000. A more modest $2,500 came from Arizona-based Republican activist Mike Schroeder. According to the *Globe and Mail*, Schroeder is the former owner of a satellite television company—a man who has advocated looser gun laws and believed the conspiracy theory that hospitals inflated pandemic figures.

"My God, the things they're doing up there," he said, referring to Canada's vaccine regulations, which kept Canadian death rates far below those in the US: "Enough is enough. These guys [the Ottawa occupiers] have stood up to it, and good for them." Schroeder also described Trudeau's invocation of the *Emergency Measures Act* as totalitarian in nature: "That's North Korea or Communist China. That's how they run it over there. I wouldn't even think about setting foot in Canada."

To be fair, another American, *Chicago Tribune* columnist Rex Huppke, wrote an open letter in which he apologized for giving Canadians "a bad case of the American stupids." Huppke summarized a few incidents, including the defacing of national monuments and the sighting of a Canadian flag featuring a swastika. Defacing national monuments while griping "is kind of our thing," he wrote, observing—rightly, I think—that the Ottawa siege was modelled on the January 6 attack on the American Capitol Building—"a deadly temper tantrum by pretend patriots in thrall to a noted huckster."

Nor was Huppke the only American to express this opinion. Steve Schmidt, a former Republican strategist for George W. Bush, spoke out on MSNBC. When the "Freedom Convoy" was happening, he described Ottawa as besieged by a fascist occupation organized and funded by the American alt-right. The Confederate and Nazi flags and other hate symbols were no accident, he said, urging those who believe in pluralism and democracy to wake up.

The storming of the Capitol, Schmidt said, was the result of "a conspiracy amongst many parties, headed by the president of the United States, to try to obstruct, destroy, obliterate the peaceful transition of power in the country." This "autocratic movement is a cult of personality," he added, "fueled by grievance and conspiracy theories." The whole toxic stew has "metastasized north of the border, and you have an insurrection underway in the capital of a very important country, our neighbor to the north, Canada."

What happened in Ottawa was an echo insurrection. Again, it calls into question the idea that Trumpism represents "isolationist fascism." The distinction is worth making because as I write, we are heading toward another US election—one in which the "Republican base" has succeeded in putting forward Donald Trump as their candidate. This despite four indictments—two on state charges and two on federal charges—encompassing a total of ninety-one felony charges. Were Trump to regain office, he would not hesitate to subvert the democratic process. He has made that clear. The man is a born autocrat. And so, like the war correspondents of the 1930s, we find ourselves crying, *Wake up! Look around! See what is happening next door!*

And that is what, if I ever see her again, I will tell that friendly American woman with whom I chatted during the run-up to the 2016 election. I will tell her that, as a Canadian, I will remain on the lookout, thank you very much, for a rough, Trumpian beast slouching toward Washington. *Vive la resistance!*

EPILOGUE

Where Is Our Churchill?

IN FEBRUARY 2024, two former diplomats came forward to urge Canadians to keep our mouths shut about the looming American election. Louise Blais, ex-ambassador to the United Nations, wrote in the *Globe and Mail* that we should not comment on the vote "other than to say that this is a domestic issue and for the Americans to support who they wish." Then David McNaughton, ambassador to Washington during the Trump years, went on record to argue that criticizing Donald Trump might well encourage "blowback" and retribution. Both were responding in part to the Trudeau government's appointment of two cabinet ministers to lead a Team Canada approach to the US—a strategy outlined in the first pages of this book. The diplomats feared the consequences of irritating the vengeful Trump.

They put me in mind of the 1930s, when British prime minister Neville Chamberlain and his Canadian counterpart, William Lyon Mackenzie King, advocated appeasement as the best way to respond to the rise of Nazism in Germany. If we keep our heads down and our opinions to ourselves, everything will be all right. Against this, we have Winston Churchill, who, even as a lowly backbencher, refused to shut up. He declared Chamberlain's ballyhooed Munich Agreement "a total and unmitigated defeat" and warned that worse would follow unless people mustered the courage to speak out.

In the House of Commons on October 5, 1938, Churchill warned, "This is only the beginning of the reckoning. This is only the first sip, the first foretaste of a bitter cup which will be proffered to us year by year unless by a supreme recovery of moral health and martial vigour, we arise again and take our stand for freedom as in the olden time."

Eleven months later, on September 3, 1939, after Hitler had invaded Poland, Chamberlain announced that Britain was at war with Germany. And on May 10, 1940, Winston Churchill replaced him as prime minister. Five days later, Churchill held the first of hundreds of strategy meetings in the Cabinet War Rooms—now one of London's most popular tourist attractions. During the Blitz, between September 1940 and May 1941, Churchill would often sleep in these spartan, below-ground rooms. In the War Rooms, Churchill lived through the "darkest hour," properly understood as May and June of 1940, the most challenging period in the early stages of the Second World War. By mid-May, more than 300,000 British and Allied troops were trapped in France on the beaches of Dunkirk.

With the German army closing in, Churchill launched the evacuation of those beaches—Operation Dynamo. Between May 26 and June 4, 338,000 Allied troops escaped across the English Channel from Dunkirk. That this miracle evacuation had proven necessary underscored Britain's vulnerability to invasion.

Soon after Dunkirk, Nazi Germany's new Blitzkrieg tactics—lightning strikes using overwhelming force—culminated in the taking of France. To the dismay of Churchill and, indeed, the whole free world, the French government surrendered to Hitler on June 22, 1940. This left Britain as the last major European power standing against the Nazis. With France defeated and occupied, a German invasion of Britain loomed as a real possibility.

At this darkest hour, Churchill had been Britain's prime minister for little more than one month. He had been appointed on May 10 after Neville Chamberlain had lost all credibility. The Nazi invasion of Czechoslovakia had proven that, despite Chamberlain's credulous assurances, formal agreements with Hitler were worth nothing.

Back in September, Churchill had spoken out, warning that the abandonment of Czechoslovakia presaged a new darkness. He reminded his audience that he had repeatedly urged Britain to rearm and develop military alliances, but those in power had undermined his every argument "on specious and plausible excuse." Churchill explained that he did not begrudge the people of Britain their spontaneous joy and relief at the thought that they faced no immediate ordeal. But he insisted that they should know the truth—that the country had "sustained a defeat without war," that "the whole equilibrium of Europe" had been deranged, and that worse was yet to come.

Sure enough, five months later, on March 15, 1939, the Nazis invaded Prague. Two months after that, Churchill became prime minister. On May 13, during his first speech as leader, he announced that he was forming as broad a government as possible. His five-member war cabinet consisted of himself as prime minister, two fellow Conservatives—Chamberlain and Lord Halifax—and two Labour Party ministers. To those who joined this government, he told the House, "I have nothing to offer but blood, toil, tears, and sweat."

Ahead, Churchill said, lay many long months of struggle and suffering. Rhetorically, he asked, what is our policy? And he answered: "It is to wage war by sea, land, and air with all our might and with all the strength that God can give us—to wage war against a monstrous tyranny, never surpassed in the dark lamentable catalogue of human crime. That is our policy." And the government's aim? "I can answer in one word: victory. Victory at all costs, victory in spite of all terror, victory however long and hard the road may be, for without victory there is no survival."

The situation on the continent grew worse. By May 25, 1940, the Germans were closing in on the Belgian army, though the remnants of two French armies and most of the British Expeditionary Force, while encircled, continued to fight. Churchill made broadcasts outlining the dire situation—more than 340,000 troops were trapped at Dunkirk—and calling on civilian boat owners to help with an emergency evacuation: small private vessels, fishing boats, pleasure craft, ferries ... All were not just welcome but needed.

Meanwhile, Churchill faced an insurrection in his war cabinet. Lord Halifax, like Chamberlain, had never ceased believing in appeasement as the only way forward. He argued that Britain would be lucky to evacuate 50,000 men from Dunkirk. The rest would all be killed. Hitler was about to destroy almost the entire British army. Then, despite the RAF, he would invade a defenceless Britain.

Churchill faced the situation squarely, acknowledging that "the whole root and core and brain of the British Army" stood surrounded at Dunkirk and seemed about to perish or be captured.

Halifax revealed that Benito Mussolini had offered to negotiate a peace agreement between the British and the Nazis. Secretly, the Italian dictator regarded Halifax and Chamberlain as "pale shadows" of those who, like Sir Francis Drake, had created the British Empire. He described them as "the tired sons of a long line of rich men" who could easily be pushed around.

Halifax threatened to resign and take Chamberlain with him, which would have sparked the removal of Churchill from office. In the Cabinet War Rooms, the crisis came to a climax on May 30, when for two hours the five men debated Mussolini's offer to negotiate. Halifax argued that France was on the verge of surrender and Britain could hardly stand alone.

Churchill agonized but could not tolerate the idea of the swastika flying over Buckingham Palace. "If they come to London," he declared, "I shall take a rifle and put myself in the pill box at the bottom of Downing Street and shoot until I have no remaining ammunition and then they can damn well shoot me." His defiance earned the support of the two Labour members of his war cabinet, Clement Attlee and Arthur Greenwood, and Halifax chose not to resign.

Meanwhile, the Dunkirk evacuation was underway. The Royal Navy had amassed a fleet of some 222 vessels, including 46 destroyers—39 British, 4 Canadian, and 3 French. Perhaps more importantly, Churchill had struck a chord with the British public. People responded to his call for help in astonishing numbers. Between May 26 and June 4, along with the navy vessels, more than 800 civilian craft shuttled across the English Channel between Dover and Dunkirk. Luckily, a thick cloud cover prevented the Luftwaffe from wreaking havoc.

By June 4, Operation Dynamo had evacuated 338,226 men from the beaches at Dunkirk. Many of them waded out into the water to haul themselves aboard the Little Ships of Dunkirk—that flotilla of fishing boats, pleasure craft, yachts, lifeboats, and merchant marine vessels—to be ferried to the larger ships and sail home. The BEF lost

68,000 men and had to abandon tanks, armoured vehicles, and equipment. But most of the army survived.

On June 4, when Winston Churchill spoke again in the House of Commons, he described the rescue as "a miracle of deliverance." But he warned the country not to regard this as a victory because "wars are not won by evacuations." Britain still faced an imminent threat of invasion. And now came the famous rallying cry that, as a clarion call to resistance, has never been bettered. Even though large tracts of Europe had fallen to the Nazis, Churchill said, Britain would not flag or fail:

> We shall go on to the end. We shall fight in France, we shall fight on the seas and oceans, we shall fight with growing confidence and growing strength in the air, we shall defend our island, whatever the cost may be. We shall fight on the beaches, we shall fight on the landing grounds, we shall fight in the fields and in the streets, we shall fight in the hills; we shall never surrender.

Now that—that is the spirit of resistance. We can all see where Big Brother might resurface. And if he does, who will lead a resistance? In recent years, Winston Churchill has come under attack from the radical left as just another British colonizer. The fact remains that but for Churchill, Hitler would have conquered western Europe before the United States entered the war.

Today's world would look very different indeed. Would Canada even exist as an independent country? Either way, would we be better off than we are? I think not. And those who would tear down statues of Churchill pay no heed to such considerations. Nor are they concerned about the emergence of any Big Brother. Those of us who think Canada worth preserving, on the other hand, gaze about and wonder, "Where is our Churchill? Wouldn't now be a good time for history to rhyme?"

Acknowledgements

ORIGINALLY, I SET out to thank all those who helped me in the writing of this book. But as the list grew and threatened to become impossible, I realized: This is crazy. I'll be like one of the winners of an unexpected Oscar, desperately racing through a foolscap list as the send-off music grows louder. And what if I miss someone?

I do want to thank the Access Copyright Foundation for sustaining my research and writing. And I wish also to thank my editors, Derek Fairbridge and Stephanie Fysh, for going the extra mile and keeping me from making a fool of myself (I think). Above all, I want to thank My Posse. Say hey to my artist-wife, Sheena Fraser McGoogan, our brilliant adult children, Carlin and Keriann, and their equally splendid partners, Sylwia and Travis. Our grandchildren, James and Veronica, are Posse Members *extraordinaire*, having distinguished themselves by hand-selling copies of my books. But one thing I need to accentuate. Without Sheena, my life-partner, my darling wife . . . long-suffering . . . seriously, I can't even imagine. Long may we run.

Endnotes and Sources

PROLOGUE AND PART ONE

BACK IN 1985, when Margaret Atwood published *The Handmaid's Tale*, I was working at the *Calgary Herald* as books editor and columnist—a position long since abolished almost everywhere. I knew her slightly from meetings of the Writers' Union of Canada and had interviewed her in 1981 for her novel *Bodily Harm*. For *The Handmaid's Tale*, I was able to take her to lunch at the Delta Bow Valley. I was mightily impressed with this extraordinary novel, and the quotes here come from a longer story I wrote.

By 2019, when Roy MacLaren's book *Mackenzie King in the Age of the Dictators* came out, I had moved to Toronto and was writing mainly books, though I would churn out the occasional review when asked. I wrote about the MacLaren book for the *Globe and Mail* and began like this: "After talking privately with Adolf Hitler in Berlin, William Lyon Mackenzie King concluded that the German Führer was a fellow mystic who spoke the truth when he insisted 'that there would be no war as far as Germany was concerned.'"

Hitler's face, the Canadian prime minister wrote in his diary, was "not that of a fiery, over-strained nature, but of a calm, passive man, deeply and thoughtfully in earnest . . . As I talked with him I could not but think of Joan of Arc." Of course I was appalled. Later, in *A First-Rate Madness* by Nassir Ghaemi, I read that John Simon, British foreign secretary from 1931 to 1935, had called Hitler "an Austrian Joan of Arc with a moustache." That made me wonder if Hitler himself, or someone in his circle, was planting this analogy anywhere he could.

MacLaren's merciless takedown of King's responses to Mussolini and Hitler found an echo in a work by Robert Teigrob entitled *Four Days in Hitler's Germany: Mackenzie King's Mission to Avert a Second World War*. Here, Teigrob recreates King's entire visit to Berlin. Painful reading.

Three books cited in the sources that follow filled in the blanks on King—one each by David Dilks, Thomas E. Ricks, and Kenneth Young. I also visited Laurier House in Ottawa and the Kingsmere estate in Gatineau, which gave me a feel for locales.

About Matthew Halton, called "Canada's greatest foreign correspondent" by Pierre Berton, I knew precious little before I began researching this book. I found the biography written by his son, broadcaster David Halton, to be remarkably even-handed. *Dispatches from the Front: Matthew Halton, Canada's Voice at War* tells the rags-to-riches story of a young Alberta journalist who finds himself in Europe reporting on what would become the most important story of the twentieth century.

Halton worked at the *Toronto Star*, as it was called, though it was officially the *Toronto Daily Star* until 1971. Another journalist who shone in Europe, American Dorothy Thompson, is the subject of two books mentioned below. The event that focuses my Chapter 11, "American Oracle Disrupts Nazi Rally," was the subject of a 2017 short documentary by Marshall Curry called *A Night at the Garden*. Now available on YouTube, it comprises black and white archival footage. *The New Yorker* called the work "as chilling and disorienting to watch as the most inventive full-length horror movie."

SOURCES: PROLOGUE

Applebaum, Anne. *Twilight of Democracy: The Seductive Lure of Authoritarianism.* New York: Signal, 2020.

Atwood, Margaret. *The Handmaid's Tale.* Toronto: McClelland & Stewart, 1985.

Campbell, Andy. *We Are Proud Boys: How a Right-Wing Street Gang Ushered in a New Era of American Extremism.* New York: Hachette Books, 2022.

Kakel, Carroll P. *The American West and the Nazi East: A Comparative and Interpretive Perspective.* New York: Palgrave Macmillan, 2011.

Liulevicius, Vejas Gabriel. *Utopia and Terror in the 20th Century.* DVD, 24 lectures. Chantilly, VA: The Teaching Company.

MacMillan, Margaret. *War: How Conflict Shaped Us.* New York: Random House, 2020.

Marche, Stephen. *The Next Civil War: Dispatches from the American Future.* New York: Avid Reader Press, 2022.

Nossal, Kim Richard. *Canada Alone: Navigating the Post-American World.* Toronto: Dundurn, 2023.

Paxton, Robert O. *The Anatomy of Fascism.* New York: Vintage, 2005.

Roberts-Miller, Patricia. *Demagoguery and Democracy.* New York: The Experiment, 2017.

Snyder, Timothy. *On Tyranny: Twenty Lessons from the Twentieth Century.* New York: Tim Duggan Books, 2017.

Taylor, Miles. *Blowback: A Warning to Save Democracy from the Next Trump.* New York: Atria Books, 2023.

Walter, Barbara F. *How Civil Wars Start and How to Stop Them.* New York: Crown, 2022.

SOURCES: PART ONE

Arthur, Anthony. *Literary Feuds: A Century of Celebrated Quarrels—From Mark Twain to Tom Wolfe.* New York: Thomas Dunne Books, 2002.

Churchill, Winston. *The Gathering Storm.* Boston: Houghton Mifflin, 1948.

Dilks, David. *The Great Dominion: Winston Churchill in Canada, 1900-1954.* Toronto: Thomas Allen, 2005.

Gage, Beverly. "Reading the Classic Novel That Predicted Trump." *New York Times,* January 17, 2017.

Glassco, John. *Memoirs of Montparnasse.* Annotated by Michael Gnarowski. Toronto: Oxford University Press, 1995. Originally published 1970.

Halton, David. *Dispatches from the Front: Canada's Voice at War.* Toronto: McClelland & Stewart, 2014.

Hemingway, Ernest. *Dateline: Toronto: Hemingway's Complete Toronto Star Dispatches, 1920-24.* Edited by William White. Toronto: Collier Macmillan, 1985.

Hemingway, Ernest. *A Moveable Feast: The Restored Edition.* New York: Scribner, 2009. Originally published 1964.

Hertog, Susan. *Dangerous Ambition: Rebecca West and Dorothy Thompson: New Women in Search of Love and Power*. New York: Ballantyne Books, 2011.

Kurth, Peter. *American Cassandra: The Life of Dorothy Thompson*. Boston: Little Brown, 1990.

Lewis, Sinclair. *It Can't Happen Here*. New York: Signet Classics, 2014. Originally published 1935.

McAlmon, Robert, revised by Kay Boyle. *Being Geniuses Together 1920-1930*. London: Hogarth Press, 1984. Originally published 1938/1968.

McAuliffe, Mary. *When Paris Sizzled: The 1920s Paris of Hemingway, Chanel, Cocteau, Cole Porter, Josephine Baker, and Their Friends*. London: Rowman & Littlefield, 2016.

MacLaren, Roy. *Mackenzie King in the Age of the Dictators: Canada's Imperial and Foreign Policies*. Montreal and Kingston: McGill-Queen's University Press, 2019.

Meyers, Jeffrey. *Hemingway: A Biography*. New York: Harper & Row, 1985.

Meyers, Jeffrey. *Scott Fitzgerald: A Biography*. New York: HarperCollins, 1994.

Reardon, Terry. *Winston Churchill and Mackenzie King: So Similar, So Different*. Toronto: Dundurn, 2012.

Reynolds, Michael. *Hemingway: The Paris Years*. Oxford: Basil Blackwell, 1989.

Sanders, Marion K. *Dorothy Thompson: A Legend in Her Time*. Boston: Houghton Mifflin, 1973.

Taylor, Frederick. *A People's History of the Coming of the Second World War*. New York: W.W. Norton, 2019.

Teigrob, Robert. *Four Days in Hitler's Germany: Mackenzie King's Mission to Avert a Second World War*. Toronto: University of Toronto Press, 2019.

Thompson, Dorothy. *Let the Record Speak*. Boston: Houghton Mifflin, 1939.

Zamyatin, Yevgeny. *We*. Translated by Clarence Brown. New York: Penguin, 1993. First published in English in 1924.

PART TWO

GEORGE ORWELL responded to the anarchistic nihilism of Henry Miller in his essays "Inside the Whale" and "Looking Back on the Spanish War." The material in this chapter comes mainly from Orwell's own books and the insightful "authorized biography" by Michael Sheldon.

Orwell is one of several figures in Part Two who inspired more than one biographical narrative. Others include Martha Gellhorn, Norman Bethune, and André Malraux. Things get interesting when the biographers disagree. The most dramatic case here is that of Malraux. Biographies by Alex Maddsen and Robert Payne, published in the 1970s, are sympathetic to their subject. The one by Olivier Todd, which appeared in 2005, verges on hostility. This might be a sign of changing times, but also Todd leans to the right politically while Malraux was a man of the left. Conflicting perspectives make sorting out "what really happened" a lot of fun.

Additional fun can be found when you turn to thinking about copyright and permissions. Rule of thumb: Here in Canada, as in the US and the UK, copyright in a book or article extends seventy years beyond the author's death. If you want to quote a substantial passage from a particular author who remained alive at some point during the past seventy years, you must track down the copyright holder (usually a publisher) and pay a permission fee.

As of 2024, according to this general rule, the work of anyone who died after 1954 is still under copyright. From Part Two, André Malraux (1976), Hugh Garner (1979), and Martha Gellhorn (1998) fall into this category. Theoretically, work by figures who died *before* 1954 (seventy years ago) have entered the public domain. This situation applies to George Orwell (who died in 1950), William Lyon Mackenzie King (1950), Norman Bethune (1939), and J.W. Dafoe (1944). So far, so straightforward.

But complications arise. Here in Canada, the federal government changed the copyright law in 2022, bringing it into line with those of the US and the UK. Before that, Canadian copyright extended not seventy but fifty years beyond the death of the author. Consider Canadian Matthew Halton, who died in 1956. Under the fifty-year rule, Halton's work entered the public domain in 2006 (1956 + 50). The changed law stipulates that there is "no revival of copyright." So, having entered the public domain in 2006, Halton's work remains there still. To quote him in Canada today, you require no permissions. But here's a question: What if you want to quote Halton substantially in a book that will also appear in the US and the UK? Logically, the situation in the country of origin would rule. This is where you need a copyright lawyer.

But if you really want to investigate a thicket of copyright madness, try writing about Winston Churchill, who died in 1965. In Part One of this book, I found myself drawing on three books—*The Gathering Storm* (essays), *The Great Dominion*, and *Winston Churchill and Mackenzie King*. Part Two brought me to *Churchill and Orwell*, and Part Four to *Churchill and Beaverbrook* and another book of essays—*Blood, Toil, Tears, and Sweat*.

Things get exciting if you wish to quote a UK parliamentary speech. All such speeches fall under a special parliamentary copyright law—or, more precisely, if like Churchill the speaker gave the speech before 1989, under Crown copyright. That law covers such expressions for fifty years from the date of creation. It prevails "notwithstanding that it [the copyright] may be, or have been, assigned to another person." Similar provisions apply in both Canada and the US.

Under these laws, the copyright in a speech Churchill gave in the British parliament in, say, 1944, would have expired in 1994. At that date, the speech entered public domain. And so today, theoretically, it can be freely quoted. I wouldn't be surprised, however, to learn that somehow, someone has asserted copyright protection over those works and expects to be paid for permissions. In any case, you can see why I refer these matters to those above my pay grade.

Hugh Garner wrote about the impact of the Spanish Civil War in a 1960 magazine series, "Depression Years," for *New Liberty* magazine. In *Hugh Garner's Best Stories: A Critical Edition*, editor Emily Robins Sharpe noted that Garner had a deep concern for the overlooked and the alienated, whether by "race, class, ethnicity, gender, age, nationality, intellectual ability, veteran status, or political affiliation."

SOURCES: PART TWO

Clarkson, Adrienne. *Norman Bethune*. Toronto: Penguin, 2009.

Garner, Hugh. *Hugh Garner's Best Stories: A Critical Edition*. Edited by Emily Robins Sharpe. Ottawa: University of Ottawa Press, 2015.

Halton, Matthew. *Ten Years to Alamain*. Toronto: J. Reginald Saunders, 1944.

Lynskey, Dorian. *The Ministry of Truth: The Biography of George Orwell's 1984*. London, New York: Anchor Books, 2019.

Maddsen, Axel. *Malraux: A Biography*. London: W.H. Allen, 1977.

Orwell, George. *The Collected Essays, Journalism, and Letters*. Volume II: *My Country Right or Left 1940-1943*. London: Secker & Warburg, 1968.

Orwell, George. *Down and Out in Paris and London*. New York: Harper & Brothers, 1933.
Orwell, George. *Inside the Whale and Other Essays*. London: Penguin, 1957.
Orwell, George. *The Lost Writings*. Edited by W.J. West. New York: Arbor House, 1985.
Orwell, George. *Nineteen Eighty-Four*. London: Secker & Warburg, 1949.
Payne, Robert. *A Portrait of André Malraux*. London: Prentice-Hall, 1970.
Ricks, Thomas E. *Churchill and Orwell: The Fight for Freedom*. New York: Penguin Press, 2017.
Sheldon, Michael. *Orwell: The Authorised Biography*. London: Heinemann, 1991.
Somerville, Janet. *Yours, for Probably Always: Martha Gellhorn's Letters of Love and War, 1930–1949*. Richmond Hill, ON: Firefly Books, 2022.
Stewart, Roderick, and Jesus Majada. *Bethune in Spain*. Montreal and Kingston: McGill-Queen's University Press, 2014.
Stewart, Roderick, and Sharon Stewart. *Phoenix: The Life of Norman Bethune*. Montreal: McGill-Queen's University Press, 2011.
Stuewe, Paul. *The Storms Below: The Turbulent Life and Times of Hugh Garner*. Toronto: James Lorimer, 1988.
Todd, Olivier. *Malraux: A Life*. New York: Knopf, 2005.
Vail, Amanda. *Hotel Florida*. New York: Farrar, Straus & Giroux, 2014.

PART THREE

TO OPEN PART THREE with a chapter about *The War of the Worlds*, first serialized in 1897, might seem an odd choice, given that *Shadows of Tyranny* draws mainly on events of the twentieth century to warn about the rise of fascism in the twenty-first. This choice derives from my earliest conception of the book, which involved incorporating relevant dystopian novels, visions of the future, into a narrative focusing on the past.

In the early drafts of this book, those I wrote between 2017 and 2020, I tried sign-posting these chapters, running them in a separate, italicized skein—adopting something like the structure Linden MacIntyre used in *The Wake*. It worked for that book but not for this one. Reluctant to jettison the whole idea, I decided to try integrating the dystopian chapters and reflections, situating them where they fit thematically in the main text.

The War of the Worlds tells the story of an invasion by an overwhelmingly powerful enemy—surely, an excellent allegory for the Nazi assaults on several European nations, including France. Already, in Parts One and Two, we have encountered the rise of the totalitarian state in *The Handmaid's Tale*, *It Can't Happen Here*, and *We*.

Part Three focuses more specifically on invasion, while Parts Four and Five treat resistance, drawing on Philip Roth's *Plot against America*, George Orwell's *Nineteen Eighty-Four*, and Jack London's *The Iron Heel*. Thematically, I think these books earn their place. I was sorry to omit Marge Piercy's *He, She and It*, Ray Bradbury's *Fahrenheit 451*, and Aldous Huxley's *Brave New World*. But they just didn't fit.

Changes kept coming, of course. Originally, I wrote chapters 23 and 24, which treat four anti-Semites, as one long chapter. But then, in the draft I submitted to editor Derek Fairbridge, I treated them in four separate chapters. Without knowing the history, Fairbridge wondered if the chapters should not be combined—either all four together, or three and one. I adopted this last approach. Always good to get a second professional opinion. Later in the book, Fairbridge nudged me into combining two more chapters and excising one other. All this improved the book and shows why God created editors.

Of those books that treat the French Resistance, I gleaned most from *The Resistance: The French Fight against the Nazis* by Matthew Cobb.

Biographer Caroline Moorehead, writing in *Gellhorn: A Twentieth-Century Life*, observed that had the wife of Bertrand de Jouvenel agreed to a divorce, Gellhorn would have married the man.

SOURCES: PART THREE

Cobb, Matthew. *The Resistance: The French Fight against the Nazis*. London: Simon & Schuster, 2009.

Grasso, Daniel. *Reading the Origins of Totalitarianism in 2020: A Short Guide to Mass Movements and Ideology*. New York: D. Grasso, 2020.

Griffiths, Richard. *France's Purveyors of Hatred: Aspects of the French Extreme Right and Its Influence, 1918–1945*. London: Routledge, 2021.

Guéhenno, Jean. *Diary of the Dark Years, 1940–1944: Collaboration, Resistance, and Daily Life in Occupied Paris*. Translated by David Ball. Oxford: Oxford University Press, 2014.

Lottman, Herbert R. *The Left Bank: Writers, Artists, and Politics from the Popular Front to the Cold War*. Chicago: University of Chicago Press, 1982.

Moody, A. David. *Ezra Pound: Poet: A Portrait of the Man and His Work*. Volume II: *The Epic Years 1921–1939*. Oxford, UK: Oxford University Press, 2014.

Moody, A. David. *Ezra Pound: Poet: A Portrait of the Man and His Work*. Volume III: *The Tragic Years 1939–1972*. Oxford, UK: Oxford University Press, 2015.

Moorehead, Caroline. *Gellhorn: A Twentieth-Century Life*. New York: Henry Holt, 2003.

Némirovsky, Irène. *Dimanche and Other Stories*. Translated by Bridget Patterson. New York: Vintage, 2010.

Némirovsky, Irène. *Suite française*. Translated by Sandra Smith. New York: Knopf, 2006.

Ousby, Ian. *Occupation: The Ordeal of France, 1940–1944*. New York: Cooper Square Press, 2000.

Roland, Paul. *Life under Nazi Occupation: The Struggle to Survive during World War II*. London: Arcturus, 2020.

Rosbottom, Ronald C. *When Paris Went Dark: The City of Light under German Occupation*. New York: Little, Brown & Company, 2014.

Sullivan, Rosemary. *Villa Air-Bel: World War II, Escape, and a House in Marseille*. New York: HarperCollins Perennial, 2006.

Weiss, Jonathan. *Irène Némirovsky: Her Life and Works*. Redwood City, CA: Stanford University Press, 2007.

Wells, H.G. *The War of the Worlds*. London: Arcturus, 2021.

Young-Bruehl, Elisabeth. *Hannah Arendt: For Love of the World*. 2nd edition. New Haven, CT: Yale University Press, 2004. Originally published 1982.

PART FOUR

IN 1989, AN obituary appeared in the *Manchester Guardian Weekly* under the headline CHURCHILL'S SPYMASTER—A MODEL FOR BOND. The story declared that William Stephenson, the Canadian spymaster whom Churchill called Intrepid, had died at his home in Bermuda on January 31, 1989, age eighty-nine. If you happen to know that he was born in 1897, you realize that you have a problem.

Thirteen years before, in a biography titled *A Man Called Intrepid*, an espionage expert had dubbed the Winnipeg-born Stephenson "the nearest thing to James Bond." The obituary added that one of the spymaster's operatives was novelist Ian Fleming, whose famous fictional character James Bond took certain characteristics from Stephenson, among them his love of gadgetry.

When another Winnipegger, Bill Macdonald, began doing research for an article, he encountered so much error and confusion, despite or perhaps because of two previous conflicting biographies, that in a bid to set the record straight, he ended up writing a biography of his own: *The True Intrepid: Sir William Stephenson and the Unknown Agents*. In this book, that is the work I tend to follow.

Sometimes truth remains elusive. About the spy Betty Pack, the best information came from *The Last Goodnight* by Howard Blum—including how, when she moved to Madrid in 1936, Pack supported Franco's Nationalists. But then, in the fall of 1937, she was denounced as a Republican spy—apparently by a woman jealous of an affair she was conducting with a Spanish priest. She moved to Paris to join the British Secret Service. Question: Did she really switch sides? More likely, perhaps, given her subsequent way of operating, she was indeed a spy and made good her escape after being found out.

The Josephine Baker chapter draws mostly on *Agent Josephine* by Damien Lewis. He described the rough Mediterranean crossing, when a trunk fell on the head of Bonzo the Great Dane.

Getting accurate figures on the sales of any book is a challenge. Regarding *Nineteen Eighty-Four*, I take my numbers from Dorian Lynskey's *The Ministry of Truth: The Biography of George Orwell's 1984*, cited above in SOURCES: PART TWO. They look to be the best supported.

On October 1, 2020, *Maclean's* magazine published the results of a recent poll of Canadians. How would they vote in a US election if they could? Overwhelmingly, Canadians supported Joe Biden over Donald Trump. In Atlantic Canada and Quebec, Biden received 90 and 89 percent support, respectively. In other provinces: Ontario, 84 percent; Manitoba and Saskatchewan, 82 percent; British Columbia, 88 percent; Alberta, 68 percent. No matter the age group, Canadians supported Biden: ages 18–34: 88 percent; 35–54: 78 percent; 55 and over, 86 percent.

SOURCES: PART FOUR

Bailey, Blake. *Philip Roth: The Biography*. New York: W.W. Norton, 2021.

Blum, Howard. *The Last Goodnight: A World War II Story of Espionage, Adventure, and Betrayal*. New York: HarperCollins, 2016.

Churchill, Winston. *Blood, Toil, Tears and Sweat: The Speeches of Winston Churchill*. First American edition. Boston: Houghton Mifflin, 1989.

Helm, Sarah. *A Life in Secrets: The Story of Vera Atkins and the Lost Agents of SOE*. Great London: Little Brown, 2005.

Hemming, Henry. *Agents of Influence: A British Campaign, a Canadian Spy, and the Secret Plot to Bring America into World War II*. New York: PublicAffairs, 2019.

King, James. *Farley: The Life of Farley Mowat*. Toronto: Harper Flamingo, 2002.

Lewis, Damien. *Agent Josephine: American Beauty, French Hero, British Spy*. New York: PublicAffairs, 2022.

Lovell, Mary S. *Cast No Shadow: The Life of the American Spy Who Changed the Course of World War II*. New York: Pantheon, 1992.

Macdonald, Bill. *The True Intrepid: Sir William Stephenson and the Unknown Agents*. Surrey, BC: Timberholme, 1998.

Mowat, Farley. *And No Birds Sang*. Toronto: Key Porter, 2003. Originally published 1975.

Richards, David Adams. *Lord Beaverbrook*. Toronto: Penguin, 2008.

Rose, Phyllis. *Jazz Cleopatra: Josephine Baker in Her Time*. New York: Doubleday, 1989.

Roth, Philip. "My Uchronia." In *Why Write? Collected Nonfiction 1960-2013*. New York: Library of America, 2017.

Roth, Philip. *The Plot against America*. New York: Vintage, 2004.

Stevenson, William. *Spymistress: The True Story of the Greatest Female Secret Agent of World War II*. New York: Arcade, 2007.

Stone, David R. *World War Two: Battlefield Europe*. DVD, 24 lectures. Chantilly, VA: The Teaching Company, 2020.

Wallace, Max. *The American Axis: Henry Ford, Charles Lindbergh, and the Rise of the Third Reich*. New York: St. Martin's Press, 2003.

Young, Kenneth. *Churchill and Beaverbrook*. London: Eyre & Spottiswoode, 1966.

Zuelke, Mark. *The River Battles: Canada's Final Campaign in World War II Italy*. Madeira Park, BC: Douglas & McIntyre, 2019.

PART FIVE

JACK LONDON'S *The Iron Heel* inspired George Orwell to write more than one essay. In July 1940, Orwell published a review of the book that later appeared as "Prophecies of Fascism" in Volume 2 of *The Collected Essays*. In March 1943, Orwell returned to *The Iron Heel* in an essay called "Jack London," published subsequently in *George Orwell: Lost Writings*. Both titles are cited in SOURCES: PART TWO, and I also draw on both in Chapter 38.

In Chapter 40, I mention that Jean Moulin, fearing that he might break under further torture, cut his own throat . . . but lived. One unsympathetic biographer, the right-leaning English writer Patrick Marnham, suggested years later that in this Moulin showed cunning, not heroism, because he cut himself near the chin, careful not to sever any major arteries.

In *Madame Fourcade's Secret War*, author Lynne Olson observes that throughout the Second World War, the woman who took the code name "Hedgehog" was known as Marie-Madeleine Méric, using the surname of her long-estranged first husband. After the war, she remarried and started using the surname of her second husband. She wrote her memoirs under that name and is known today in France by Fourcade. To avoid confusion, Olson uses Fourcade throughout her biography, and to me that seems a sound decision.

The most useful book on Odette Sansom proved to be *Code Name: Lise: The True Story of the Woman Who Became WWII's Most Highly Decorated Spy*, by Larry Loftis.

"This guy is a collaborator and, therefore, a coward." Lucie Aubrac told this story in a 1997 interview with *European Magazine*.

Roy Cohn is depicted in *Angels in America*, a Pulitzer Prize–winning play by Tony Kushner, as going to his grave denying the truth that he was dying of AIDS.

SOURCES: PART FIVE

Argyle, Ray. *The Paris Game: Charles de Gaulle, the Liberation of Paris, and the Gamble That Won France*. Toronto: Dundurn, 2014.

Aubrac, Lucie. *Outwitting the Gestapo*. Translated by Konrad Bieber and Betsy Wing. Lincoln: University of Nebraska Press, 1993.

Cobb, Matthew. *Eleven Days in August: The Liberation of Paris in 1944.* London: Simon & Schuster, 2013.

Dargie, Richard. *Hitler's Last Day: The Final Hours of the Führer.* London: Arcturus, 2019.

Haley, James L. *Wolf: The Lives of Jack London.* New York: Basic Books, 2010.

Humbert, Agnès. *Resistance: Memoirs of Occupied France.* Translated by Barbara Mellor. London: Bloomsbury, 2008.

Kershaw, Alex. *Jack London: A Life.* New York: St. Martin's Griffin, 1997.

Loftis, Larry. *Code Name: Lise: The True Story of the Woman Who Became WWII's Most Highly Decorated Spy.* New York: Gallery Books, 2019.

London, Jack. *The Iron Heel.* New York: Macmillan, 1908.

Lottman, Herbert R. *The Fall of Paris, June 1940: A Dramatic Narrative of the Final Weeks in Paris before Its Capture by the German Army.* New York: HarperCollins, 1992.

Magida, Arthur J. *Code Name Madeleine: A Sufi Spy in Nazi-Occupied Paris.* New York: W.W. Norton, 2020.

Marnham, Patrick. *Resistance and Betrayal: The Death and Life of the Greatest Hero of the French Resistance.* New York: Random House, 2000.

Moore, Bob. *Resistance in Western Europe.* New York: Berg, 2000.

Olson, Lynne. *Madame Fourcade's Secret War: The Daring Young Woman Who Led France's Largest Spy Network against Hitler.* New York: Random House, 2019.

Rees, Sian. *Lucie Aubrac: The French Resistance Heroine Who Outwitted the Gestapo.* Chicago: Chicago Review Press, 2016.

Riding, Alan. *And the Show Went On: Cultural Life in Nazi-Occupied Paris.* New York: Knopf, 2011.

Sebba, Anne. *Les Parisiennes: Resistance, Collaboration, and the Women of Paris under Nazi Occupation.* New York: St. Martin's Press, 2016.

Smith, Jean Edward. *The Liberation of Paris: How Eisenhower, De Gaulle, and Von Choltitz Saved the City of Light.* New York: Simon & Schuster, 2019.

Weitz, Margaret Collins. *Sisters in the Resistance: How Women Fought to Free France 1940-1945.* New York: John Wiley, 1995.

PART SIX

STEVE SCHMIDT, A former Republican strategist, spoke of the Ottawa siege on MSNBC on February 21, 2022. He made his case on *The Last Word*, hosted by Lawrence O'Donnell, and was quoted on CBC-TV and other news outlets.

MacLean, Nancy. *Democracy in Chains: The Deep History of the Radical Right's Stealth Plan for America.* New York: Penguin, 2017.

Santucci, Robert. *The Chronology of Chaos: The Mistakes, Missteps, Mishaps, and Missed Opportunities during Donald Trump's Reign as POTUS.* Robert Santucci, 2020.

Tye, Larry. *Demagogue: The Life and Long Shadow of Senator Joe McCarthy.* New York: Houghton Mifflin, 2020.

Wells, Paul. *An Emergency in Ottawa: The Story of the Convoy Commission.* Toronto: Sutherland House, 2023.

Wicker, Tom. *Shooting Star: The Brief Arc of Joe McCarthy.* New York: Harcourt, 2006.

Index

on Churchill, 59, 66; declaration of war,
135; on Hitler, 58, 60, 61–62, 134, 290;
Mackenzie King in the Age of the Dictators
(MacLaren), 60, 61, 290; position on
Spanish Civil War, 114; and the royal tour,
117; spiritualism of, 59, 60
Kirov, Sergei, 45, 266
Koestler, Arthur, 72, 160, 219, 220
Kopp, George, 101, 102, 103
Korean War, 198, 215, 269
Ku Klux Klan, 8–9, 153

Lais, Alberto, 197–198
Lenin, Vladimir: and anti-Semitism, 83;
control of workers, 56; cult of personality,
40–41, 42; illness and death, 42; on
Stalin, 266
Lewis, Sinclair: *Babbitt*, 49; *Elmer Gantry*,
49; *It Can't Happen Here*, 24, 50, 56–57,
130, 176, 224, 268; *Main Street*, 49; and
Thompson, 49–50, 51
liberalism, 53
Libération (newspaper), 244, 245
Librairie Gallimard, 146. *See also* Gallimard,
Gaston
Lindbergh, Charles, 176–177
Lippman, Walter, 36
London, Jack, 224–**225**–227; *The Call of the
Wild*, 224; *The People of the Abyss*, 74–75
Long, Huey, 51, 268
Loustaunau-Lacau, Georges "Navarre,"
236, 237, 239
loyalty, 40, 43, 44, 166. *See also* disloyalty
Lynch, Charles, 259, 261
Lynskey, Dorian: *The Ministry of Truth:
The Biography of George Orwell's 1984*,
218, 219, 268, 273, 296

MacLaren, Roy, 61
MAGA, 13, 224, 276
Malraux, André, 79–86, 251–257; acquiring
aircraft for the Spanish Civil War, 84–85,
93; on authoritarianism, 83; captured
by Nazis, 253–254; communist factions
fighting for Russia and not France, 257;
and d'Astier, 243; and de Gaulle, 218,
232, 253; and Drieu La Rochelle, 142, 252;
early life, 80; eulogy for Moulin, 232;
formation of air squadron, 107; and the
"Gangster Brigade of Colonel Malraux,"
255–256; and Hemingway, 85, 86; Josette
(common-law-wife), 252; leadership
qualities of, 253; and Orwell, 218; in
prison, 254–255; prisoner in Front Stalag,
251–252; on spread of fascism on Europe,

119; stolen artifacts in Cambodia, 81–82,
84; unease over rise of Nazi party, 82;
and *The Wilderness of Zin* (Lawrence), 81.
See also Todd, Olivier
Malraux, André, works by: *The Conquerers*,
82; *Man's Fate*, 83; *Man's Hope*, 86, 255;
The Royal Way, 82; *The Walnut Trees of
Altenburg*, 253
manipulation of the truth: historical
revisionism: in dystopian fiction, 219–220
Marx, Karl, 226; *Das Kapital*, 26
Marxism: Benjamin, 157, 161; and Drieu La
Rochelle, 142; Garner reading, 113; and
Lenin, 40; and Stalin, 41; and Trotsky, 43.
See also communism
McCarthy, Joseph, 39, 268–**274**–275; Army-
McCarthy hearings, 272–273; compared
to Buzz Winthrop, 268; death, 273;
in-group condemnation, 273; purges of,
270–271; and Trump, 273–274; use of
smear tactics, 159, 204, 269, 270; and
Winchell, 204
McInnes, Gavin, 13
McNair, John, 100, 101
mental health: battle exhaustion (combat
fatigue), 209; *The Cult of Trump* (Hassan),
40; depression, 102, 173; insanity, 153;
institutionalization, 226; narcissistic
personality disorder, 152–153; of Pound,
152, 153; shell-shock (PTSD), 117;
suicidal crises, 82, 141, 143, 229–230.
See also death by suicide; Pound, Ezra
Miller, Henry, 143, 216; Orwell on, 99–100,
292; *Tropic of Cancer*, 99
Morocco, 104, 216, 235, 256
Moulin, Jean, 84, 232–234, 244, 245;
arrest of, 246, 249
Mowat, Farley, 206–210; *And No Birds
Sang*, 206, 207; *People of the Deer*, 210;
The Regiment, 206; *Sea of Slaughter*,
206, 210
the Munich Agreement, 61, 63–64, 65, 134,
139, 181, 183
Murrow, Edward, 271
Mussolini, Benito: aid to Franco, 43–44;
alliance with Germany, 203; death
of, 266; Hemingway profile on, 18;
and Hitler, 25, 29, 170; King and, 60;
Manifesto of Race, 151; similarity to
Trump, 12; support for Poland, 149

narcissism, 40, 152–153, 268. *See also* cult
of personality
Nazi collaboration, 138–147; *La nouvelle
revue française (NRF)*, 140, 142, 252